Inhuman Citizenship

Inhuman Citizenship

*Traumatic Enjoyment and
Asian American Literature*

Juliana Chang

UNIVERSITY OF MINNESOTA PRESS
MINNEAPOLIS • LONDON

The University of Minnesota Press gratefully acknowledges financial assistance provided for the publication of this book from the English department, the Office of the Dean of Arts and Sciences, and the Provost's Office at Santa Clara University.

An earlier version of chapter 1 was previously published as "Melancholic Remains: Domestic and National Secrets in Fae Myenne Ng's *Bone*," *mfs: Modern Fiction Studies* 51, no. 1 (Spring 2005): 110–33.

Epigraph to the Introduction, "Ming the Merciless," copyright 2002 by Jessica Hagedorn. Reprinted by permission of City Lights Books.

Copyright 2012 by the Regents of the University of Minnesota

Published by the University of Minnesota Press
111 Third Avenue South, Suite 290
Minneapolis, MN 55401-2520
http://www.upress.umn.edu

Library of Congress Cataloging-in-Publication Data

Chang, Juliana.
   Inhuman citizenship : traumatic enjoyment and Asian American literature / Juliana Chang.
   Includes bibliographical references and index.
ISBN 978-0-8166-7443-5 (hardback) — ISBN 978-0-8166-7444-2 (pb)
1. American literature—Asian American authors—History and criticism.
2. Asian Americans in literature. 3. American literature—20th century—History and criticism. 4. American literature—21st century—History and criticism. 5. Identity (Philosophical concept) in literature. 6. Melancholy in literature. I. Title.
   PS153.A84C465 2012
   810.9´895073—dc23

                                    2012030015

Printed in the United States of America on acid-free paper

The University of Minnesota is an equal-opportunity educator and employer.

20 19 18 17 16 15 14 13 12   10 9 8 7 6 5 4 3 2 1

for Russell

Contents

Introduction

Inhuman Citizenship

> king of the lionmen
> come dancing in my tube
> sing, ming, sing
> blink sloe-eyed phantasy
> and touch me where
> there's always hot water
> in this house
>
> . . . .
> ming, merciless ming
> come dancing in my tube
>
> —JESSICA HAGEDORN,
> "Ming the Merciless"

Why is the alien villain Ming the Merciless so captivating and arousing to the speaker in Jessica Hagedorn's 1981 poem? Why do we love to hate, and hate to love, such grotesque and outlaw figures? I begin *Inhuman Citizenship* with this poem because it so provocatively evokes the three major themes of this study: traumatic enjoyment, the racial inhuman, and the domestic. Taken together, these three concepts provide an intriguing entry into understanding the psychic lives of the U.S. nation-state and its subjects. Throughout this book, I employ a psychoanalytic reading of Asian American texts, focusing especially on the affect of traumatic enjoyment. Traumatic enjoyment is my translation of Lacan's "jouissance," a violent yet blissful shattering of the self. I find that Lacanian psychoanalysis offers compelling alternative epistemologies and ethics as we think through and navigate our relationship to power. I am especially interested in the ways that Asian American domestic narratives unexpectedly surface tropes of the racial other as inhuman, figures that threaten the boundaries of the human and evoke the trauma of jouissance for the normative national subject.

1

Ming the Merciless, as highlighted in Hagedorn's poem, is a marvelously suggestive example of the racial inhuman that is apprehended through the domestic ("my house") and that gives shape to national jouissance. Racialized by his name and appearance as Asian, Ming the Merciless is the alien arch-enemy of the all-American superhero Flash Gordon, a character made popular in the United States in the 1930s through comic books and film.[1] A fantasy figure of Oriental treachery and empire, Ming the Merciless was a variation on the Asian arch-villain archetype most popularly known through Sax Rohmer's fictional creation, Dr. Fu Manchu.[2] As the embodiment of pure evil, these Asian arch-villains were racialized as inhuman, and Ming's extraterrestrial status simply literalizes this inhumanity. What I find daring about Hagedorn's poem, which was published in a fairly early period of Asian American consciousness, is its unabashed embrace of what I call the racial inhuman.[3] The poem does not take part in the more common gestures of protesting the "de-humanization" of the Asian and insisting that the Asian is as human as any American. Rather, it revels in the pleasures and enjoyment of the inhuman, as we can see from the speaker's diction and tone. Addressing Ming as "king of the lionmen," the poem makes Ming into a royal hybrid of human and animal, a creature with the aura of the divine, with its nobility accented by the rhyme of "king" with "ming." Elsewhere in the poem, apostrophic addresses convey a tone of awe and fascination at this divine creature, magically morphing into the sacred and the prehistoric: "o flying angel/o pterodactyl."[4]

Interrogating the nature of Ming's inhumanity allows us to comprehend why and how Ming generates such delicious enjoyment on the part of his audience. As the dastardly villain and despot, Ming sadistically enjoys power and evil for their own sake. As we see from his moniker, Ming the Merciless, he is not bound by conscience, that is, he exempts himself from social law and morality. He not only lacks compassion for the suffering of others; he revels in and enjoys such suffering. This enjoyment is what makes him inhuman: unethical, irrational, enjoying for no reason other than for enjoyment itself.

A superhero story, so the saying goes, is only as good as its villain. The villain delights and electrifies us in two major ways. First, as imaginary victims, we are not only traumatized by him, but we may masochistically enjoy this trauma. Second, we secretly wish we could *be* him. Because we are bound by law in our everyday lives, we fantasize that breaking the law would be exhilarating, providing us with a rush of utter freedom. We enjoy identifying with the villain, and then find ourselves traumatized by this enjoyment of what we otherwise vilify; for does it not call into question our own status as ethical and rational beings, as human? This is why we love to hate and hate to love the villain, the outlaw, the inhuman, because of this nexus of trauma and enjoyment.

Let us further investigate the subject who enjoys Ming so much: the speaker of the poem. The speaker's appeal to "touch me where / there's always hot water / in this house" can be read as a reference to female sexual arousal. In this reading of the speaker as feminine, her seductive invitation to "come dancing in my tube" coyly suggests the rhythmic pleasures offered by sexual intercourse, but also the pleasures of performance that are beamed through television. The metaphor of the tube conjoins the speaker's erotic desire with mass culture in the United States. This brings us to the question of the speaker's racial identification. Is she Asian American, like the author? If so, then the poem's provocation lies in the way that the Asian American does not reject or separate herself from Orientalist fantasy. Instead, she ardently embraces the "bad Asian," and resignifies the terms of his hypnotic appeal.[5] But indeed, if the speaker rearticulates mass fantasy, might we understand her not only as Asian American but more broadly as the U.S. subject-citizen? While the poem appears to go against the grain of mainstream American morality, does it not in fact uncover the enjoyment—the traumatic enjoyment—that underlies this national and imperial fantasy of race? Finally, let us note how the American spectator's enjoyment of the racial inhuman makes her into a thing as well: a cyborg vagina-television; an aroused, animated house. The house and the television, icons of twentieth-century American domesticity, are rendered uncanny amalgams of the human and the inhuman.

I have explicated Hagedorn's poem at length in order to tease out the key concepts of this study: traumatic enjoyment, the racial inhuman, and the domestic. Throughout the book, I show how Asian American domestic formations may be read as symptoms of America's relationship to its national fantasies, and to the jouissance that both threatens and underlies these fantasies. Jouissance is the affect that must be excluded in order for the nation and its subjects to stage its ideal versions of identity, for jouissance shatters any coherent sense of self or structure. At the same time, jouissance promises a sublime and ultimate satisfaction, providing an irresistible "kick" of affect that helps to anchor fantasy. In the national imaginary, racial subjects are often perceived as the source of jouissance, which they supposedly embody through their excesses of violence, sexuality, anger, ecstasy, and so on—excesses that threaten to overwhelm the social order. We might say that racial subjects function as symbolic placeholders for jouissance. Jouissance itself is an impossible condition, but the fantasy that the racial subject embodies jouissance covers over this impossibility. And the shape that is often given to racial subjects as the site of enjoyment is the racial inhuman. Just as jouissance is the surplus and support of the symbolic, the inhuman can be found in what exceeds the human within the human itself. The flying angel of Hagedorn's poem, for example, amalgamates the human and nonhuman, like the lionmen over whom Ming rules. One of the central arguments of this book is that we should not automatically reject these figures of the racial inhuman as false and harmful. Instead, what if we accept and assume, impossibly, the condition of the inhuman? What if we bring to the surface the otherwise buried enjoyment of the racial inhuman? How might this teasing out of national jouissance crack open the fantasies of the nation? This is what I mean by inhuman citizenship: the ethical practice of assuming responsibility for the racial symptoms, fantasies, and unconscious of the U.S. nation-state.

I have found that domesticity, the interior and "private" site of home and family, proves to be a most apt site for the covering and uncovering of these secrets of nation. If family, like nation, functions as a fantasy of coherence and harmony, then highlighting what I call "family business" helps to unpack this fantasy. By family business, I mean to suggest both the economic and social dimensions of sustaining the family: financial business and the business of caretaking. The child plays a pivotal role in Asian American family business, and we need to understand her affective labor, and especially her traumatic enjoyment, in sustaining the fantasies of family and nation. The national fantasies with which this study is most concerned are the mythology of American exceptionalism and the ideology of neoliberalism, both of which dovetail interestingly with the fantasies of Asian American family formation. American exceptionalism, in my definition, is the belief in the uniqueness and distinctiveness of America's moral superiority, a belief that buttresses the nation's claim to global hegemony.[6] One of the fundamental tenets of this belief is the nation's democratic and economic openness to all, regardless of race or national origin. The establishment of Asian immigrant and Asian American families would appear to confirm such openness, indicating that immigrants are drawn not only by work opportunities, but by the opportunity to find a new home.

Neoliberalism, which gained ascendency in the United States in the 1980s and 1990s, shares with American exceptionalism a belief in the good of universalizing freedom in its incarnation as free-market practices. The racial formation of Asian Americans as model minorities posits them as exemplary neoliberal citizens who depend not on the state or the public sector for survival, but rather on the private realm of other family members.

The four novels that I investigate in this book unsettle these national fantasies of American exceptionalism and neoliberalism. Each novel features as its protagonist a second-generation Asian American whose citizenship, or mode of belonging and unbelonging to the nation, is mediated by his or her role in family business and is permeated by traumatic enjoyment. The characters in Fae Myenne Ng's *Bone*, living and dead, practice a melancholic citizenship in which a history of labor exploitation remains animated. In Brian Ascalon Roley's *American Son*, the Sullivan family may be apprehended through the lens of a shameful citizenship that produces an animalistic jouissance for the U.S. nation-state. Chang-rae Lee's *Native Speaker*, meanwhile, features romantic citizenship as the practice of generating a fantasy of the nation as exceptionally lovable and loving. Finally, Suki Kim's *The Interpreter* proposes perverse citizenship as an overacquiescence to power that consequently distorts and wields power differently.

RACE AND TRAUMATIC ENJOYMENT

The act of reading multicultural literature, when performed by an ethnic-racial subject, is conventionally interpreted as a practice of identity politics. In the most reductive understanding, this reader seamlessly and harmoniously identifies with the protagonist of the narrative, thereby strengthening and reinforcing her ethnic-racial identity. Indeed, I found myself drawn to the study of Asian American narratives because they promised a particular resonance with my life experiences and with the stories of those who were closest to me. But far from providing the reassuring comfort that one might assume, these texts proved to be the most traumatizing of any that I had read. This was not only because I reexperienced, along with the characters, the psychic pains of displacement, loss, and epistemic violence. It was also because of the ethical conundrums with which these stories confronted me. What did it mean, for example, that I derived a sadistic satisfaction from the narrator bullying the "quiet" Chinese American girl in Maxine Hong Kingston's *The Woman Warrior*? That I so gleefully relished the brutal revenge that concludes Brian Ascalon Roley's *American*

Son? Was there something inhuman about my enjoyment of another's trauma, my inability to sympathize with human suffering? How could I explain such extravagant heartlessness, and indeed, how could the absence of heart produce such an overflow of affect?

When I initially conceived of this book, I framed it as a study of national *haunting* by the racial inhuman. Like many critical race, American studies, and critical theory scholars, I was struck by the pervasiveness of loss, death, and absence in late twentieth-century cultural forms such as Asian American writing.[7] I was drawn to characters who were grappling with profound voids in their lives, and with the disarray that such holes generated. As I considered their narratives more carefully, however, I came to realize that the paradigm of haunting did not fully capture the dominant affect of these novels. While haunting connotes a presence that is structured by absence or lack, I found instead that these novels were sites of excess and shock. Not only were they narratives about trauma, but they also produced trauma. They rendered Asian Americans not only as the objects but also as the vehicles and agents of inhuman suffering. An implicit assumption often governs race and ethnic studies: the objects and victims of racism are positioned on a higher moral plane than the perpetrators of such injustice. I was disturbed but strangely exhilarated—disturbed *because* I was exhilarated—by these characters who were indeed objects of racism, and yet I also inhumanly enjoyed their suffering and the suffering of others.

One example of this enjoyment in Asian American literature is the well-known "torture incident" in Maxine Hong Kingston's *The Woman Warrior*.[8] Stigmatized for not speaking up in the classroom, the narrator discharges her humiliation by aggressively cornering another Chinese American "quiet girl" in the school bathroom. She chastises, insults, and physically assaults the girl, ordering her to say something, anything, even one word. In Sau-ling Wong's explication of this incident, the quiet girl serves as the narrator's alter ego. The narrator interprets the girl's quietness, so like her own, as a racial stain, a "residue of racial difference" that threatens the narrator's own hopes for assimilation.[9] Thus the narrator's torture of the girl conforms to a logic of self-punishment and self-discipline. If the quiet girl can speak, the narrator believes, so too can the narrator assert herself and prove her social belonging.

We perceive how the suffering of both girls results from the degradations of gendered racial formation. What is more difficult to acknowledge is the enjoyment that is produced by these degradations. Consider our commonsense moral response to this story. We "know" that the narrator, as perpetrator of violence, is in the wrong. But what was involved in arriving at such a judgment? Keep in mind that narratives are typically structured to enable readerly identification with the narrator. This means that the reader sympathizes with the narrator's desire to speak as a form of self-validation. We feel the desperation of the narrator to make the quiet girl prove that verbalization is possible. Needing to discharge this fear and dread, we transfer our excess affect into contempt for the quiet girl: How hard can it be to say just one word? We start to enjoy the narrator's sadistic treatment of her; then, taken aback by our enjoyment, we cover over this disturbing gratification by switching the objects of our identification and judgment. Now we morally condemn the narrator, which means that *we enjoy our own superior morality* in our identification with the innocent victim. Our moral judgment is simply a shift in enjoyment. The narrator, too, judges herself guilty. "The world is sometimes just," she remarks, by way of explaining why she is subsequently struck by a mysterious illness that lasts for eighteen months.[10] As readers, our satisfaction at this resolution is also a form of enjoyment. We enjoy the narrator's punishment, in the guise of safeguarding justice, morality, and law. Indeed, one of the key insights of psychoanalysis is that enjoyment is the very mode of an ostensibly neutral structure of social law.

Although Lacanian theory has understandably been critiqued for its abstruse quality and its universalist deployments, I nevertheless find that its models and concepts offer a compelling alternative epistemology of race, nation, and capital, for these are not only sociopolitical forces but also powerful subjective and affective formations. Much of our analysis of structural racism has proceeded along the axes of what Lacan termed the Symbolic (culture, language, and law) and the Imaginary (visuality and binary relations). To understand the visceral power of racial hegemony, however, we must also engage with Lacan's third dimension of the Real: what is foreclosed from and disrupts the Symbolic. In this book I will emphasize how jouissance, an element and affect of the Real, is crucial to understanding the politics of race and nation. Racial, national, and imperial modes of jouissance are the very forces through which hegemony secures consent—sometimes enthusiastic consent—from its subjects. Jouissance helps to explain the otherwise puzzling question of why subjects act or believe against their rational self-interest. Christopher Lane elaborates on the insights of psychoanalysis for studies of race, nationalism, and colonialism:

Studies that aim to resolve urban strife and ethnic warfare often . . . anticipate that people locked in conflict want an end to struggle in order to secure the material gains they can achieve only in times of peace. To this perspective, psychoanalysis adds a difficult truth: When people and groups are locked in conflict, they are—beyond their immediate interest in securing sovereignty over another land or people—*already* experiencing intangible gains. . . . For instance, a group's "gain" might consist of the pleasure received in depleting another's freedom.[11]

These kinds of dynamics explain why white working-class Americans may resent black welfare recipients, Latino "illegal immigrants," or workers in India to whom jobs are "outsourced" to a much more volatile degree than the bankers or politicians they could otherwise hold responsible for their suffering. These fantasmatic racial figures are caricatured as parasitic masses, not quite human. If the racial inhuman is the other for the normative, white, American citizen-subject, then psychoanalysis helps us to understand this relationship by highlighting the contradictions and excesses of this national subject, as well as its objects and abjects.

As Antonio Viego and other critics have noted, hegemonic understandings of race and nation are in fact already undergirded by certain versions of psychology, namely, ego and social psychology. Lacan's key intervention here is his trenchant critique of ego psychology, which posits a normative, whole, and healthy ego as the cure for pathology.[12] Instead, Lacan saw the ego as an illusory fantasy of wholeness and mastery that precisely covers over contradictions and excess. In addition, Lacanian theory removes the stigma of pathology from psychic symptoms and conditions by refusing the model of the normative healthy ego. In this vein, I too insist that the racial inhuman is not a pathology that must be cured or redeemed. Instead, we should understand the racial inhuman as a mode that interrogates hegemonic forms of humanity and nation. In this way, Lacanian analysis provides a framework for understanding the power and ethics of the racial inhuman.

In my reading, jouissance is the affect in which our senses of reality and selfhood become traumatically scrambled. As I will outline in chapter 3, for example, the Korean domestic worker Ahjuhma performs such a function when she knocks the narrator off balance. Ahjuhma is the monstrous, maternal Thing for young Henry, utterly opaque in her recalcitrant Korean ethnicity. The Thing is the name given to the surplus of the subject; it is the primal object from which we detach in order to become Symbolic subjects. Derived from Freud's notion of *das Ding,* the Thing is a term that is meant to evoke the inhuman. We are fascinated by the Thing, but we are also terrified by the way that it threatens to bring us outside of law, language, and the realm of the human. For Henry, Ahjuhma's stubborn and atavistic Korean ethnicity is the dimension of the Real, what exceeds the Symbolic order through which we comprehend reality. What is the difference between reality and the Real? Although we commonly think of reality and fantasy as oppositional categories, Lacan aligns reality with fantasy while opposing both to the Real. Fantasy, that is, gives coherence to our symbolic reality, whereas the Real exceeds symbolic reality. Indeed, the intrusion of the Real annihilates the coherence of our reality. Ahjuhma's Korean ethnicity, like the silence of the quiet girl, is experienced by the second-generation Asian American narrator as the Real, the racial residue that shatters one's symbolic reality and produces the affect of jouissance.

"Jouissance" is often translated into English as "enjoyment." The term "enjoyment," however, does not capture the violent ambivalence of jouissance. Jouissance is experienced as a traumatic intrusion that brings pain as well as pleasure. This is because jouissance goes beyond the pleasure principle: experiencing such an excess of pleasure that the pleasure becomes painful and unbearable. In this unbearability, it is a sensation that threatens the very foundation of the subject. Lacanian theory formulates jouissance as the excruciating convergence of suffering and satisfaction, in which one finds satisfaction in one's suffering as well as suffering in one's satisfaction.[13] Jouissance stands for that elusive, primordial sense of being that we sacrifice in order to enter into the Symbolic order of law, language, and culture. The abstractions of the Symbolic, particularly in the form of linguistic signifiers, alienate us from primal being. Compelled toward this primal sense of being, we unconsciously seek jouissance despite—or perhaps because of—the suffering-satisfaction that it promises.

Because we are ever separate from, yet ever seeking, this primal enjoyment, we imagine that others have access to this enjoyment, and we envy them. Lacan describes this visceral envy:

> This register of a jouissance as that which is only accessible to the other is the only dimension in which we can locate the strange malaise that, if I'm not mistaken, only the German language has managed to point to— along with other psychological nuances concerning the gap in man—with the word *Lebensneid.*

Lebensneid is not an ordinary jealousy, it is the jealousy born in a subject in his relation to an other, insofar as this other is held to enjoy a certain
form of jouissance or superabundant vitality, that the subject perceives as
something that he cannot apprehend by means of even the most elementary
of affective movements.

Imagining that others have stolen our enjoyment, our envy becomes resentment and aggression.[14] These others are often figured across social
differences such as race, ethnicity, class, gender, or sexuality. In an article
from the 1990s, Tim Dean explains how subordinate others frequently
bear the blame for the privative effects of the Symbolic order:

One example of this may be seen in the conservative discourse about
welfare mothers, a discourse that paradoxically manages to represent some
of the most disenfranchised members of our society as effectively robbing
the rest of us; although it is the Other that steals our jouissance through the
privative effects of language on the human body, the persistent misidentifi-
cation of social others with the Other permits conservatives to credibly
claim that young, impoverished African American women are in fact stealing our jouissance.[15]

Dean uses the specific example from the 1980s and 1990s political discourse that stoked racialized resentment against welfare recipients. This
racial resentment was both an effect of and an impetus for neoliberal restructuring; stripping welfare benefits was part of a larger dismantling of
the welfare state and a move toward privatization.[16] In the post–9/11 era,
figures who steal enjoyment from "us" include the radical Muslim terrorist, the illegal immigrant, and the gay/lesbian subject bent on destroying
"traditional" (heterosexual) marriage. These are tropes whose function is
to maintain the fantasy that "our" enjoyment is possible but has merely
been displaced. As Dean highlights, the paradox of this formulation is
that it represents the "disenfranchised" as "robbing the rest of us"; in Lisa
Cacho's formulation, disempowerment has been criminalized.[17] A prime
example of such essentialist criminalization is the prevalent reference to
undocumented migrants as "illegals," as if they are transgressive of law
in their very being. The stigma of criminalization derives not only from
the formula of the racial other as "thief." Enjoyment itself is outside the
Symbolic law, and in this way the racial or sexual other is deemed lawless

simply for enjoying, that is, enjoying his difference. And even more primally, the racial other who enjoys is conceived of as the Thing, the inhuman.

THE RACIAL INHUMAN

"Underneath, we are the same; we are all human beings." "There is only one race: the human race." A curious feature of these statements of color-blind sentiment is the fact that they are articulated so automatically and so ubiquitously—in other words, they are repeated so often that they become mechanical and de-individualized, thereby belying their humanistic content. And the content of these utterances is assumed to be so virtuous in their universalizing identification and sympathy that no further elaboration is necessary. Indeed, these axioms are meant to end conversations, not to start or continue them. Let us consider how these declarations of humanist universalism are in fact structured and permeated by undercurrents of inhumanity. The systematic and impersonal nature of these assertions, however heartfelt their intentions, illuminates their instrumental purpose in reinforcing hegemonic ideology and structures. In fact, it is the very sincerity and authenticity of sentimental desire that sutures hegemonic ideology to its subjects. And the content of these seemingly benign avowals enacts an inhuman cruelty by traumatically nullifying the psychic realities of racial subalterns—a cruelty that is masked by hegemony's claim to the status of common sense and the reasonable.

In this section, I explicate the problems of claiming human status for the racial subaltern, for, as I note above, humanist ideology is already permeated by inhuman means and ends. I argue instead that we should recognize the racial inhuman as a powerful trope and force of counter-hegemony. While there is now a burgeoning body of posthumanist scholarship that interrogates our received assumptions about humanism and the humanities, less developed has been a sustained and substantial analysis of race together with posthumanist study.[18] In the book, I use the framework of critical race studies to query our axiomatic beliefs about the human.

Racial violence and violation have historically been rationalized by the exclusion of racial others from the category of the human as that which merits respect and protection. The most obvious strategy for rectifying such injustice, then, would consist of claiming human status for racial subjects. Paul Gilroy's *Postcolonial Melancholia* is characteristic in his call for a "planetary humanism," an updated naming of universalism. Observing how colonization produced racial groups as "sub- or infrahuman," Gilroy advocates for a universal "right to be human."[19] Within the liberal paradigm that Gilroy invokes, the human is in fact conceived of as one who has the right to rights. What Gilroy's plea highlights, then, is the a priori exclusion of the racial subaltern from this human condition of the rights-bearing subject. This fundamental elision explains why the ostensible protections of civil rights still remain fraught and fragile. How can specific legal rights be negotiated when the very question of the right to have rights remains ideologically suspended?

Within Enlightenment modernity, humanity is generally understood as deriving from a rational and ethical struggle for self-determination and freedom. The practice of freedom, in this formulation, consists of overcoming the limitations of one's immediate existence.[20] What presumably distinguishes the human from other animals and beings are the abilities to reason, to transcend the self by sympathizing with others, and to remake the world through symbolic culture.

Let us consider the implication of terms used by Gilroy and others such as "sub-human," "infrahuman," and "dehumanization." What would it mean to subtract or extract humanity from the racial other? Subtraction or extraction would result in a lack of humanity and a subsequent alignment with other beings that lack human characteristics: animals, plants, inanimate objects, machines, and so on. While racial others can be degraded as subhuman and reduced to material embodiment, however, let us remember that they can also be abstracted as superhuman spirits, such as angels or demons—magical divine beings who use their supernatural forces for good or evil.[21] Whether sub- or superhuman, however, these figures *lack* the normative features of the human: higher functions of rationality in the case of the subhuman; an innate sympathy for human frailty in the case of the superhuman.

If European humanism was a construct of a liberal modernity that emancipated one from the bonds of tradition and traditional authority, then the positing of racial others as primitive meant that they had not yet entered into the category of the civilized human: the self-possessed, self-governing, and rational subject. Indigenous, colonized, and enslaved peoples were historically made into reason's other, bound by instinct, tradition, and superstition. This framing of temporal underdevelopment or lack led to the "solution" of civilizing such peoples into an ethical and rational humanity. Indeed, this was the purported goal of colonization: to bring the non-Western world into modernity, civilization, and "the family of man."

Precisely because the norms and ideals of the human have been used not only to exclude and exterminate, but also to violently include and incorporate, it is essential that we refuse the gesture of arguing that racial others are just as human as white subjects. We must go beyond the simple diagnosis of racism as dehumanization, because it is far too easy to turn to rehumanization as remedy—a solution that chillingly resonates with the civilizing aims of colonization. The presumable end goal of educating, assimilating, and Christianizing natives or migrants is achieved through deploying military and paramilitary forces of the imperial state to "pacify" and "regulate" such populations. Thus, while postcolonial critics like Gilroy rightly decry the "bloodstained workings" of racist dehumanization, let us observe that the apparent redress of rehumanization—that is, civilizing the other—has its own histories of violence.[22]

To comprehend the problem of race as a problem of lack means, simply, that "adding" humanity and its attendant rights would fix the problem. Our received notions of humanity, including the implicitly racialized, Eurocentric norms of the human, remain intact in this model. Aspiring to this predetermined ideal means reinforcing such norms and still excluding those who do not or cannot achieve legibility as human. In effect, a few of us become tokenized as human and rendered exceptions to the general mass (who are deemed inhuman precisely because they are a de-individuated mass) of racial others—exceptions that prove the general rule of racial inhumanity. Instead of proving ourselves human and thereby accepting the terms of such humanity, my purpose here is to claim the epistemologies, ethics, and aesthetics of the racial inhuman.

What is overlooked by the paradigm of racialization as a lack of humanity is the way that racial others are produced as an *excess* of humanity. By inhuman, then, I mean something far more disturbing and ominous than the nonhuman. Slavoj Žižek explains the distinction between the nonhuman and the inhuman by way of Kant's philosophy:

> In his *Critique of Pure Reason*, Kant introduced a key distinction between negative and indefinite judgement: the positive statement "the soul is mortal" can be negated in two ways. We can either deny a predicate ("the soul is not mortal"), or affirm a non-predicate ("the soul is non-mortal"). The difference is exactly the same as the one, known to every reader of the Stephen King, between "he is not dead" and "he is undead." The indefinite judgement opens up a third domain that undermines the distinction between

dead and non-dead (alive): the "undead" are neither alive nor dead, they are precisely the monstrous "living dead." And the same goes for "inhuman": "he is not human" is not the same as "he is inhuman." "He is not human" means simply that he is external to humanity, animal or divine, while "he is inhuman" means something thoroughly different, namely the fact that he is neither human nor inhuman, but marked by a terrifying excess which, *although it negates what we understand as humanity, is inherent to being human.*[23]

Unlike the subhuman, the inhuman does not correspond to a lack of human attributes. Nor is the inhuman analogous to the superhuman, for the superhuman's condition is exceptional: she is superhuman precisely because she is elevated above humans. In contrast to these other categories that leave the norms of humanity intact, the inhuman threatens the very foundations of human identity. It is the alien obscenity at the very heart of the human, an innate "monstrosity."[24] It inspires dread and horror not only because we find it strange but also because we find it overly proximate. It terrifies and exhilarates in its threat and promise to deform the human, to devastate our sense of ourselves as rational and benevolent beings. The inhuman is the alien that permeates the human, and the human that finds itself alien.

In the chapters that follow, I will attend to the significance of four instantiations of the racial inhuman: the living dead, the animal, the antifetish, and the death drive. These four tropes are manifestations of excess: the living dead as surplus life substance; animal enjoyment that is unbound by law; the antifetish that shatters national romance; the death drive that destroys even as it rebirths. I interpret jouissance as the affect generated by the racial inhuman, an annihilating sensation of terror, trauma, and ecstasy. As I noted, one of the key attributes of the human is its capacity for transcendence. Jouissance, however, is precisely that which blocks transcendence. Embodying substance without sense or meaning, resisting symbolization or dialecticization, jouissance pulls one into a sensation of overembodiment and overembeddedness. The purpose of this study is to sharpen our awareness of how the racial inhuman and its attendant affect of jouissance both disrupt and sustain the prevailing ideologies and fantasies of the U.S. nation-state. The fantasy of liberal citizenship, for instance, which is ostensibly grounded in a shared human condition, covers over the monstrous inhumanity of a nation-state that wields the power of "organized death" against its racial and imperial others.[25] Moreover, as I note in my earlier critique of color-blind universalist discourse, the dream of a shared humanity not only veils, but *is also enabled by,* a secret kernel of inhumanity.

THE UNCANNY DOMESTIC

As scholars of Asian American studies have established, Asian American racialization comprises two major facets. First, Asian Americans are model minorities whose putative success and assimilation is pointed to as evidence of America's color-blind meritocracy and openness. Second, Asian Americans are construed as perpetual foreigners, seen as alien to American culture regardless of nativity or citizenship. Using a psychoanalytic schema, we might view these two facets as different elements of national fantasy. The notion of Asian Americans as the model minority is used to support a certain vision of American exceptionalism: its openness to the world in providing limitless opportunity regardless of race or national origin. The perception of the Asian as alien, however, creates a frisson of jouissance: one is both traumatized by and enjoys the status of the Asian as utterly outside. In this fantasy, the normative American subject achieves his own coherence by projecting alterity onto the Asian other, who presumably enjoys by virtue of not being subjected to the norms of Western civilization. My focus is on the domestic and undomestic incarnations of such racial fantasy and jouissance. The belief that Asian American families conform to American heteropatriarchal norms is one aspect of model minority formation. Asian Americans are considered an acceptable presence so long as they align themselves with "family values" and contribute to the fantasy of the nation as itself a harmonious family.[26] What my study proposes, however, is a reading of Asian American literature through the lens of *family business,* rather than family per se. Where the paradigmatic family is the site of nationalist fantasy, the lens of family business allows us to deconstruct these fantasies of nation and to uncover the jouissance of imperialist nationalism. Where family is sentimentalized as the site where we are most human, family business allows us a glimpse into the impersonal and inhuman forces that permeate our most intimate relationships.

This book is a study of Asian American domestic narratives—stories of private homes and families. However, as scholars of American studies, feminist theory, and postcolonial studies have established, it is impossible to separate the notion of private domesticity from the concept of nation as domestic space.[27] "Home" and "family" serve as powerful metaphors for the nation, such that seemingly primal desires and fantasies become transferred from the private domestic sphere to the public sphere of the nation. Lauren Berlant, for example, explains how national citizenship, often understood as an abstract and technical form, produces powerful instinctual affects: "In return for cultural, legal, and military security, people are asked to love their country, and to recognize certain stories, events, experiences, practices, and ways of life as related to the core of who they are, their public status, and their resemblance to other people. This training in politicized intimacy has also served as a way of turning political boundaries into visceral, emotional, and seemingly hardwired responses of 'insiders' to 'outsiders.'"[28] It is this polarization of interior and exterior, as well as the security promised in exchange for love, that links the two connotations of domestic as home and nation. In both instances, the domestic signifies interiority, a condition that is not only bounded and separate from the outside but indeed needing dire protection from threats coming from outside. Against the exterior as a source of strife, danger, and conflict, the interior space of home or nation is imagined as a realm of safety, harmony, and love.

Home and family, of course, are more than metaphors for the nation; they are also sites of subject and cultural formation for the nation. Ann Laura Stoler contends that the study of intimate relations does not detract from an understanding of rule by an imperial nation; rather, it enables us to understand what Foucault called the microphysics of such power.

> To study the intimate is not to turn away from structures of dominance but to relocate their conditions of possibility and relations and forces of production. . . . Refocusing on the intimate opens to what haunts those social relations, to the untoward, to the strangely familiar that proximities and inequalities may produce. . . . [I]t reminds us how central the emotional economy of sexual access, parenting, and domestic arrangements have been to colonial politics of labor recruitment and pacification.[29]

If ideological norms of domesticity are posited as crucial to the health and stability of the nation, then private homes and families become sites of surveillance, knowledge production, discipline, and regulation. In this way, apparently deviant domestic formations are subject to regimes of hypervisibility. And as Avery Gordon elucidates, hypervisibility can shade into invisibility: the deviant are relegated to the margins of peripheral vision and become objects of disavowed visibility or even blindness.[30] In chapters 2 and 3, I refer to this oscillation between racial hypervisibility and invisibility as "deviant visibility." This oscillation between visual excess and visual lack may be understood as a symptom of what Stoler refers to as the haunting of structures of dominance by the intimate. To put this in the terms of my study, I interpret private domestic realms, such as Asian American family business, as the underside of U.S. national formations of ideology, politics, the economy, and citizenship. As the obverse of U.S. national fantasy, Asian American family business can support such fantasy as well as disrupt and shatter it. As I will elaborate in chapter 1, Asian American family business is a kind of secret of the nation. It is an open secret when it supports fantasy in its guise as the model minority, but it becomes disavowed in its more threatening form: the racial inhuman. Reassuring yet alien, Asian American family business is an incarnation of the national uncanny.

Like Hagedorn's figure of the inhuman as an indeterminate amalgam of thing and person, some of Freud's most salient examples of the uncanny include objects that generate "intellectual uncertainty" as to their categorization as human or nonhuman, such as dolls or automata.[31] The uncanny is not disturbing, Freud points out, simply because it is unfamiliar, but rather because it is both strange and familiar at once. In the case of the doll, for example, its human features seem familiar to us even as its inanimate status renders such human features unsettling. Homi Bhabha has reminded us that the German term *unheimlich*, which Freud references in his theory of the uncanny, more literally translates to "unhomely."[32] In this formulation, the ambivalence of the uncanny derives from the ambivalence of the domestic. What is this ambivalence of the domestic? Explaining that the connotations of *heimlich* (belonging to the house) and *unheimlich* shade into one another, Freud quotes from Grimm's dictionary to theorize the ambivalence of the home: "From the idea of 'homelike,' 'belonging to the house,' the further idea is developed of something withdrawn from the eyes of strangers, something concealed, secret."[33] Interiority, the very quality of the home that produces familiarity, also produces secrecy. That is, it produces what is known and what is unknown. What haunts the home, as in gothic fiction, is this enigma: something intimate yet estranged, familiar yet alien. The crucial point here is that the strangeness produced by apparent exclusion may be more accurately understood as produced by inclusion. Exteriority here is not the opposite of interiority, but its doubling: the interior of the interior. In a similar manner, I will discuss how the apparent alienness of Asian Americans is produced by incorporation and intimacy as well as exclusion and alienation.

It is not surprising that a postcolonial critic like Bhabha would recall the etymological root of the uncanny as unhomely, for colonialism is a condition in which the familiarity of home is made strange, while the strange is made intimate and domestic. Taking a cue from Bhabha, let us also recognize the etymological relationship between "familiarity" and "family." The uncanny's simultaneous familiarity and unfamiliarity references a feeling of kinship that is also estrangement. And as Freud's example of the doll illustrates, this kin relation may also be the "family of man." The inhuman is uncanny not only because it is not human, but because it bears a family resemblance to the human, thus generating the disturbance of intellectual uncertainty. Keeping in mind these links between the uncanny, the un-family, and the inhuman, we see how colonialism precipitated encounters with unfamiliar peoples whose racial strangeness was interpreted as un-family and inhuman. And often it was the nonconformity of native cultures with modern regimes of domesticity that was understood as a distance from civilized humanity and proximity instead to a primitive state of nature.

Bhabha alludes to the intimacies of imperial violence in his statement that "'the recesses of the domestic space become sites for history's most intricate invasions."[34] Grace Cho's *Haunting the Korean Diaspora* provides an exemplary study of how imperial secrets become interred within families and homes. Cho posits that the Korean war bride, the Korean woman who marries a U.S. serviceman and migrates to America, "operates as a figure for the disappearance of geopolitical violence into the realm of the domestic." She then goes on to ask, "What better place to bury a social trauma than in the closely guarded space of the family?"[35] Again, the very characteristics of home and family that render them protective—interiority, insularity—also produce the conditions for incubating and reanimating traumatic secrets. And as in Cho's example of the Korean war bride, critical race studies scholars have elucidated how imperialism, migration, and domesticity converge in U.S. national formations of race. We may thus look to narratives of racial domesticity for symptoms of national expansionism and incorporation.

For Lisa Lowe, the uncanniness of Asian immigration derives from the history of U.S. military and imperialist interventions in Asia: "The material legacy of the repressed history of U.S. imperialism in Asia is borne out in the 'return' of Asian immigrants to the imperial center."[36] I would like to place this interpretation of racial migrants as a symptom of U.S. imperialism in conversation with Amy Kaplan's essay "Manifest Domesticity." Kaplan observes how ideologies of domesticity in nineteenth-century U.S. women's writing helped to structure discourses of expansionism and imperialism as civilizing practices: "The 'Africanist presence' throughout *Uncle Tom's Cabin* is intimately bound to the expansionist logic of domesticity itself. In the writing of Stowe and her contemporary proponents of woman's sphere, 'Manifest Domesticity' turns an imperial nation into a home by producing and colonizing specters of the foreign that lurk inside and outside its ever shifting borders."[37] The American home and the American nation were construed as mutually constitutive civilizing forces. As the doubled interiority of home creates uncanny effects of intellectual uncertainty, so too does the nation's "ever shifting borders" of interior and exterior create uncanny effects. National expansion, which included the recruitment of racial migrants to work on U.S. nation-building and home-making, as well as extraterritorial colonization, meant interiorizing the formerly exterior, blurring the boundaries between the alien and the intimate.

Like the uncanny, the Lacanian concept of the "extimate" also captures the affect of alterity that is produced by Asian American racial formation. The extimate is the external-intimate, the intimate that is radically other, the zone of alterity at the heart of the self.[38] Deviations of race, religion, national origin, gender, sexuality, and class comprise some modes of the national extimate. The notion of the racial extimate gives us insight into one of the most widespread and confounding experiences for second-generation Asian Americans who have come of age in a post–civil rights, ostensibly color-blind era: born and raised in the United States, identifying mainly with American culture, why are they nonetheless treated as cultural aliens? Why are they perceived as so external to Western civilization and its legacies of liberal humanism that they are construed as less than, or more than, human? I will focus on narratives of Asian American family business, especially in its working-class and petit-bourgeois formations, to explain how the children of Asian immigrants inhabit and practice an inhuman citizenship.[39]

Asian American Family Business

Brian Carr begins his essay "At the Thresholds of the 'Human'" with an epigraph from Ridley Scott's 1982 film *Blade Runner,* an exchange between humanoid replicant Rachel and replicant-killer Deckard:

DECKARD: Shakes? Me too. I got 'em bad. Part of the Business.
RACHEL: I'm not in the Business. I am the Business.

Along similar lines, *Inhuman Citizenship* considers how the children of Asian immigrants not only participate in family business but *are themselves family business*. *Blade Runner*, as Carr elaborates, questions and troubles the boundaries between human and nonhuman through its android replicant characters, humanlike machines that are implanted with memories. If our sense of personal identity is constituted by the continuity of our memories, the film implies, then why wouldn't Rachel also identify as a person, a human? Indeed, Rachel, Deckard, and the audience all assume at first that she is human, and we subsequently share in her traumatic realization that she is a replicant, a machine, because of the way that it renders insecure our own assumed human status. The significance of the quoted exchange between Deckard and Rachel, for Carr, is Rachel's pointed reminder to Deckard of her nonhuman, subaltern, and endangered status. She is the object, not the subject, of the Business—the deadly Business of distinguishing human from nonhuman.[40]

Business has been yoked to family through much of Asian American history. Facing racialized barriers to entry in many occupational fields, a significant number of Asian immigrants turned to small business enterprises that could benefit from the unpaid labor of family members.[41] While nineteenth- and twentieth-century industrialization in the United States and Europe produced modern forms of domesticity separate from work, Asian immigrant families, including children, often worked together in a common economic enterprise. To reformulate *Blade Runner*'s distinction, these children are *in the business* and they also *are the business*.

I define Asian American family business as denoting two meanings: (1) the economic and entrepreneurial practices that produce financial resources for sustaining the family; and (2) the ideologies and practices that go into maintaining the family itself as a cohesive institution. In contrast to modern domestic norms of childhood as a time of innocence from economic imperative, Asian American family business permeates the child with financial and ideological demands. The child participates in family business as productive labor, and the child embodies family business as reproductive labor—labor that includes the production of the self as a commodity of cultural capital.[42]

The involvement of children in family business and their status as objects of family business render Asian American domesticity deviant, and even inhuman. The imbrication of family with business taints the ideal of family as a site for cultivating human sentiment. If families are ideally structured by personal emotions and acts such as unconditional love, care, and nurturance, then impersonal conditions such as profit, loss, and competition can only degrade and dehumanize the family. Colleen Lye has noted how an Asian presence in the United States is identified with "the social costs of unbridled capitalism."[43] Asian American family business keenly shows how these social costs include the loss and contamination of an ideal, sentimental, and human family.

The novels in this study narrate how second-generation Asian American subjects are formed by and as family business. As children of immigrants, they mediate and sometimes translate between private and public spheres, between parents and public institutions. With one or both parents working long hours, older children may take on the role of helping to raise younger siblings (reproductive labor), and children may be expected to "help out" with family business through service or manual work (productive labor). erin Khuě Ninh has aptly called Asian immigrant families "cottage industries" for the production of model children—children who generate economic and cultural capital for the family.[44] These second-generation children are objects as well as subjects of production and reproduction. Ninh's term "cottage industries" highlights how Asian American domesticity is the site of such production, deviating from the separate-spheres ideal of home as a location that is uncorrupted by the impersonal realm of political economy (the "haven in a heartless world," in Christopher Lasch's well-known phrase).[45]

In *Consuming Citizenship,* an ethnographic study of children of Asian immigrant entrepreneurs, Lisa Park uses the terms "premature adulthood" and "prolonged childhood" to refer to the particular temporality of development for children who participate in Asian American family business: "Premature adulthood is the placement of an individual who is considered a child (as indicated by age and developmental level) in adult-like roles with adult responsibilities. Conversely, then, a prolonged childhood is the placement of an individual who is socially considered an adult into child-like roles with child-like responsibilities. The importance of both phenomena lies in the fact that they are out of synch with the larger, socially determined concept of adulthood and childhood."[46] Park also expresses a more concise formulation of these developmental phenomena as "children who grow up too fast and, as young adults, never age."[47] Premature adulthood seems readily understandable, referring to children taking on the adult responsibilities of work in the family business. However, the simultaneous state of prolonged childhood requires some explanation: How is the premature adult also an over-mature child? Although prolonged childhood might seem to be the inverse of premature adulthood, in fact both conditions result from the same dynamic. Many immigrant parents depend on their children, who are more linguistically flexible, to sustain the family; this includes translating and mediating for the parents in the public sphere. Immigration often means a downward shift in social status due to the devaluing of one's language, education, and racial status. Because of this low social status, and sometimes because of the conditions of low-wage immigrant work, children of immigrants are keenly aware of their parents' vulnerability and disempowerment. This is why the work that children of immigrants do to support the family business includes the emotional work of worrying about their parents.[48]

The child of immigrants who participates in family business is thus rendered deviant in temporality, simultaneously over- and underdeveloped. She is foreclosed from normative citizenship and indeed normative humanity by this simultaneous excess and lack. On the one hand, this is the child who knows too much, who is not innocent enough to embody the hopeful futurism of the potential citizen.[49] On the other hand, even as an adult, she remains childlike in her attachment to her parents and her ethnic culture. She has not achieved "appropriate" maturity and individuation, and thus lacks the capacity for autonomous self-governance. This lack of individuation and autonomy means that she is not fully developed as human, even as a premature exposure to adulthood produces a traumatic knowingness that marks her as excessively human.

Most of the novels in this study devastatingly refute the hegemonic notion that the child of U.S. immigrants represents a hopeful future. In national mythologies of immigrant romance, multiracial democracy, and American exceptionalism, the child represents the future in the sense of ethnic succession. This idea of ethnic succession installs a belief that the child of immigrants embodies the ethnic and national progress of an Americanization figured as a full human self-actualization. In immigrant mythology, the immigrant "sacrifices" so that her child may have an American future. This is a teleological narrative or fantasy of the nation: America as the natural endpoint for all persons. While the immigrant is imagined as hoping and dreaming of the future, the child is the site where dreams are supposed to be realized, actualized. Put simply, the child is the very telos of America. But what if these novels provide not narratives of subject formation, but narratives of subject antiformation? What if the child develops not into a fully human citizen-subject but into the inhuman?

INHUMAN CITIZENSHIP

I deliberately mean for my book title, *Inhuman Citizenship*, to evoke the contradictions of the racial nation-state. Referring to major concepts of political modernity such as citizenship, the state, and democracy, Dipesh Chakrabarty observes that these political formations assume a "universal and secular vision of the human."[50] If citizenship in a liberal democracy is based on the "inalienable rights of man," the rights that accrue to those of human status, then how does racialized deviation from human status put this citizenship into crisis? How might citizenship not only exclude, but also be supported by, the racial inhuman? And how can we conceive of inhuman citizenship as a form of agency that is not quite human? That is, inhuman citizenship is not only a condition that is imposed by power. It is also a redeployment of power and even an ethical claim.

For Lacan, ethics involves the subject's relationship to her symptom and her fundamental fantasy. One of Lacan's many counterintuitive theoretical moves was to denaturalize what we assume to be the subject's most personal property: her unconscious. Instead of embodying the subject's innermost truth, he posited, the unconscious is a most foreign element, consisting of signifiers from the Other as the Symbolic order. The unconscious is conceived here not as individual, but as *trans*individual.[51] And contrary to popular fears that psychoanalysis absolves individual responsibility because of its emphasis on the unconscious, a force beyond our will and conscious control, Lacanian ethics do demand responsibility for the unconscious, although indeed its formations are beyond our control and not our own. Lacanian psychoanalysis asks the subject not to identify with his ego, but instead with his symptom, with the Thing that is most foreign and most intimate. This act of "subjective destitution" constitutes the end of analysis, for the subject can no longer constitute himself in the same way as before.[52]

Lacan specifically uses the term "act" to refer to this ethical undertaking, the assumption of responsibility for the unconscious and for the symptom. I would like to think of Lisa Lowe's phrase "immigrant acts," which she uses to denote Asian American cultural production, in conjunction with this Lacanian meaning of the act:

> By insisting on "immigrant acts" as contradictions and therefore as dialectical and critical, I also mean to emphasize that while immigration has been the *locus* of legal and political restriction of Asians as the "other" in America, immigration has simultaneously been the site for the emergence of critical negations of the nation-state for which these legislations are the expression. . . . "Immigrant acts" names the *agency* of Asian immigrants and Asian Americans: the acts of labor, resistance, memory, and survival, as well as the politicized cultural work that emerges from dislocation and disidentification.[53]

While acknowledging the disenfranchisement produced by the racialization of native-born Asian Americans as alien and immigrant, I would like to continue with Lowe's expansive definition of "immigrant acts" to include all Asian Americans.[54] One of the insights of a politicized psychoanalysis is the way that trauma is transmitted transgenerationally, so that children may experience memories of what never happened to them.[55] This is a prime example of how the unconscious is transindividual, and we may consider how the agency and acts of the children of immigrants are also transindividual. In *Inhuman Citizenship,* the work of Asian American cultural production is interpreted as immigrant and ethical acts that contribute to the subjective destitution of the nation; such acts practice and compel a collective assumption of responsibility for the unconscious symptoms of the U.S. nation-state. This undoing of the national subject is achieved through breaking the spell of its fundamental fantasy of American exceptionalism: the notion of America as an exceptional site of color-blind democracy, equal opportunity, and universal citizenship. In the novels that I examine, the children of Asian immigrants come to terms with this fundamental fantasy of the nation. Their mode of subjective destitution entails identification with the symptom of this fantasy: the racial inhuman as the site of traumatic enjoyment. In this ethical act of acceding to the position of the racial inhuman—identifying with the national symptom—they assume responsibility for a national unconscious that is all too often disclaimed.

The first chapter, "Melancholic Citizenship," provides a template for my study, demonstrating how domestic secrets and symptoms may be understood as signs of inhuman citizenship. I consider Fae Myenne Ng's novel *Bone* as a narrative of domestic restructuring during the early phase of late twentieth-century neoliberalism. The emergence of Chinese Americans into heteronormative domesticity would seem to augur their entrance into "reproductive futurism," Lee Edelman's phrase for the temporality that forms the horizon of political legibility. This normative family formation, so distinct from the early twentieth-century legacy of Chinese immigrant bachelor societies, presumably signals the arrival of full citizenship and national belonging. We find, however, that the impossibility of life for Ona, who as the Child signifies the hope of reproductive futurism, repeats the impossibility of life for the old bachelors. Ng also indexes the forestalling of the future through her structure of reverse chronology, in which the novel moves backward in time. The peculiar temporality of *Bone* means that we cannot incorporate its characters into modern, developmental paradigms of racial assimilation and national progress. Instead, I demonstrate how they inhabit a suspended, extraneous state that I call the living dead. As noted in my earlier citation of Žižek, the undead are neither living nor dead. Rather, they are a strange surplus of life, exceeding the Symbolic order of a national, capitalist modernity. We must look to the supernatural for an understanding of the book's inhuman epistemology of counting those who are unaccounted for in the nation's Symbolic economy.

Like *Bone,* Brian Ascalon Roley's novel *American Son* also strikes at the foundations of modernity, in particular at law and the gaze of power. In chapter 2, "Shameful Citizenship," I demonstrate how racial shame is produced for the enjoyment of the hegemonic gaze of the nation. By revealing this traumatic enjoyment as the obscene underside of modernity, *American Son* critiques the assumption that modern power is neutral, impersonal, abstract, and universal. In tandem, the novel also interrogates the human as a hallmark of modernity by highlighting its imbrication with animal jouissance. *American Son* narrates a trajectory that the Filipino American narrator, Gabe Sullivan, unsuccessfully resists—what Deleuze and Guattari have termed "becoming-animal." The novel's cathartic climax finds the narrator transformed into a lawless brute. Thus, my formulation of the term animal jouissance refers not only to the Sullivan family business of selling attack dogs, but also to the enjoyment derived from the hegemonic rendering of the indeterminate brown subject as primitive and lawless. Citizenship is an agreement to submit to the rule of law, as well as a claim to the agency of shaping the law. Because the Sullivans are deemed lawless, they are excluded from legitimate citizenship. However, I argue that their condition and practices of shameful citizenship do serve the purposes of nation and capital as well as threaten them. I conclude the chapter by meditating on how the Sullivan family business of animal jouissance derives from legacies of U.S. imperial nationalism—including the colonization and neocolonization of the Philippines—as itself also a family business, writ large, of producing jouissance.

If *American Son* is a novel about the Asian American subject "becoming-animal," then Chang-rae Lee's *Native Speaker* is a narrative about the Asian American "becoming-human." The Korean American narrator, Henry Park, is figured as alien to American culture in his emotional opacity; within the first few pages, his white wife Lelia calls him an "emotional alien." If citizenship is a status that can accrue only to humans, as those with the right to rights, then Henry must transform himself from an affect alien to a sympathetic human in order to be recognized as a legitimate subject of the nation.[56] In chapter 3, "Romantic Citizenship," I interpret family business in *Native Speaker* as the production of national fantasy, taking the form of romance between the immigrant and the nation. By teasing out the private and public modes of romantic citizenship, I hope to illuminate the psychic vicissitudes of U.S. nationalist feeling. The narrative presents us with two major blocks to romantic citizenship: the recalcitrant migrant woman worker, and the underground economy organized around undocumented migrants. Both are sites of too much enjoyment, rendering them opaque to the hegemonic gaze. Henry's job is to render these migrants transparent and knowable in the public sphere, while his marriage requires him similarly to open himself up in the domestic sphere. Offering his heart to his wife and to the nation, Henry humanizes himself by practicing romantic citizenship.

While I loosely consider the previous novels to be narratives of domesticity, I would call Suki Kim's *The Interpreter* an antidomestic narrative. The protagonist, Suzy Park, does not feel settled or secure in her apartment, instead treating it as a temporary shelter from unknown dangers. She relinquishes her claims on family, and she contravenes the bonds of marriage by seeking affairs with married men. How can we explain Suzy's antidomesticity, in which she not only avoids, but actively destroys, domestic forms and connections? What might this antidomesticity reveal about gendered racial citizenship and U.S nation-state formation? In chapter 4, "Perverse Citizenship," I theorize Suzy's antidomesticity as a manifestation of the death drive. This death drive, it turns out, is a legacy of her family business, in which her parents served as informants to the U.S. state, resulting in the deportation of numerous co-ethnic migrants. Drawing from Lacan's notion of the pervert as the instrument of the Other's jouissance, I argue that the Park family's perverse citizenship reveals the violence and enjoyment that underlie national fantasies, especially the myth of America as an exceptionalist and innocent site of new beginnings. In its tropes of perverse rebirth, *The Interpreter* suggests how U.S. nation-statehood is structured by the death drive, by tendencies toward destruction that produce race not as lack but as surplus: life that exceeds the Symbolic.

I conclude the book with a meditation on the infectiousness of enjoyment. While I note throughout how Asian American characters assume their status as the embodiment of enjoyment, my coda illustrates how they also transmit and circulate enjoyment. In circulating jouissance, they confound human status not only for themselves but also for the normative citizen-subject and indeed for the nation itself.

1 Melancholic Citizenship

The Living Dead and Fae Myenne Ng's Bone

"What makes their ugliness so alive, so thick and impossible to let go of?" (35). Leila, the narrator of Fae Myenne Ng's novel *Bone*, describes the marital strife of her mother and stepfather as a live, unseemly profusion to which both parties are painfully attached. The chronic heartache of family life, and its most obvious manifestation in the suicide of Leila's sister, Ona, accounts for the pervasive tone of grief and sorrow throughout the novel. Yet Leila herself often displays a flat affect in her narration. She explains this repression of her feelings in a passage on managing family trauma: "I'd been worried about Mah and Leon and I hadn't given myself time to feel. . . . All the duties had kept me occupied, safe from the true emotion" (151, 153). How does Leila's role in her family business explain this gap between her emotionally sparse narration and the novel's dominant affect of sadness? What is the relationship between the submergence of Leila's feelings and the too-live traumas of Mah and Leon's marriage? How, in other words, is second-generation Asian American affect impacted by the sticky, adhesive quality of immigrant parental pain in *Bone*? How, in other words, does the sticky, adhesive quality of immigrant parental pain in *Bone* have an impact on second-generation Asian American affect? I examine this intergenerational dynamic using the psychoanalytic paradigm of melancholia, a practice that accounts for the jouissance of working-class Chinese American domesticity by animating what would otherwise be left for dead. Leila, as the narrator and the translator for the family, generally transforms the too-live Real into the deadness of the Symbolic. Her sister Ona, however, is not given any such mandate. Inheriting the traumatic enjoyment of her parents' lives, she performs her legacy as an excess of life. This chapter will consider Ona and

28

other characters as the living dead: the living who are left for dead as well as the dead who should be living.

Leila is frequently startled and taken aback by her own behaviors. "My harsh tone surprised me. . . . The mug hit the table harder than I intended. . . . I was surprised at my accusing tone. . . . I didn't realize my force, but I dropped it" (48, 62, 97, 144). Such mundane, everyday shocks are eruptions from her unconscious that demand recognition. I will explore this unconscious affect as encrypted secrets, not only at the level of the personal and domestic but the national as well. *Bone* presents us with a second-generation narrator who must manage her immigrant parents, resulting in the burial of her own emotions and desires. Leila's domestic responsibilities form a kind of grave for her suppressed feelings, covering over and encrypting any emotion that is judged extraneous to family survival. While growing up, Leila finds that her subconscious is colonized by family worries. After the death of Grandpa Leong, an adolescent Leila lies in bed at night while Mah does her sewing work and consults Leila about family plans.

> At home, late at night, she would ask me: Should we have a wake, too? What kind of coffin? Should it be open or shut? What to write on the gravestone? How to pick a burial site? Was Nina too young to go? Should we all wear hemp? Who would sing the lament songs? Should we hire a professional mourner?
>
> My bedroom was also the sewing room, so I lay in bed, listening to all Mah's worries. . . . All I remember is staring up at the ceiling, waiting for sleep, wishing for the right answer. (79–80)

Leila's bedroom is the site of family business in its dimensions of both economic survival (Mah's sewing work) and the support of family as an institution (decision making about family rituals). In *Bone*, the domestic sphere is not a space that protects the child from the hardships of the economic sphere. For the three daughters in the novel, but most notably for Leila, domestic space is one of reproductive and productive labor. As the eldest, Leila is interpellated as the parentalized child, the child who assumes the worries and burdens of a parent. Structurally responsible for her family as the bilingual eldest daughter, Leila cannot afford to acknowledge her own feelings because she must manage those of her family members. Such emotions and concerns take the form of the unspoken, a remainder that is encrypted. In one of the novel's many convergences of the literal and metaphorical, this scene provides us with images of coffins, gravestones, and burial sites, even as Leila's unspoken feelings become interred by the imperative to listen to Mah. As a novel haunted by death and loss, it seems especially appropriate to read *Bone* through the critical lens of melancholia, a concept that has become paradigmatic in postcolonial and critical race studies.[1]

While melancholia, like its companion concept, mourning, is commonly understood as a response to loss, this chapter demonstrates the importance of understanding how an epistemology of melancholia allows us to comprehend *excess* as well as loss. Melancholia is a practice of animating the lost object, imbuing this absence with a presence that should not be. I use the trope of the living dead to reference how melancholia keeps alive what is otherwise abandoned for dead. The living dead are not simply alive; they are a disturbing surplus of life substance, a category beyond the continuum of living and dead. A reading of Ng's novel through the lens of melancholia allows us to understand racial labor exploitation as constituting this kind of superfluous life.

The recruitment and exploitation of Chinese male labor in the late nineteenth and early twentieth century was an integral part of U.S. nation-building during the period of continental and imperial expansion. We can see how the Chinese were racialized as alien and temporary workers by immigration laws and practices that discouraged the formation of Chinese immigrant families. In the late twentieth century, such racial labor exploitation became less obvious, with the apparent shift to more "open" immigration policies that permitted the formation of Chinese American families and thus an acceptance of Chinese as potentially permanent members of the nation. However, we will see how such family formation does in fact facilitate racial labor exploitation in the service of late Cold War imperial nationalism, albeit in a different form.

Through an understanding of how the sorrows of racial domesticity are formed in a melancholic citizenship, *Bone* helps us to apprehend the encrypted secrets of a liberal and emergent neoliberal nation-state formation. In particular, I will focus on how forces of neoliberalism, including the "openings" of immigration in the 1960s, restructure the national economy in its dimension as an economy of sacrifice. By sacrifice, I mean the transformation of a social antagonism or contradiction into an ejected surplus, so as to reconstitute the social as coherent and whole. In my analysis of *Bone,* I consider how racial immigrant workers are figured as this sacrificial surplus. This status means that they become surplus to the national Symbolic, even as their labor is extracted to build American economic power. Posited as the excess of the Symbolic, they are the nation's living dead.

Bone is dedicated to Ng's great-grandfather, Ah Sam. In interviews and remarks about *Bone,* Ng often refers to similar grandfatherly figures—the "old-timers" of San Francisco Chinatown. Such frequent references to a historical and elderly generation of men are especially striking and even puzzling when we consider that the novel centers on the travails of three contemporary young women. Indeed, the very first sentences of *Bone* would seem to invite a reading that aligns it with famous Chinese American woman-centered narratives, such as Maxine Hong Kingston's *The Woman Warrior* and Amy Tan's *The Joy Luck Club:* "We were a family of three girls. By Chinese standards, that wasn't lucky" (3). Chinese American woman-centered texts are often understood within a liberal multicultural feminist framework as narratives of ethnicized female subordination and liberation. Like liberal nationalism, however, liberal feminism presumes its own kinds of teleology, understanding racial-ethnic women as oppressed by ethnic and white patriarchies, and achieving self-actualization through practices of freedom and autonomy. Under this paradigm, the lives of young Chinese American women would seem quite discontinuous from those of the old bachelors. While the grandfather figures may be considered remnants of an old-world patriarchy or of a long-ago racist era, these young women are understood as figures supplanting such anachronisms. Ng's dedication and comments provoke us to question, however, how the lives of these young Chinese American women resonate with, not merely against, those of the old bachelors.

The novel is set at a key historic moment, when large numbers of this younger generation are coming of age and as families become more established in Chinatown. In this chapter, I will highlight how this domestic restructuring is produced by the emerging forces of global capital and neoliberal state formation. In this way, I interpret Ng's narration as an examination of how the prehistory of neoliberalism restructured Chinatown domesticity.

Histories of neoliberalism posit its ascendance in the period of the early 1980s, when the policies of Ronald Reagan and Margaret Thatcher intensified the dismantling of the welfare state and the consolidation of the deregulated, privatized market economy.[2] *Bone*'s historical setting roughly corresponds to this period, at the very beginnings of neoliberal consolidation.[3] When we analyze the novel's narration of Chinatown's domestic restructuring, we can already detect some elements of an emergent neoliberalism. Specifically, we see that the support and management of racial migrant labor takes place in the private sphere of family, not the public sphere of government. Put another way, governmentality and biopolitics have already been shifted into the private sphere for racial communities, even in this very early, emergent phase.

Neoliberalism structures family business in both its economic and institutional forms. While all members of the family work to sustain the family economically, it is Leila who assumes the greatest responsibility for maintaining the family as an institution. This means that Leila, as the child of immigrants, becomes accountable for the management and support of migrant labor. The opening excerpt depicting Leila as her mother's interlocutor and consultant is just one example of such family management. Because of the imperatives of collective survival, there is no room for Leila's individualized desires. This is not to say that such desires do not exist; rather, they are rendered as excess and transformed into secrets. Indeed, Leila even uses the form of the secret to transform the burden of her obligations into a sticky enjoyment: "I was afraid my secret guilt would start to grow sweet, and I would never want to spit it out" (106).

Bone reveals the secret guilt and enjoyment not only of its main character but also of the U.S. nation. Even as it is haunted by the racial labor exploitation that is both at the heart of its economy and in excess of its official mythos, the nation also enjoys it. For example, as I will discuss below, the old bachelors of Chinatown are hegemonically perceived as a kind of repellant, obscene surplus of the nation. They are sites of a racial jouissance that allow the nation to disavow its own inner antagonisms and to displace the disturbing affect of antagonism onto the Imaginary other.

Dominant narratives of the modern nation-state are structured by Enlightenment values of development and progress. They are modern in the sense that they are linear and accumulative, rather than cyclical and recursive. In the post–civil rights and late Cold War era, the American version of this national fiction took the form of an exceptionalist myth of multiracial democratic openness. The United States claimed a unique and exceptional status in basing its offer of full citizenship on consent rather than descent. In this developmental paradigm, racial migrants and racial subjects would progress along an arc of ever-higher socioeconomic maturity, thus enabling American democracy to become evermore complete. Such a linear, sequential account of national modernity enabled the late Cold War formation of U.S. global hegemony. The United States relied on this claim to exceptional multiracial democracy for its mantle of moral leadership: it proclaimed itself the exemplar and arbiter of liberal openness, economic progress, and human rights.

Because capitalism and liberal democracy are fused together in this mythos, where freedom is equivalent to the free market, the capitalist ideology of progress is tied to this notion of progress. A foundational myth of U.S. capitalism is that everyone, of all socioeconomic strata, has an equal opportunity to accumulate. In the ideology of 1980s Reaganomics, for example, the accumulation of wealth in the upper classes will "trickle down" to everyone else. Through deregulation of the market, in which the "freeing" of economic activity uses the trope of political liberty, all participants presumably become unencumbered so that their choices and their opportunities to accumulate become limitless. Such material achievement acquires a spiritual and transcendent dimension by being fantasized into the American Dream.

Let us clarify further the relationship between racial migrant labor and the emergence of neoliberal and imperial nation-statehood. The ascendance of U.S. global hegemony, its economic preeminence and might, relied upon the surplus value extracted from a cheap and mobile migrant labor force. In tandem, the ideological enfolding of racial migration into multiracial exceptionalism formed part of the apparatus for recruiting such migrant labor from around the world. As a result of the 1965 Immigration Acts, family reunification became the major category for the recruitment of this type of labor, which meant that new migrant populations were both supported by and subject to regulation by their families and communities. In this way, they were outside the modern (impersonal, bureaucratic) rationality of industrialized labor. In other words, support and management of racial labor became privatized, the realm of the private spheres of family and community, not the public spheres of work, the formal economy, or the state.[4]

Within a national mythos of multiracial democratic progress, the domestic restructuring of Chinatown is understood as an incorporation of racial subjects into full citizenship. In Lee Edelman's terms, the production of families as signaled through the reproduction of children would mean that

Chinese Americans have entered into the normative temporality of "reproductive futurism," the mode through which we understand politics as such. In *No Future*, Edelman argues that political decision making, as well as politics itself, is circumscribed by the ideology of the ideal, mythical child as the figure of the future. To the extent that queerness is excluded from such reproductive futurism, it is excluded from politics and indeed from sociality. Edelman's critique, however, presupposes a universal figure of the child, a trope of privilege whose whiteness is unstated. My analysis of *Bone* reveals how the racial child and heteronormative family do not in fact represent reproductive futurism. Instead, they animate the past and produce the inhuman figure of the living dead.[5]

Bone is not a ghost story in the conventional sense. While Ona is a haunting presence, she does not appear in spectral form to address Leila directly. However, the questions ignited by Ona's death are clearly the driving force of the narrative, which repeatedly turns to the problems of meaning and cause. One chapter ends with a literal repetition that turns the question from one of meaning into a performance of linguistic jouissance: "Why. Why. Why. Why. Why?" (133). Even in trying to find a rational cause for Ona's death, Leila's articulation cannot escape the senselessness of her profound and traumatic loss.

In Avery Gordon's formulation, the ghost is the figure that demands justice and seeks balance amid the chaos of historical trauma.[6] I address this ghostly demand for justice through a supernatural interpretation of the novel, an epistemology distinct from that of secular modernity and humanism. Through this supernatural interpretation, I show that Ona activates an alternative economy. This economy is supernatural because it counts and values the living dead: the surplus to the modern, rational, national Symbolic order; the excess produced by a neoliberal, imperial nation-state.

A psychoanalytic reading of *Bone* illuminates how Chinatown family business requires the encryption of secrets and also how it *is* an encrypted secret. First let me address how relations between family members demand the production of secrets. Mah's affair and Ona's transgressive romance cannot be spoken of because of the pain that they cause Leon, while Leila's feelings and emotions are routinely buried because she must first attend to the caretaking of others. Leila's role as second-generation caretaker, as manager of migrant labor, requires that her own feelings become encrypted secrets: the unspoken.

I interpret such domestic secrecy as a symptom of racial citizenship. Domestic secrets in *Bone* reveal a concealed kernel at the heart of the nation-state: the continuation of racial sacrifice in the form of labor exploitation. This is how Chinatown family business *is* an encrypted secret. In the mid- and late twentieth century, Chinese immigration patterns shifted so that families, rather than "bachelors," came to constitute Chinatown and other Chinese immigrant communities.[7] This shift, which was largely facilitated by the immigration category of family reunification, has been presumed to mean that the Chinese have assimilated into national norms of domesticity and liberal citizenship. What we learn in *Bone*, however, is that family becomes a primary site of labor, both productive and reproductive. In this way, racial labor exploitation continues to live on, past the period in which it has presumably expired. Chinese American family business, as both economic practice and social institution, as the business of providing and managing low-wage and informal labor for the nation, becomes an encrypted secret, disavowed because it is not incorporable into myths of multiracial equality, universal citizenship, and American exceptionalism.

I will consider the significance of the living dead as embodied variously by *Bone*'s characters. And I will investigate how melancholia acknowledges and produces the living dead, and how this figure of the inhuman calls for us to rethink racial citizenship as one of surplus. As examples of such surplus, I highlight three tropes from the novel: secrets, bones, and the old bachelors of Chinatown. Surprisingly, Leon, the family man, practices a lifestyle similar to these old bachelors; though they signify a social existence on the wane, their way of life (and excess of life substance) eerily continues in Leon. Our contemporary frameworks of Asian American studies allow us to comprehend the old men as workers who were hyper-exploitable by their racial disfranchisement, which expressed itself partly through exclusion from heteronormative domesticity. Mah and Leila, as wife and daughter, are supposed to signify the progress made by U.S. multiracial democracy in accepting the Chinese as full and permanent citizen-subjects. However, I interpret Mah and Leila as encrypted secrets of the nation: the continuation of racial labor exploitation in the form of women, children, and family.

MELANCHOLIA

At first glance, it would appear that we could read *Bone* as a sequel of sorts to Louis Chu's 1961 novel *Eat a Bowl of Tea*. If *Eat a Bowl of Tea* charts the tumultuous transformation of New York Chinatown from "bachelor society" to "family community" in the middle of the twentieth century, *Bone* would seem to represent the late twentieth-century result of that transformation. *Eat a Bowl of Tea* portrays the waning years of Wang Wah Gay and his fellow Chinatown "bachelors," men whose labor was recruited by the United States and who ended up unable to establish families. The homosociality of this bachelor society, whose members are past their productive years, is marked in Chu's novel by gendered practices of gambling, gossiping, joking, and cursing. The settling of Wang's son Ben Loy with his new bride in Chinatown represents the hope of renewal for a community previously unable to reproduce itself through conventional family formation: the old men wait anxiously and collectively for a grandchild to signify a sense of future they have otherwise been denied.[8] *Bone* features Leila Fu, just such a grandchild of an old "bachelor," as its narrator.[9] Moreover, Ng's novel is set in San Francisco, the city where the newly married couple of *Eat a Bowl of Tea* must relocate to start anew. Indeed, *Bone* also begins with a newly married couple: Leila and Mason have just eloped in New York City and have returned to San Francisco. Rather than a site of regeneration and reproductive futurism, however, Ng's San Francisco Chinatown proves to be the site of loss and melancholia. While in *Eat a Bowl of Tea*, family represents the potential for moving forward into the future, in *Bone*, family and narrative remain haunted and traumatized by the past. The novel's very structure, its reverse chronology, takes us increasingly into this past.

Therefore, rather than reading Chu's and Ng's texts according to a logic of sequential, historical time in which the present naturally follows and fully replaces the past, I propose instead a temporal paradigm based on the notion of text as palimpsest, as multilayered. *Bone's* narrative is structured palimpsestically, in a chronology that moves back in time to reveal what lies underneath the events that Leila narrates in the novel's beginning. This palimpsestic composition is characteristic of melancholia, a condition in which an object that should be relegated to the past is instead psychically kept alive in the present. By comprehending how time is layered such that the past is not erased but remains alive in the present, a palimpsestic reading practice offers an alternative to modern conceptions of time and history as horizontal, linear, and continuous. Benedict Anderson observes that this "homogeneous, empty" time of modernity is also the time of the nation, and that subjects of the nation are constituted within the horizontal simultaneity of this national time.

In this chapter, I show how Ng's melancholic temporality critiques the myths of American exceptionalism that facilitate the country's global hegemony. The historic changes in domestic configurations that we see in *Bone* appear to herald the entrance of Chinese Americans into the modernity of national citizenship, as well as the making of the United States into a premier site of racial and global openness. However, in the novel we see how the contemporary, heteronormative domesticity of Chinatown is haunted and traumatized by earlier histories of deviant domesticity and labor exploitation. This haunted domesticity enables us to understand the structure of Asian American citizenship as melancholic, and this melancholic citizenship reveals what is in excess of the national Symbolic, what remains after history is told through nationalist narratives of development and multiracial incorporation.

As the subject of the nation, the citizen is defined by a certain kind of relationship to time: she participates in recalling the collective memory that has been narrated as national history. This memory is selective, consisting of events that provide ideological support for nationalism, so that memory also means "remember[ing] to forget."[10] Remembering (to forget) is a process of incorporating the past into the Symbolic of national history. And, as psychoanalytic theory reminds us, symbolization always produces its remainder or surplus—in this case, the forgotten. Unassimilated and unresolved, the remainder becomes a secret kernel that returns to haunt the Symbolic. Nicolas Abraham and Maria Torok build upon Freud's theory of melancholia to elaborate on this haunting of the remainder. According to Freud, melancholia is the condition of unresolved mourning, in which the subject internalizes the lost object, rather than acknowledging the loss and breaking attachment to the object. Abraham and Torok use the terms "introjection" and "incorporation" to differentiate between mourning and melancholia. Introjection is a process in which the loss of the object is acknowledged and assimilated by the subject, while incorporation refers to an imagined "swallowing" of the object itself (126). Refusing to acknowledge the loss, the subject keeps the object alive in a psychic crypt, and the incorporated object assumes the status of an encrypted secret within the subject's psyche.

Abraham and Torok further theorize that secrets can be encrypted and transmitted across generations: their term for this transmitted secret is the "phantom" (171–86). In this theory, the crypt preserves the lost object in order to disavow the loss, but the disavowed trauma of the loss is then passed on to the next generation. This conceptualization of traumatic re-pression as transindividual is useful for understanding how psychic phenomena operate not only at the level of the individual subject but also at the level of groups and nations. The notion of the phantom, of a psychic condition that is not entirely one's own, challenges modern and liberal notions of the subject as autonomous, whole, self-identical, and self-possessed. While the proper subject of the nation-state must *remember* the past, assimilating it into the national Symbolic, the melancholic and phantomatic subject *embodies* the past, improperly keeping alive what has not been symbolized. Abraham and Torok refer to this materialization as "demetaphorization," taking literally what is meant figuratively (132). If introjection means assimilation into the Symbolic, then incorporation is accompanied by a failure of language: "The crucial move away from introjection . . . to incorporation is made when *words* fail to fill the subject's void and hence an imaginary thing is inserted in the mouth in their place" (128–29). In *Bone,* this melancholic demetaphorization becomes a strategy of making palpable what has been encrypted by the subject and the nation, the remainder that is subtracted to form the national Symbolic. Ona Leong, whose suicide and powerful absence haunt the novel, is the most obvious subject of melancholia. We will see, however, how this melancholia does not only belong to her but is also a condition that she inherits from her father, Leon, from her racial community, and from the nation-state itself.[11] This haunted citizenship, a condition of being possessed by a trauma that is not one's own, decidedly departs from the norm of the self-possessed subject of liberal citizenship. National histories live on and linger, traumatizing racial citizenship.

In a palimpsestic reading of *Bone,* we can observe how Ng's contemporary representation of Chinatown manifests traces of earlier inscriptions of it. Nineteenth- and early twentieth-century U.S. immigration laws and policies resulted in a Chinese immigration population that was overwhelmingly male. Chinese men were recruited for their labor, and Chinese women were largely excluded by the enforcement of laws that construed them as "imported" for "immoral" purposes.[12] Discouraging the formation of Chinese families in the United States ensured a cheap and mobile labor force and allayed national anxieties about the potentially permanent settlement of an "alien" race. In the middle of the twentieth century, however, the United States faced international scrutiny for its racially exclusionary immigration policies because it promoted itself during World War II as an exemplar of democratic openness. During the Cold War, this democratic representation of the United States was considered a premier ideological weapon as the United States battled the Soviet Union for global hegemony. In order to don the mantle of moral leadership, the United States rescinded and reformed its exclusionary immigration laws. Such changes permitted the entry of Chinese women in far more substantial numbers, and greater numbers of Chinese American families were established, beginning in the 1950s.[13] Thus, Chinese American history is conventionally narrated in terms of domesticity, as a trajectory from "bachelor" to "family" sociality. We can see in *Bone*, however, how the contemporary formation of a heteronormative family in fact embodies traces of earlier "bachelor" histories. My psychoanalytic reading of domesticity in *Bone* observes how the intergenerational transmission of encrypted secrets structures family formation and family business. In reading these encrypted secrets at the level of domesticity, we also find an encrypted secret at the level of the neoliberal nation: its construction of and reliance on the hyperexploitation of racial immigrant labor, which, I argue, constructs these workers as the living dead. Immigration laws that permitted Chinese American family formation did not end the racial labor exploitation signified by Chinatown bachelor sociality; rather, they restructured such racial labor exploitation to include women as well as children of immigrants. In this way, the business (as preoccupation) of Chinese American families became Chinese American family business (as economic occupation).

During the Cold War era, racial difference was ideologically introjected, or assimilated, into the national Symbolic as evidence of an exceptional, multiracial democratic openness. According to this national narrative, the racial immigrant enjoyed the freedom provided by the equality of opportunity, and this freedom allowed her to follow a trajectory from initial hardship to eventual fulfillment and belonging. What was subtracted and covered over by this developmental narrative was capitalist exploitation on behalf of an imperial, and emergingly neoliberal, nation-state. The interests of capital and nation-statehood demanded minimal wages for labor so that profits could be maximized, thereby providing an economic basis for the global hegemony sought by the United States. And such exploitation of labor, enabled by the disfranchisement of racial populations, was unowned, disavowed, and covered over by national ideologies of exceptionalist democratic equality. Indispensable yet unacknowledged, the exploited racial worker was thus produced as the secret melancholic object of the

U.S. nation-state. By secret, I mean the concealed and buried heart of the nation—its hidden core utility and enjoyment. This essential possession is at the same time an excess, disavowed and expelled from the national Symbolic.

As a number of critics have demonstrated, modernity and modern nation-statehood are often articulated through tropes of family and sexuality.[14] If the premodern primitive or savage is interpreted as a figure of unregulated sexuality, then the modern family, as the site of legitimate and reproductive sexuality, stands as a sign of civilization and humanity, modernity and nation. From the mid-nineteenth century to the mid-twentieth century, Chinatowns were perceived as racial ghettos inhabited primarily by male "bachelors," and secondarily by a far smaller number of female "prostitutes." The absence of heteronormative nuclear family formation had the effect of inscribing Chinatown morality and sexuality as lewd and debauched: perverse, drug-addicted, pedophilic, syphilitic. Chinese men and women were represented as morally and medically endangering the health of white families, and by extension, the health of the United States as a white, Christian nation. As Nayan Shah's *Contagious Divides* demonstrates, San Francisco Chinatown was represented as a threatening and sensationalistic site of "queer domesticities" and "perverse spaces."[15] In this way, the deviant domesticities of Asian migrants meant exclusion from the modernity of the nation and even, in the figuring of the Chinese as germlike contagions, exclusion from the category of humanity.[16]

If the absence of the heteronormative family in early San Francisco Chinatown signified racial difference as an uncivilized sexual deviance and pathology, then the subsequent historical emergence of families in Chinatown would seem to signal the potential assimilation of the Chinese American into modernity, civilization, and national belonging. As Jennifer Ting points out, this transition to "'normal' heterosexuality . . . is not only a marker of assimilation achieved, it is itself a means of assimilation."[17] The heteronormative nuclear family, as a signifier of modernity and Americanization, serves as a structure enabling the legibility of its members as national citizen-subjects. The family at the center of *Bone*—mother (Mah), (step)father (Leon), and three daughters (Leila, Ona, and Nina)—would seem to represent development and progress in the racial community (from immature bachelors to mature families) and nation (from incomplete democratic incorporation to fulfilled democracy). This family would thus seem to signify and enable the assimilation of the Chinese American subject into modernity and national citizenship. However, the apparent heteronormativity of the Leong family turns out to be haunted and traumatized by earlier histories of domesticity inscribed as deviant and pathological. Leila begins her narrative by telling us that her family is judged as a "failed family" (3). Rather than reading such failed domesticity as a symptom of incompletion and unfulfillment, I interpret it as a sign of excess. The failure of this racial domestic form encrypts the secret heart of the neoliberal nation-state: its reliance on racialized domesticity as a mode of labor, even as this reliance must "fail" to be incorporated and must be made excess to the national Symbolic. *Bone*'s melancholic domesticity subverts the interpretation of Chinese American family formation as signifying an exceptionalist multiracial democracy. This melancholia alerts us to what lives on in the transition from bachelor to family domesticity: a sacrificial economy marked by the exploitation of racial labor, which now includes the affective labor of the child managing and supporting her working immigrant parents.

What Lives On

The suicide of the middle daughter, Ona, may be understood as a spectacular display of melancholia: she jumps from the "M" floor (the thirteenth floor) of a building in Nam Ping Yuen, a housing project in Chinatown. We learn about Ona's suicide at the very beginning of Leila's narration. The remainder of the novel is organized in a reverse chronology, whereby each subsequent chapter takes place at a moment prior to the events of the preceding chapter. Thus, for example, we learn that Leila marries Mason before she narrates his proposal; Leila describes her current job as a liaison between school and community, then a later chapter features her colleague maneuvering to get her this job. We know that Ona continued a forbidden romance with Osvaldo Ong, but the narrative bides its time in presenting the harrowing reasons for bad blood between Ona's and Osvaldo's families. Lisa Lowe explains the significance of this reverse chronology:

> One effect of the reverse narration is that *causality* as a means of investigation is disorganized. Although Ona's death appears initially as the originating loss that would seem either to motivate the reverse chronology or to resolve a progressive one, when the event of the suicide is at last reached, it dissolves, apprehensible not as an origin but as a symptom of the Leong family's collective condition.... [W]e learn that the painful divide between

the parents precedes the death and is the result of the steady rhythm of loss that has been the mainstay of their lives.[18]

In other words, because effect precedes cause in the novel, the reader expects the eventual, climactic revelation of the cause of Ona's suicide. What we find instead is not a singular cause, but rather the diffuse unfolding of hardship, sorrow, and endurance.

Mah and Leon employ the superstitious paradigm of "bad luck" to explain the death of their child: "[B]eyond Ona there was the bad luck that Leon kept talking about. What made Ona do it. Like she had no choice" (50). Younger sister Nina's attribution of blame appears more rooted in the "real" world, but it turns out to be just as vague: "Nina blamed us, this family. Everybody. Everything. Salmon Alley. The whole place" (51).[19] As Leila realizes, these nebulous or superstitious family narratives are illegible within a framework of modern rationality in which effect is explained by a concrete cause. This framework is represented by the report that the police officer submits about Ona's death.

> He didn't get it. He was looking at the typical stuff. He was looking at now. Maybe I could have said something about how . . . Ona was the middle girl and she felt stuck in the middle of all the trouble. I could have given him Leon's explanation that it was because Grandpa Leong's *Bones* weren't at rest. . . . But I didn't say any of this; it wasn't anything he could use for his report. (139)

The narrative is full of excess knowledge—"I didn't say any of this"—that cannot be spoken because it does not fit into hegemonic needs and demands. Leon's supernatural figure of restless bones and his paradigm of bad luck are dismissed within Western modernity as irrational superstition and Old World fatalism, while Nina's location of cause in "everything" appears useless. The novel does, however, permit us to make sense of these explanations. The bad luck that Mah and Leon attribute to their lives represents the hardship and suffering that U.S. racialization naturalizes, and Nina's "everything" alludes to the impossibility of separating out into discrete units the multifarious social, economic, and historical pressures on the Chinatown subject.

The police officer's epistemological framework of "looking at the typical stuff" and only "looking at now" limits what he can perceive and comprehend. This is why Leila's narration follows a movement back into the past, instead of forward into the future. Rather than unfolding into the future, that is, locating the story in an ever-present "now" that is caused by, and replaces, events that move unquestionably into the past, *Bone* disturbs this linear temporality of modernity and national history. Instead of an inevitably arriving future, it is the past that we are propelled into, a past that remains unknown and radically open. These contrasting concepts of time correspond to Freud's distinction between mourning and melancholia. Mourning is a process that exemplifies progress. It acknowledges loss so that the attachment to the lost object may be removed, and the subject may thus achieve closure and move on. Melancholia, in contrast, signifies an improper attachment to the past, palimpsestically keeping alive what should be left behind. *Bone's* lack of closure manifests this melancholic temporality of deferral, a temporality that Leon learns from his days at sea: "Leon told us that sorrow moves through the heart the way a ship moves through the ocean. Ships are massive, but the ocean has simple superiority. . . . *Forward and forward and then back, back*" (145, emphasis in original). If normative mourning is marked by a linear arc and resolution, Leon's metaphor of the ship and ocean recognizes the recursive nature of sorrow and affect, which may depart only to return.

In her chapter "Decolonization, Displacement, Disidentification: Writing and the Question of History" in *Immigrant Acts*, Lisa Lowe explains how Asian American novels prompt us to reconsider questions of history by presenting alternatives to the realist aesthetic of historical narrative. In her reading, texts such as *Bone* "excavate the material histories that have been subjugated or erased by" orthodox historical representations.[20] She cites *Bone's* reverse chronology as enabling an elaboration of Chinatown space as a "repository of layers of historical time."[21] I would call Ng's reverse chronology, as an alternative to dominant national history, a temporality of the remainder. Like Benjamin's angel of history, to which Lowe refers in her chapter, *Bone's* backward gazing reader perceives the catastrophic piling of "wreckage upon wreckage."[22] Ng's temporality of the remainder acknowledges what is left behind by national history, and what is covered over by history's transformation of racial sacrifice into the exceptionalist myth of national democratic progress and openness.

Lowe notes that Asian American texts, which emerge out of contradictions produced by race, capital, and nation, offer a material memory that "dialectically returns" to pressure dominant versions of history.[23] Psychoanalysis enables us to comprehend how these contradictions produced by national narratives result in, and result from, ambivalent layers of psychic affect at the level of both subject and nation. Like the Marxist notion of contradiction, the psychoanalytic concept of excess, or the remainder, highlights the nontotalizing nature of the structures that govern our lives, and points to opportunities for rearticulating these forces. *Bone* evokes several figures of excess and remains: unspoken secrets, bones, and old men. These remains are produced by conditions of political and economic contradiction, the provocative affects—furtiveness, pathos, and dread—of which melancholia allows us to understand. Here I discuss these figures of excess and analyze Leon as the main character in the novel who embodies these affects of traumatic enjoyment.

According to Abraham and Torok, the formation of the psychic crypt in which the lost object is buried alive is accompanied by an encryption of language that they describe as silence and demetaphorization. *Bone's* narrative is littered with these encryptions of language, moments at which language becomes unspoken, buried: "I wanted to say: I didn't marry in shame. I didn't marry like you. . . . I wanted to shake [Mah] and ask, what about me? Don't I count? Don't I matter? . . . I should have asked Ona, Why are you crying, What are you sad about? . . . We didn't talk about Leon's bruised and swollen face or his limp" (23, 91, 137, 171). As I have mentioned, Leila's feelings and concerns often remain buried in deference to her family caretaking responsibilities. But even as we readers are privy to Leila's thoughts of aborted speech, we feel that she withholds from us as well. Her narrative style is ascetic, staccato, unsentimental.[24] Her sentences are bare skeletons of subjects and verbs: "I could endure. . . . Nina's couldn't. She yelled back. She said things. She left" (25). The briefest job definitions suffice to convey whole lives of the immigrants that she encounters on her job: "Both parents work. Swing shift. Graveyard. Seamstress. Dishwasher. Janitor. Waiter. One job bleeds into another" (16).

Leila's narrative sparseness can be explained by her experience as the family translator, a childhood burden in which "every English word counted" (17). Responsible for mediating between her parents and public institutions, Leila's English-language skills are a precious resource that must not be squandered, for each word can make a difference in her family's survival. Linguistic elaborations are luxuries that the family cannot afford. An economy of efficiency is also practiced by Mah, who cooks inexpensive meals of pigeon for the girls, then sucks everything from the bones so there is no waste: "Mah always sat alone in the kitchen sucking out the sweetness of the lesser parts: the neck, the back, and the head. 'Bones are sweeter than you know,' she always said. She came out to check the bag. 'Clean bones.' She shook it. 'No waste'" (30–31). But just as this economy of efficient consumption does produce its remainder—bones—so too does Leila's aesthetic of efficient articulation produce its remainder: the unspoken. Leila tells us, "Ona has become a kind of silence in our lives. We don't talk about her. We don't have anything more to say" (15). Clearly, however, this family silence results not from having nothing to say, but rather from having too much to say. The silence, like Ona herself, is not so much an absence as the symptom of an excess. What remains unspoken by the family, what is kept secret, is what exceeds family survival and family business. Ona is also a figure for what remains unspoken and encrypted by national narratives of multiracial exceptionalism: the price paid for immigrant-family survival. Silence appears to cover over the encryption of a secret, but if we learn how to interpret silence symptomatically, we can uncover the remains of the unspoken.[25] Later I will return to how Ng allows us to comprehend these remains through strategies of demetaphorization, in which the metaphoric function of language is subtracted to reveal the excess that remains after symbolization by the nation-state.

But first, let me explain that while my analogy between bones and the unspoken may seem incongruous, I consider both as remainders from the past that have a certain heft in the sense that they exert pressure on the present. By titling the novel *Bone,* Ng signals such remainders as pivotal narrative forces. In Leon's belief of supernatural causality, Ona died because Grandpa Leong's bones remain animated, haunting and cursing the family. Leon's status as a legitimate subject of the U.S. nation derives from his fictive relationship to Grandpa Leong, who claimed Leon as a "paper son." During the era of exclusion, Chinese migrants were able to partly circumvent strict exclusion laws by assuming fictive identities as children of U.S. citizens.[26] Having purchased these identity papers, Leon has paid off an economic debt to Grandpa Leong, but he still owes him a moral debt, which takes the form of a promise to accompany Grandpa Leong's bones back to China for burial in their final resting place. We can think of Leon's failure to keep this promise as a repetition of other failures in his life, or, in Leon's cosmology, we may also see this failure as a cause for other failures. Leon's unpaid debt is both a symbol of incompletion (an unfulfilled promise) and of excess (an animated and haunting specter taking the form of bones).

Ng has commented on the desires of Chinese migrant "old-timers" to have their bodily remains repatriated. "The book's title honors the old-timers' desire to have their bones sent back to China for proper burial. I wanted to remember the old-timers buried here against their wishes. As I wrote *Bone*, I was conscious of their regret, so I wanted to create in the language of the book an English that could serve as the fertile and final resting place for my memories of the old-timers."[27] The old-timers' longing for burial in China derives from a need for appropriate rites, symbolic completion, and final belonging. Finding themselves aging and unwanted, they have discovered too late that the ideology of the United States as a site of fulfilled promise obscures an economic system that recruits and then discards them as cheap, exploitable labor. If the "social death" of racialized marginalization denies them a sense of belonging,[28] then actual death could at least promise a sense of belonging that they imagine as literal incorporation into their country of origin. Instead, because they do not have family members in the United States who can fulfill these wishes, their bones are literally incorporated into a nation that does not symbolically assimilate them as living subjects. The literality of this incorporation is its key characteristic, for as Ng shows, even the bones cannot be assimilated into the symbolic order. In the novel, the bones are disinterred, then mixed together and reburied, so there is no way to claim them as belonging to particular individuals (76–78). The unassimilability of these bones into the symbolic order marks their status as the demetaphorized remains that accompany the encryption of a secret. This national secret is the recruitment and exploitation of racial labor, which is necessary to nation building, but must be disavowed by exceptionalist myths of democratic openness and equal opportunity.

We see from the animated and haunting quality of Grandpa Leong's bones that such bones are metonyms for the old bachelors at the margins of the text. No longer productive, their aging bodies are what remain from a sacrificial economy of underpaid and exploited labor. This history of exploited labor is covered over by developmental narratives of multiracial equality, so that the old men's stories remain incomprehensible within the symbolic frameworks of modernity, capitalism, and nation. Their mumbling makes them inarticulate; their loss of memory means that they are lost to whatever families or friends they may have; they waste time because they have been rendered waste by time (84, 6, 7). To Leila, the old men look like "dark remnant scraps of fabric" (8). The old bachelors are the illegible and illegitimate remainders of national history, cast aside in trajectories of national development, rendered surplus after the extraction of surplus value from their labor. Unassimilated into the national Symbolic, their status as demetaphorized remains consigns them to the space of living death: their bodies have material existence but no symbolic value.[29] As mentioned earlier, living death is more than a liminal space between life and death. Rather, living death is the condition of an excess of life substance in which this animated materiality cannot be recognized by the symbolic order. The living dead are figures of jouissance, or traumatic enjoyment: they have no symbolic existence and can only register as disturbing and repellent entities.

These old men are shadowy figures hovering at the margins of *Bone's* domestic drama; in this context, Leon oscillates between deviant "old man" and normative "family man." As a figure of oscillation, Leon embodies the contradictions of a Chinatown domesticity structured by the racialized demands of older and newer forms of national hegemony. Leon is a figure of jouissance; his excessive enjoyment cannot be domesticated, and it traumatizes his family. The "problem" of Leon is that he is not productive. He obsessively initiates new projects of entrepreneurial innovation or technological domesticity but does not complete them. In this way, Leon represents the jouissant underside of neoliberal capitalist fantasy, a traumatizing enjoyment that is in excess of productivity.

Ona is the central figure of absence in the novel, but Leon functions as a strong secondary figure of absence, for he is constantly on the verge of disappearing from domestic space. This is hard to perceive at first because he is such a colorful figure of jouissance: the junk collector who makes a mess, the spectacularly wounded husband, the emotionally volatile immigrant. In fact, these are the very qualities that contribute to his frequent disappearances—into secondhand stores to look for parts, shipping out to sea after discovering Mah's adulterous affair, skipping dinner to violently confront a duplicitous business partner. For Leila, the parentalized child, Leon is the unruly "problem parent" (18) that she must manage in her neoliberal role as child-manager of migrant labor.

At the beginning of the novel, Leon has moved out of the family home. He and Mah are still married, but his lifestyle and network are structured by the homosociality of bachelor society. He lives in a small room in the "old-man hotel" called the San Fran, eats at places like Uncle's Café, where "every single table is an old-man table," and cooks up schemes with other old-man "time-wasters" and "fleabags" (7, 7, 16). Leila's use of terms like "old man," "time waster," and "fleabag" to refer to the subjects of bachelor sociality indicates how the bachelor is a figure of decay and decomposition.

Leon's continued life as a bachelor, even after marriage and reproduction, calls into question the paradigms of modern citizenship, in which the racialized subject presumably develops from a premodern domestic deviance to a modern domestic norm. Initially we believe that Leon moved out because of the family crisis precipitated by Ona's death, but we come to realize that Leon's long and consistent absences from the domestic space of the family have marked his and Mah's marriage from the very beginning. Leon's work in the service sector of the shipping industry requires frequent forty-day absences from his family when he ships out to sea. Leon returns to this compulsive mobility during moments of domestic crisis; immediately after Ona's death, for example, he avoids his home by sleeping over in the homes of other families before moving to the San Fran hotel. We can see here how the demands of capital and the nation structure racial domesticity and citizenship as melancholic. Leon's oscillations between presence and absence in domestic space metonymize his ambivalent formation as a national subject, poised between presence and loss. On one of her many quests to find Leon, Leila notices a lost old man in the lobby of the San Fran who cannot remember his identity. The hotel manager, upon seeing Leila, inquires, "Leon lost, too?" When the manager suggests that Leila look for Leon at Portsmouth Square, Leila tells us, "I hated looking for Leon at the Square, seeing him hanging around with those time wasters, so I went and checked a couple of other places first" (7). Leila's fear of finding Leon at Portsmouth Square rests precisely in the dread of seeing him as yet another "old man," another "time waster," wasted by time. Leila is afraid of losing Leon as a legible subject, afraid he will become as illegible as the other mumbling, lost old men, that he will disappear into the morass of human waste.

Chapter 6 begins simply, "Leon lost. Leon found" (62). Leon's status as the (step)father and husband that the family repeatedly loses marks his formation as a melancholic subject. In his theory of melancholia as unresolved mourning, Freud posits that melancholia can result not only from the loss of a specific love-object but also from loss of faith in "fatherland, liberty, an ideal, and so forth" (164).[30] For Leon, this lost ideal is America, a nation of broken promises:

[H]e blamed all of America for making big promises and breaking every
one. Where was the good job he'd heard about as a young man? Where was
the successful business? He'd kept his end of the bargain: he'd worked hard.
Two jobs, three. Day and night. Overtime. Assistant laundry presser. Prep
cook. Busboy. Waiter. Porter. But where was his happiness? "America," he
ranted, "This lie of a country!" (103)

What Leon has lost is his faith in America as the site of promises fulfilled,
of completion and belonging, of full citizenship. We can thus interpret his
breaking his promise to repatriate Grandpa Leong's bones as repeating
the broken promise of America itself. Leon encrypts within himself this
lost ideal of America, a status of melancholic citizenship. Ona, the child
who is most like Leon and who is emotionally closest to Leon, has inherited this melancholic phantom, this encrypted secret of a failed America.
Maria Torok explains the concept of the phantom that she and Nicolas
Abraham formulated: "In general terms, the 'phantom' is a formation in
the dynamic unconscious that is found there not because of the subject's
own repression but on account *of a direct empathy with the unconscious or
the rejected psychic matter of a parental object.*"[31] As Leila tells us, neither
Mah nor Leon "could believe that Ona's unhappiness was all her own"
(104). While Leon's broken promise to Grandpa Leong mimics the broken promise of America, Ona's shattered body materializes this broken
promise. Ona is the child who no longer signifies the promise of the future
but literalizes—demetaphorizes—the losses of the past. In this materialization that exceeds the Symbolic, Ona becomes an agent of jouissance.

ENCRYPTED SECRETS AND LIVE BURIAL

The novel's central question, "Why did Ona kill herself?" leads us to ex-
pect the revelation of a secret at its narrative climax. What we find instead
is that secrecy is not an exceptionalist, isolated event, but a general structural condition of the family. "Don't have to worry. I keep a secret good,"
says Leon reassuringly, when Leila confides in him about Nina's love life
(11). Leila remembers Leon colluding with ten-year-old Ona to keep her
act of shoplifting a secret. Identifying with Ona in her act of transgressing
the law, and defiantly dismissive of the store manager as an authority figure, Leon refuses to discipline Ona. In fact, he rewards her by taking her
out for a treat of ice cream, and says, "Don't tell Mah. Our secret. It was
only a little thing. Only lipstick" (140). In the present, Leila wonders if she

could have had a talk with Ona that would have kept her from committing suicide. Nina shakes her head and says, "Ona could keep a secret better than anybody," to which Leila responds, "We're all pretty good at it" (111–12). In her narration, Leila continues, "We learned it from Mah and Leon. They were always saying, Don't tell this and don't tell that. Mah was afraid of what people inside Chinatown were saying and Leon was paranoid about everything outside Chinatown" (112).

As Freud suggests in "The Uncanny," the very structure of domestic interiority generates secrecy, a condition of keeping things hidden and concealed. We see in *Bone*, however, how an especially acute domestic secrecy derives from a legacy of racial and gendered surveillance. Leon's status as a paper son means that he must keep his original identity a secret, for fear of deportation. Mah's secrecy results from the gendered demands of respectability. Already inscribed as a fallen woman because her first husband (Leila's father) abandoned her, Mah marries Leon, only to then commit adultery with her boss and landlord, Tommie Hom. As the above quote suggests, Leon's and Mah's distinct forms of secrecy seem divided according to a gendered spatial economy, whereby Leon is threatened in the public sphere by a repressive state apparatus, and Mah bows to the more private pressures of an ethnic community. Indeed, Leon says to Mah, "You don't know. You're inside Chinatown; it's safe. You don't know. Outside, it's different" (181). Upon further analysis, however, this apparently gendered distinction between external and internal threats proves to be more complex. Mah's need for respectability is tied to the legitimacy of her status as a national subject. When her first husband leaves, she marries Leon for his green card, so that her own status as subject of the U.S. nation-state will remain secure. Mah's status as a husbandless, fallen woman makes her an illegitimate national subject, and she must restore her legitimacy through remarriage. Meanwhile, Leila discovers that Leon has not only kept his identity a secret from government authorities; he has also hidden his shameful histories of rejection and failure from his family. Leon constructs a facade of national belonging in order to maintain his image as a heroic family man in the domestic sphere. While Mah's secrecy manifests itself in response to her ethnic community, her domestic status is in fact formulated by the demands of the nation-state. Leon's negotiation of his public persona serves the purpose of maintaining secrecy within the domestic sphere of the family. We can see in these examples how the public sphere structures the secrecies of domesticity, and thus how these domestic secrets might in turn reveal secrets of the national public sphere. An example of this dynamic is the traumatic open secret of Ona's forbidden romance with Osvaldo Ong.

Leila describes the daughters' transition into adulthood as a "graduat[ion]" from keeping their parents' secrets to keeping their own (112). In fact, however, Ona disregards her sisters' advice to keep her forbidden romance a secret.[32] Her transgression is not so much the romance itself as what it reveals. In conducting an open romance with Osvaldo, Ona exposes the status of Leon's relationship with Osvaldo's father, Luciano, as similarly structured by romance. Luciano Ong functions as an ego-ideal for Leon, embodying a confident masculinity that symbolizes wealth, success, and belonging. In other words, Luc signifies the promise of America as the site of material and social fulfillment, of full national citizenship. "Leon talked about Luc all the time. Every story he heard Luc tell at the Square he repeated for us at dinner. Luc tipped Paul Lim twenty dollars for parking his car. Luc bought snakeskin shoes at Florsheim. Luc had a gold Rolex. Soon Luc was going to buy a new Cadillac (165)." Luc's conspicuous consumption of commodities is read as evidence of his entrepreneurial talent, his fulfillment of the American Dream, and his full citizenship in the nation. A source of perpetual fantasy, Luc comes up with grandiose business plans that seduce Leon. The plans are almost ready to go; all they need are a thousand or more dollars, or one more man to give a final push. Leon's desire to be Luc's "last man" (165), to complete Luc, functions as a fantasy of his own completion, fulfillment, and success: "Ong and Leong. . . . Their names fit together like a pair of chopsticks that they could eat with for the rest of their lives" (165, 166). Their search for a joint business venture is described like a courtship. "I never saw Leon happier. Every morning he got up early and put on his double-breasted blue suit and his luck-red tie. He polished his shoes until they shone almost as brightly as Luc's. Before the sewing ladies arrived for work, Leon was at the front of the alley" (166).[33]

Leon's feminized position in dressing and waiting for Luc is repeated when their business partnership is actualized in a laundry business.[34] Leon agrees to serve as the "inside man," the operations manager, while Luc assumes the position of the "outside man," presumably drumming up business while remaining unaccountable to his partner. Leon's subsequent betrayal by Luc, whose nonpayment of bills results in the closure of the business, reveals how Leon's desire is not reciprocated, which inscribes him as incomplete, a subject of lack. The unrequited romance with Luc, however, is only a particular instantiation of the catastrophic, failed romance between Leon and the United States.[35] Thus we must read Ona's transgressive romance not only at the level of the domestic—the betrayal of an individual patriarch—but also at the level of the nation, betraying the secret of America as the site of failure. Again, Ona is the agent of de-metaphorization: her romance with Osvaldo literalizes and makes palpable Leon's unconscious romance with Luc as a symbol of America. Leon is driven to the edge not just by the loss of his daughter to a rival family, but by the surfacing of his own failed romance with, and betrayal by, the U.S. nation: " [E]very time he saw Osvaldo, he remembered his whole past, every job he got fired from, every business that failed. . . . Leon look[ed] after Ona as if he was watching everything he'd ever hoped for disappear" (173, 175). Ona has inherited from Leon the melancholic condition of oscillation between presence and loss.

The bachelor is a figure of both incompletion and excess: a man without a family to complete him, a man in excess of family. However, we see in *Bone* that family itself is a mode of incompletion and excess. The Leong family cannot complete a full banquet table, for example, and is introduced to us from the beginning of the narrative as "failed" (29, 3). They exceed models of comprehensible cohesion, as when the police officer reporting on Ona's suicide does not understand why Ona and Leila have different last names. In late twentieth-century Chinatown, heteronormative domesticity is not so radically different from early twentieth-century formations of "deviant" domesticity.

What has remained from these earlier formations, covered over by developmental narratives of the nation-state? Evelyn Nakano Glenn's historical analysis of Chinese American domesticity can help us think through this question. In Glenn's formulation, distinct forms of domesticity have prevailed in different moments of Chinese American history: split-household, small-producer, and dual-wage earner. Split-household arrangements, in which production was separated from other domestic functions, were common in the early period of Chinese immigration (1850–1920), when the wives of Chinese migrant laborers were excluded from the United States and remained in China. Small-producer households were established in the middle period (from 1920 to the mid-1960s) by Chinese American families with limited economic options. In this domestic arrangement, all members of the household, including children, worked together in a small business. The dual-wage-earner household, largely comprised of post-1965 immigrants, consists of husbands and wives pooling together their wages from work in the secondary labor market of service and small manufacturing sectors. In each of these eras, Chinese American domesticity is structured by the sometimes contradictory, sometimes converging, demands of capital and of the nation-state. The split-household arrangement ensured the low cost of maintaining a cheap, mobile labor force, while the exclusion of Chinese women alleviated racial fears of an alien population settling in the United States. The unpaid family labor of the Chinese American small-producer household enabled maximum production at minimum cost and provided the appearance of a national openness to racial difference as well as transnational trade. Workers in the dual-wage-earner household fill the low-wage jobs of the national economy. Because these parents often work long hours, reproductive labor is shifted to older children, who care for younger siblings as well as themselves.

What is notable about the family in *Bone* is that it has taken on all three of these historical configurations: split-household when Leon ships out to sea; dual-wage earner when he finds odd jobs on land, while Mah continues work as a seamstress; and small producer when parents and children work, first in a grocery store and then in the ill-fated Ong and Leong laundry business. In *Bone*, domesticity is not an autonomous sphere of stability and privacy; instead, it shifts and pulsates according to the racialized and gendered forces of capital and the nation-state. Keeping "past" formations alive in the present, this melancholic domesticity reveals that family formation represents not the fantasy of citizenship (its freedom and rights), but the continuing constraints and traumas of labor exploitation.

We can see that gendered demands of proper domesticity *enable* this exploitation of labor. In *Bone*, changes in domestic formation are motivated by the desire to redeem Mah from her fallen-woman status. Having been abandoned by her first husband, Lyman Fu, Mah marries Leon partly because of the peripatetic nature of his job, feeling that the regularity of Leon's absences will give her a better sense of expectation and control over husbandly absence. Mah accepts their split-household arrangement in order to maintain legitimate status in the community and the nation while easing into a marriage that she might not otherwise have chosen so quickly. However, Mah's subsequent affair with Tommie Hom indicates that this domestic arrangement does not meet Mah's emotional needs, and Leon attempts to find employment on land in order to stabilize the domestic sphere through his presence. Their household temporarily assumes the dual-wage-earner configuration, but in the meantime Mah recognizes that she needs to redeem herself from fallen-woman status for a second time. She finds that the small-producer-household configuration enables her to do this because she can put distance between herself and her boss, Tommie Hom, while working at the grocery and then the laundry with her husband and children.

Linking gendered demands for respectability with capital's demands for exploitable labor, Leila notes first that Mah "married Leon to be saved from disgrace," and then ironically continues that Mah is "saved to work" (34). Mah's ceaseless toil to provide wages and respectability for her family raises the question of whether she has been saved *from* (disgrace) or *for* (her labor). The gendered discourse of salvation that accompanies a woman's "fall" is here also a racial and imperialist discourse of salvation, in which the immigrant woman is presumably saved from being deported back to the harsh conditions of the Third World. But what conditions does Mah face in the United States? "Every night, Mah sat down at the Singer with dinner rice still in her mouth. When we pulled down the Murphy bed, she was still there sewing. . . . [T]he street noises stopped long before she did. And in the morning, before any of us awoke, she was already there, at work" (34). Practices in the garment industry such as subcontracting and homework enable corporations to circumvent laws intended to protect workers from hyperexploitation. The pay structure of sweatshops, whereby wages are paid according to units produced rather than hours worked, means that seamstresses like Mah constantly work overtime, sometimes at home, sometimes impressing their children to work, simply to make their deadlines.[36] "Work was her whole life, and every forward stitch marked time passing. She wanted to get out before her whole life passed under the stamping needle" (163).

Entrapped by a racialized labor structure that provides the only means for her family's survival as well as her own, Mah's salvation does not translate into the freedom or fulfillment promised to properly gendered citizen-subjects of the U.S. nation-state. Laura Kang articulates the fallacy of equating U.S. national subjecthood with salvation from "Third World" conditions: "In light of the similarities of their labor status and work conditions to women in Asia, it is difficult to argue that living and working in the late capitalist United States assures a better, more modern, and liberated existence for Asian/American women."[37] The discourse that would represent Mah as a privileged subject saved from disgrace and from Third World status covers over the real subject of this saving, which Leila reveals in her formulation of Mah being saved "to work." Mah's exploitable status as a racialized immigrant worker—generating profit, inexpensively managed by her daughter—translates into a substantial savings for U.S. and transnational capital. The paradigms of gendered respectability and racialized immigration as equivalent to salvation and progress not only cover over but also enable this gendered racial labor exploitation.

The maintenance of gendered respectability is an integral component of family business since it constitutes the social capital of the family's reputation. Mah is spooked by Ona's ashes because they remind her of her moral debt, the cost of her ill-fated affair with Tommie. Nina tells Leila that Mah feels she is "paying" for her adultery (127). Ona's literalized status as sacrificial object reveals how Mah is symbolically positioned by a gendered and racialized moral economy as the fallen, Third World woman who must sacrifice herself to pay off her moral debt. But Mah's status as a racialized immigrant worker means that she can never wholly redeem herself by achieving the properly gendered domesticity that signifies legitimate citizenship. Mah's domestic space cannot be a pure site of sentimental, feminine maternal care, for it is penetrated and contaminated by capitalist relations of production. Thus Mah's moral debt cannot be fully paid off, and she must continue to sacrifice and pay. Mah articulates the shameful affect of debt during the period in which she must rely on community members to help her with Grandpa Leong's funeral because Leon is at sea: "It was all the asking: Mah said she felt like she owed everyone; that was what humiliated her" (79). As a subject of debt, Mah is excluded not only from the self-possession of liberal citizenship because others have claim upon her; she is also excluded from the dignity of the human in her abjection and humiliation.

This shame makes Mah want to hide (6); in this way, Mah herself becomes an encrypted secret, undergoing a kind of live burial. Notably, all the other characters have some mode of escape, a form of mobility that gives some measure of freedom. For Leon, it is the ocean; for Nina, her occupation as a flight attendant; for Leila, driving with Mason. Ona's falling to her death is imagined as a flight (150), a common association of death with transcendence and freedom.[38] Only Mah, the racialized migrant woman worker, is rendered immobile, fixed in domestic space by the demands of labor and gendered respectability. Mah's attempt to escape her pain through an affair with Tommie Hom only renders her more captive to her indebted situation, increasing not only her moral debt to society but also her financial debt when she leaves Tommie's business, only to have Luciano Ong wipe out the family finances. Mah is an obverse figure to Ona. Ona is made into a spirit, while Mah is all too embodied and embedded. "It wasn't just death that upset Mah," Leila notes, "it was life, too" (82). Like the old men, Mah is also a figure of the living dead, embodying an excess of life substance that cannot be incorporated into the national Symbolic. Mah's status as the living dead is less obvious, however. Her incorporation into heteronormative domesticity would seem to render her more socially intelligible than the old men, yet this very incorporation into heteronormative domesticity turns out to be a kind of materialized introjection, a fixating paralysis. Consumed and sacrificed by the demands of work and gendered propriety, Mah becomes fixed into a domestic workspace, sealed into her life with no escape.

For both Mah and Leon, life is equivalent to labor: "Work was [Mah's] whole life. . . . [Leon] said that life was work and death the dream" (163, 181). Leon's dreams are not only figuratively but also literally stolen by work: he works double shifts and has little time to sleep. Yet somehow this excess of work translates into lack. Leon's quantification of his labor— "as much as I could"—is equivalent to "not enough" wages to sustain the household (181). Mah and Leon's only hope is to frame this economy of excess work and lack of money within a narrative of sacrifice for and investment in the future, in the form of their children. Speaking of the difficulties and tensions that plague her parents' marriage, Leila says, "They both worked too hard; it was as if their marriage was a marriage of toil—of toiling together. The idea was that the next generation would marry for love" (33). In this imagined economy, Mah and Leon sacrifice and pay with their bodies, their health, and their lives, in the hope that their daughters will receive the return on these investments. Romantic love functions here as a trope for fully realized desire, agency, and subjectivity. The daughters represent the generation that can presumably realize and fulfill their choices. That is, "marriage for love" is a trope for liberal modernity, for the freedom and belonging that liberal citizenship promises. Although excluded from this promise of citizenship, Mah and Leon hope that their daughters will fulfill this promise.

Leila does marry for love, and her relationship with Mason does indeed signify freedom and belonging for her. With Mason, Leila has one escape from the caretaker role; as my students say, Mason is the perfect, support-ive partner. However, Ng subverts the conventional marriage plot, which climactically resolves social contradictions in a satisfying and fulfilling nar-rative conclusion. Because of the narrative technique of reverse chronol-ogy, Leila's wedding ceremony at New York City Hall is presented at the *beginning* of the novel, in an unglamorous and anticlimactic fashion. "My way wasn't exactly fun. Last minute, like refugees, a strange city. Hurried. A borrowed dress. No rings. Just yes, yes" (18). The connotations of choice and consent represented by the "yes, yes" of the wedding cere-mony is undercut by the constraints of time and place. Leila's figure of the refugee connotes the involuntariness of escape and dislocation, rather than the voluntariness and leisure that the figure of a tourist, for example, would connote. The dark-suited man who marries them has the distracted expression of a sweatshop presser: marriage is still tied to labor and toil—to business rather than romance (36). For the clerk, the wedding is less a sacred and timeless ritual and more an obligation of work that is con-strained by time because of the demands of having to perform more cere-monies in the service of efficiency and productivity.

The first chapter of *Bone* stages Leila's confession to Mah about her elopement and Mah's angry reaction to the news. Mah chastises Leila, "Marriage is for a lifetime and it should be celebrated! Why sneak around, why act like a thief in the dark?" (23) Why, in other words, must the sec-ond generation still be the site of encrypted secrets? Mah's disappoint-ment in Leila's furtive elopement is due not only to being reminded of her own marital shames. Mah also interprets Leila's elopement as a sign that her moral debts have not been paid off. Leila knows that Mah would have liked to have thrown a wedding banquet for other community members in order to pay them back for inviting her to their banquets. This settling of financial debts would in fact be a pretext for the spectacle of settling a moral debt. The display of an honorably married daughter would demon-strate that Mah has finally achieved respectability in the domestic sphere.

The economy of parental sacrifice and filial fulfillment is predicated upon filial debt. Leila is initially reluctant to move in with Mason because she feels obliged to give Mah her everyday companionship and support: "I just feel like I owe her," she expresses to Mason (184). As Leila ex-plains to the reader, "Mah and Leon forced themselves to live through the humiliation in this country so that we could have it better" (140). Even more poignant than the unending work that Mah and Leon perform is the sacrifice of their very humanity through the degrading subordination of service work and the stigmatization of working-class powerlessness. In Mah's fantasy of the wedding banquet, Leila would pay off her filial debt by helping her mother pay off her moral and financial debt. What this structure of the child helping to pay off the parent's debt reveals is the hidden way that children of immigrants are the objects of sacrifice, not just the parents.

SUPERNATURAL COUNTING

As the child of immigrants, Ona is expected to redeem her parents' sacrifices through the exercise of full citizenship, with the freedom and opportunities that such citizenship promises. Ona is expected to "marry for love," to exercise the kind of choice that her parents could not. Yet Ona is placed in an untenable position when her romantic choice threatens to expose the secret of a failed America. For the Leong family, the fantasy of romance shades into the threat of a traumatic excess. I have argued that the traumatic excess of Asian American family business constitutes an encrypted secret of an emerging neoliberal nation-state. Yet the burial of a secret does not mean its death. If *Bone* teaches us anything, it is how secrets defy death to live on and animate the present, and how the supernatural provides an epistemology for understanding what cannot be understood through the secular knowledge of the modern nation. The very title of the novel, *Bone*, gestures to Leon's belief that his family is cursed by Grandpa Leong's unburied bones. We may think of Leon as a member of the older generation who is imbued with "old world" values and superstitions, but the novel is in fact replete with Leila's superstitions as well. She touches the carousel pony by her mother's store for luck, for example; and when she gets married, she is gratified by the rain, which signifies good luck (20, 37).

Let us recall Leon's association of Ona's suicide with bad luck: "What made Ona do it. Like she had no choice" (50). To what extent was Ona able to exercise freedom of choice in her life or death? Is it possible to separate Ona's act of suicide from her parents' verbal threats of suicide (31, 188), from Leon's symbolic suicide in taking on the identity of a paper son, or from the historical notion of Chinatown itself as marked for death?[39] Ona's "choice" of death over life belies the national narrative of ethnic succession. In this narrative, immigrant hardship becomes transformed into second-generation fulfillment and full citizenship. Ona's suicide traumatically reveals the fallacy of Mah and Leon's imagined economy, in which their sacrifices are figured as investments whose returns their children will embody. In the transitional period of *Eat a Bowl of Tea*, the figure of the child would appear to signal a hopeful future for men who previously had only their own deaths to anticipate. On the surface, the restructuring of Chinese American domesticity into heteronormativity seems to indicate a national temporality of progress and development. Such a developmental narrative promises a multiracial liberal citizenship and a multiracial democracy. This is the fantasy of Asian American family business at the level of national mythmaking: the interpretation of Asian American family formation as a signifier of American exceptionalism. What Ona reveals is the traumatic underside of family business, in which sacrifice of the racial subject continues in the figure of the child. The trauma of Asian American family business is that the child represents not a break from a sacrificial economy of debt and labor exploitation, but the *continuation* of such a sacrificial economy in a restructured form.

The notion of ethnic succession is a key component of the nationalist myth of American exceptionalism. Under ethnic succession, the child of racial migrants is the site of projection for the fantasy of universal and multiracial liberal citizenship. The melancholic suicide of Ona, in whom the figure of the child (as hopeful future) and female (as potential reproductive agent) crystallize, critiques this myth of national exceptionalism. Having broken with the finitude of life, Ona's various demetaphorizations also open up a realm that counters the knowledge frameworks of Enlightenment humanism and liberal citizenship, a realm of the supernatural and the sacred.

Dipesh Chakrabarty refers to the incommensurabilities of "the time of history" and "the times of gods": "In effect, we have two systems of thought, one in which the world is ultimately, that is, in the final analysis, disenchanted, and the other in which humans are not the only meaningful agents."[40] Sylvia Wynter refers to these two systems of thought as "natural causality" and "supernatural causality."[41] If national narratives and national myths are constituted by the universal, secular time of liberal modernity, how might a melancholia cognizant of that which lives on after death "blast open the continuum of history"?[42]

The only parental dream that Ona can realize is that of death (Leon's "life was work and death the dream"). Given the interfamilial permeations of debt and melancholia, Leila cannot comprehend Ona's suicide as an act of autonomous agency. Leila remembers an old village chant that matched ten living things to the first ten days of the New Year. This counting rhyme ensured that all forms of life were acknowledged and recognized. Counting the days after New Year's, Leila considers the significance of the fact that the memorial service takes place on the Day of Thieves. "Someone stole Ona. Ona hadn't wanted to go" (121). Mah and Leon fear that Ona's death was the price they paid for the guilt of their moral debts. In saying that Ona was stolen, however, Leila underscores that the debts are *not legitimate*. Racial migrants are hegemonically figured as owing a debt of gratitude to the United States as a "generously" and exceptionally open nation. But in showing how Mah and Leon hope their children can collect on their sacrifices, *Bone* recognizes that these migrant workers are *owed* a debt.[43] Through its practice of supernatural counting, *Bone* proposes an alternative economy. Countering hegemonic ideologies that would position migrant workers and their children as owing a debt to the nation, this alternative economy recognizes the sacrifices that migrants and children have already made as extractions of surplus value. Such extraction may become abstracted in the form of capital, but the remainders of this extraction are all too materially embodied, a visceral excess of the national Symbolic. *Bone's* alternative economy recognizes sacrificial remains as the living dead, who are owed a debt of recognition and value.

As the novel's primary haunting presence, Ona enters the realm of the supernatural. As Leila recalls, Ona had always wanted to be a "smart old goddess" (88), and so she is transformed through death and through her family's memorials into one of those gods and goddesses that she and Leon honored in their makeshift New Year's ceremonies: the Eight Holy Immortals, the Goddess of Mercy, the God of War, Jesus, Confucius (107–8).[44] Ona's realm is counting:

> She counted the one hundred and forty times our pet rooster crowed in his short life; she tried to keep count of the number of culottes Mah sewed one summer (Mah sewed faster than Ona could keep count). She counted off the days till Leon was coming home, and then she stood at the mouth of the alley, counting the cabs that went by. Every night that Leon was gone, she'd count out ninety-nine kisses to keep him safe, to bring him back. (88)

Counting up to the Day of Thieves, Leila uses Ona's epistemological ritual to both recognize and critique the sacrificial economy of debt and exploitation that steals Chinatown life and dreams. In my interpretation of the novel's cosmology, Ona becomes the Goddess of Counting, living on, offering an alternative to a national economy that would disavow its sacrificial remainders. "Inside all of us, Ona's heart still moves forward. Ona's heart is still counting, true and truer to every tomorrow" (145). While Leon wonders at all the dead buried in the cemetery, Leila ponders, "If Ona were here, she would count the living; Ona would tell us that there are more living than dead" (89). In my interpretation, Ona allows us to see the life in those who are left for dead. Leila meditates in her conclusion on "the secrets we hold in our hearts," positing "the unspoken between us" as "a measure of our every promise to the living and to the dead" (193). Ona's heart is one of these "secrets we hold in our hearts," animating our core feelings. Her heart allows ours to count, value, and honor the living and the dead, and the living dead as the excess who otherwise remain discounted and uncounted.

2 Shameful Citizenship

Animal Jouissance and Brian Ascalon Roley's
American Son

A sudden and disturbing flash of heat spreading through one's body; a racing pulse; the urgent need to avert one's eyes. These and other involuntary, physical manifestations of shame occur with such conspicuous frequency in Brian Ascalon Roley's novel *American Son* that they categorically demand our readerly attention, even as we might be uncomfortable at witnessing so many scenes of humiliation. Why is shame the dominant affect in Roley's novel about two mixed-race Filipino American brothers living in 1990s Los Angeles? How can we interpret the text's many interactions that result in embarrassment? Why do the Sullivan brothers embody such different responses to racial shame, such that the narrator, Gabe, wants to hide while his older brother, Tomas, shamelessly flaunts racial otherness? And why is the reader repelled, yet attracted, by these scenes in which racial debasement is produced? In other words, what is the relationship between traumatic enjoyment and racial shame?

In my reading of *American Son,* racial shame is produced and consumed in order to provide enjoyment for the hegemonic gaze of a racial and imperial nationalism. By revealing this traumatic enjoyment as the obscene underside of law, Roley's novel critiques the modern notion of law as neutral, impersonal, abstract, and universal. My aim in this chapter is to undo the myth of neutrality that underlies and legitimates modern institutions such as law, democracy, and citizenship. Instead, I show how these apparently impersonal forms of modernity are highly affective, interested, and invested sites of racial and imperial power. This affective investment assumes the form of racial and imperial jouissance.

What is the political significance of the Lacanian concept of jouissance? Understanding racial and imperial modes of jouissance is important to the study of race and nation because they are the forces through which hegemony secures consent—sometimes enthusiastic—from its subjects. Jouissance helps to explain the otherwise puzzling question of why subjects act against their rational self-interest. As I discussed in the introduction, jouissance refers to an experience in which meaning, language, and law collapse. Jouissance, or traumatic enjoyment, is the affective dimension of the Real, the excess that is not incorporable into the Symbolic order. Because of the primal sense of being and wholeness that we give up in order to become Symbolic subjects, we are both drawn toward and repelled by this surplus of the Symbolic—an excess that promises to restore our wholeness, to return us to this primal state. While we surrender our jouissance to the Other in order to become subjects of Symbolic law, language, and culture, we are also compelled toward this traumatic enjoyment. The trauma of jouissance is its lawlessness, its senselessness, and the enjoyment derived from its mixture of pain and pleasure, suffering and satisfaction.

Although our entry into the Symbolic Other demands this surrender of jouissance, we wish to believe that this jouissance is nevertheless accessible. As I discussed in the introduction, socially subordinated others become construed ideologically as the site of this imagined enjoyment. For subjects of U.S. national hegemony, these projected sites of jouissance may include imperial, racial, sexual, classed, and nonhuman others. In this way, the national Symbolic needs socially subordinated subjects like the Sullivans to produce jouissance: to displace attention away from the way the hegemonic Other siphons jouissance from its subjects. Instead, these social others become the scapegoated site of envy and resentment for hegemonic subjects.

Language and law are generally conceived of as the main functions that distinguish the human from the animal. Jouissance, then, as the failure of these functions, represents the "reversion" of human into animal, the rational into the carnal, disembodied abstraction into material substance. American Son narrates a trajectory in which fifteen-year-old Gabe attempts to escape, but eventually succumbs to, a condition we might call "becoming-animal," to borrow Deleuze and Guattari's term. His brother Tomas serves as his sadistic tutor and initiator into an "animal jouissance" demanded by imperial and racial hegemonies.

In my reading of American Son as a narrative of "becoming-animal," I conceive of the animal jouissance permeating the Sullivan brothers as a legacy of U.S. imperial relations with the Philippines. Conquest and colonization of the Philippines at the turn of the twentieth century was rationalized by the construction of Filipinos as racially "unfit for self-government." Seen as uncivilized, Filipinos were degraded by some as bestial savages, and condescended to by others as "little brown brothers" in need of tutelage by Americans into liberal democracy. In both cases, they were seen as driven by instinct rather than reason, aligned with nature rather than civilization. Deemed incapable of higher human reason, they were animalized: irrational, immoral, the site of lawless enjoyment.

I interpret the Sullivan family business as the production of racial animal jouissance for the nation. In using the term "animal jouissance," I mean to evoke Tomas's actual business of selling attack dogs, but also the enjoyment derived from the hegemonic racial formation of the indeterminate brown subject as primitive, brutal, and lawless. This chapter traces how the Sullivan family business of animal jouissance derives from the legacies of U.S. imperial nationalism—including the colonization and neo-colonization of the Philippines—as itself also a family business, writ large, producing jouissance.

In *American Son*, Gabe and Tomas live with their Filipina mother in South Santa Monica, an economically liminal area bordering poorer as well as richer neighborhoods. Tomas has learned to capitalize on both their economic liminality and their racial liminality to generate surplus-value for their family business. Specifically, Tomas understands that the socially degraded is the site of symbolic capital, which can be converted into economic capital. The Sullivan household is considered deviant and "broken" because the brothers' white American father, who met their mother in the Philippines while serving in the U.S. military, abandoned them several years ago. The very conditions by which the Sullivan family has come into being, then, are those of U.S. imperialism, which necessitates military deployment at strategic sites around the world in order to maintain its global hegemony. We can thus understand the Sullivan family as one site of the "intimacies of empire,"[1] an imperial domesticity marked by the white American patronym, Sullivan, that continues to name its members long after the departure of the individual father. This chapter develops an understanding of racial shame and racial jouissance as modes of such imperial intimacy.

While 1980s and 1990s multiculturalism highlighted domestic, nation-based understandings of race and ethnicity, scholars of Filipino American studies during this period emphasized the importance of U.S. empire as a framework for interpreting Filipino American culture. The work of Oscar V. Campomanes, especially his 1995 article "Afterword: The New Empire's Forgetful and Forgotten Citizens," was especially influential in inaugurating a paradigm shift in the way that we comprehend Filipino American, Asian American, and American literature and culture. As Victor Bascara puts it, Asian American cultural politics has provided the conditions for U.S. empire to become newly recognizable.[2] It is the newness of this recognizability that I want to underscore here. While many American studies and Asian American studies critics have become familiar with this scholarship on U.S. empire, such a context is not as readily discernible for more casual readers of *American Son*, precisely because of the historical unrecognizability of empire that Campomanes and others have pinpointed. Many of the scenes that I quote and analyze from the novel can be comprehended—quite rightfully—within nation-based understandings of race. They depict everyday encounters between differently racialized subjects, staging interpersonal dynamics that are shaped by palpable inequalities in power and privilege. It is imperative, however, that we also understand how racial formations are themselves imperial formations. The limit of nation-based frameworks is precisely their erasure of imperial dynamics. In a nation-based frame, the "solution" to racism is understood within liberal constructs such as civil rights, and the state is seen as the guarantor of such rights. Within the framework of empire, we see more explicitly the state's interest in attaining hegemonic power over other states. Such global hegemony is enabled by the restructuring of capital and labor and by militaristic force, which in *American Son* take the form of imperial intimacies that are also racial formations. I especially want to emphasize how the children of U.S. migrants are formed by such imperialism. It is not only migrants, immigrants, and neocolonial subjects inside and outside the U.S. territory, in other words, that should be studied as transnational subjects, but also the "successive generations" of racial migration that would otherwise be understood within models of Americanization. Within the paradigm of multicultural or multiracial Americanization, assimilation into the U.S. nation is viewed as the ultimate and logical endpoint, albeit achievable only by overcoming obstacles and barriers, for global populations. Such a model is the very mythos of American exceptionalism that ideologically undergirds U.S. global hegemony. Instead, we must understand the experiences of these successive generations as legacies and "linger[ing]s" of imperialism.[3] From this perspective, Gabe and Tomas are the remains of U.S. empire, the progeny of a family formed by U.S.-Philippine neocolonial relations. Remains are of course also excess, and the family survives in the United States by capitalizing on their status as excess: as generators of a surplus-enjoyment that converts into surplus-value.

I begin this chapter by explaining the significance of shame as the primary mode of citizenship and domesticity for the Sullivan family. I then focus on the two main dimensions of family business in *American Son*. First, I discuss the economic dimension of family business: Tomas's marketing of attack dogs. I then consider the maintenance of family as institution, in which the sons understand their filial responsibility as absorbing the racial and gendered shame of their Filipino mother. In the same way that economic family business generates jouissance in the service of law, so too does the family business of shame generate jouissance for the hegemonic gaze. Understandably, Gabe wishes to flee the trauma of such family business, so he runs away to Northern California. I analyze the central, lengthy "interlude" depicting Gabe's escape, which takes the form of a fantasy of white masculinity, a mythos of white maleness as whole and free from animal jouissance. Such a fantasy cannot be sustained indefinitely, however, and its own permeation by shame and jouissance are revealed in the end. Finally, I examine Gabe's fate in "becoming-animal" as a legacy of indebted racial citizenship, structured by imperial jouissance.

SHAMEFUL CITIZENSHIP

Racial shame is the predominant mode of citizenship and domesticity in *American Son*. This shameful citizenship is a paradoxical incorporation into the nation that is structured by the nonrecognition of national belonging. Recognition and its negation are primarily figured in *American Son*, and in the phenomenon of shame more generally, through the fields of visuality and corporeality. Shame is the feeling that one is bare, vulnerable, and exposed to the gaze of the Other. And as if one did not already feel overexposed, the body betrays itself with the heat of blood that rushes perceptibly to one's face, visibly blushing as if to solicit even further scrutiny. Humiliated, one feels hypervisible, and in turn wishes to protect and cloak oneself in invisibility, even to disappear altogether. Yet, confronted by this desire for disembodiment, the body hotly asserts itself with a vengeance. How can we think about this self-betrayal? Helen Lewis explains shame as "the vicarious experience of the other's negative evaluation."[4] The object of shame internalizes the gaze of the social other as the judgment of the

Other who wields power. As an embodied response to such scrutiny and evaluation, shame is a mode of self-punishment and self-regulation. We can also see, however, an excess in shame's response that is not entirely incorporable into its hegemonic functions. Even as the body submits itself to further scrutiny, it forcefully asserts its existence in the face of a verdict demanding that it disappear itself.

Shame can arise, then, from the awareness that one is the object of a juridical gaze. Contrary to the myth of juridical impartiality, this gaze is obscene. It is not neutral; rather, it sadistically derives enjoyment from this scene of debasement. The effect of this sadistic gaze is an intensified, self-conscious embodiment of the object. Earlier I referred to temperature, heartbeat, and eye contact as bodily elements that are transformed by embarrassment. Other physiological symptoms triggered by humiliation in *American Son* include tears, nausea, and a choked voicelessness. Especially in combination, such symptoms indicate a sense of self-endangerment: the debasement of shame threatens the self. Yet, if one does not want to call further attention to oneself, if one wishes to escape the gaze by holding still in the hopes of disappearing, then these physical symptoms may be more paralyzing than energizing, producing a feeling of entrapment in the body. Put another way, the embodiment of shame makes embodiment itself an excess, a substance that should not be. If we define obscenity as offensiveness to the senses, then the obscenity imputed to the debased object derives from this excess, this overly full, repellant, supersaturating substance in the fields of sight and the other senses. From this obscene excess of shame, the hegemonic gaze derives an overstimulating, almost unbearable enjoyment. My focus here is on the racial shame that is produced for the jouissance of the imperial, white supremacist gaze.

Psychologists find that a forerunner of shame occurs in infancy, "when the circuit of mirroring expressions between the child's face and the caregiver's recognized face . . . is broken: the moment when the adult face fails or refuses to play its part in the continuation of the mutual gaze."[5] As Eve Sedgwick suggests here, shame is an affect arising from the nonreciprocity of recognition in the field of vision, in which one's expectation of and desire for connection and affirmation is thwarted. In a related formulation, Silvan Tomkins finds that shame arises in a visual encounter with the strange or the stranger. Shame might be triggered, he says, "because one is suddenly looked at by one who is strange, or because one wishes to look at or commune with another person but suddenly cannot because he is strange, or one expected him to be familiar but he suddenly appears unfamiliar, or one started to smile but found one was smiling at a stranger."[6] Let us consider Sedgwick's and Tomkins's insights together. Why would shame be triggered by looking into the face of someone who has turned strange? Because the stranger cannot confer the comforting recognition that one desires from the loved one. The stranger is not recognized as one who can recognize. Tomkins has been credited with the insight that an affective investment such as interest, desire, or love is necessary for the production of shame.[7] And reciprocity of this affective investment is necessary for one to feel acknowledged and recognized, such that the thwarting of this desire for reciprocity is experienced as negation of the self. Note that an encounter between two strangers per se would result only in indifference. What produces the trauma of shame is the interaction in which an expected familiar turns strange. And the stranger's nonrecognition in turn produces the self as also strange and foreign.[8]

We can now consider how citizenship and domesticity are racialized, gendered, and sexualized as shameful in *American Son*. Taught that America as a globally protective force to its neocolonial subjects, and as the land of equal opportunity for its racial migrants, will recognize and include them, the Sullivans are bewildered when the face of America "fails or refuses to play its part in . . . the mutual gaze." Histories of colonization and neocolonialism have produced America as the site of libidinal and fantasmatic investment for its global and migrant subjects. America is expected to be familiar, but it turns out to be a stranger in its refusal of recognition. And the gaze of the stranger-nation in turn produces the racial migrant as foreign, as excess to the national Symbolic. As surplus and thus unrecognizable by the national Symbolic, the racial migrant becomes the site of jouissance. Obscene and offensive to the senses, the hypercorporealized racial subject cannot be abstracted into universal citizenship. Although they are excluded from this abstract citizenship, I will show how the Sullivan family members are indeed incorporated into the nation as commodity and excess on one hand, and as labor and absence on the other. The shameful citizenship of the Sullivans indexes the paradox of such nonuniversal incorporation, a belonging structured by excess.

Allan Isaac's reading of the momentarily infamous case of Andrew Cunanan from the 1990s allows us to understand how the racial unrecognizability of the Filipino American, which derives from the nonrecognition of U.S. empire, is a form of enjoyment for the hegemonic gaze. Isaac recalls in his introduction to *American Tropics* how Cunanan attracted the national media spotlight in 1997, when he was discovered to be the instigator of a series of murders, most notoriously that of fashion designer Gianni Versace. Print and television newsmagazines led us through the national "manhunt" for Cunanan, culminating in Miami's South Beach. Along the way, we delved into Cunanan's gay "underworld," fascinated by his chameleon-like, ever-changing appearances. Of Filipino and Italian descent, Cunanan had occasionally passed as Mexican and Jewish, and he was often described as a white male. As Isaac puts it, the mainstream media's obsession with Cunanan's unrecognizability, referenced in the figure of his various "masks," "not only laid bare American dis-ease with homosexuality . . . but signaled the blind limits of the U.S. racial imaginary and its misreading and incomprehension of its imperial history."[9] Isaac posits the Cunanan case as a prime example of the "unrecognizability of the Filipino and the Philippines in larger U.S. narratives,"[10] an unrecognizability that other scholars of U.S. empire have commented on for the past two decades.[11] My argument is that racial jouissance and shame in *American Son* are the legacies of imperial blindness: the nonrecognition of empire producing the racial other as an excess of the national Symbolic.

Scholars of U.S. empire have enabled a critique of purely domestic understandings of nation. Thus, we see how the deviant visibilities of the Sullivan family are produced not only by domestic national frameworks of white privilege and power, but also by the blindness to and blindness of U.S. empire. In addition to this connotation of the domestic-as-national, I would like to point to a second way in which the "domestic" helps us understand the shameful citizenship of the Sullivans. Here I refer to the ways in which domesticity as a regime of heteronormativity also determines the conditions of legibility and recognizability. Isaac recounts the sensationalism of Cunanan's media portrayal as fixated upon his ever-changing alterity, an unrecognizability conditioned by racial hybridity and imperial blindness as well as the deviance of gay homosociality from a stable, knowable, and respectable domesticity. The hegemonic gaze is both traumatized by and enjoys such unknowability, drawn to yet dreading the other as the site of enigma and potentially traumatic revelation. That is, in its very disavowals of colonization and queerness, the national gaze is titillated by the other, who tickles and threatens to expose the secret excesses of the nation.

Along similar lines, we must attribute the shame of the Sullivan household to racial difference as it is figured by deviance from heteropatriarchal norms. In other words, the Sullivans' deviance from heteropatriarchy renders its racial difference all the more salient. Furthermore, they are a "broken" family because of their abandonment by the white American husband and father. It is this abandonment that renders their racial and immigrant status newly conspicuous, as they are "unhomed" in the nation without the legitimating anchor and alibi of the U.S. military father. I deliberately use the word "alibi" here, for the borderline legitimacy of the Sullivan family positions them perilously close to the borders delineating lawful presence from lawless presence. If kinship to the American patriarch legitimated their migration to and continued presence in the United States, then the severing of this kinship threatens to de-legitimate their presence. As a "broken" family with an overworked, ineffectual single mother and two adolescent males engaged in illicit activities, the Sullivan household is considered the site of domestic dysfunction and pathology. Such pathology means that the Sullivans oscillate between hypervisibility and invisibility. They are hypervisible because they must be surveilled and morally judged. But they are also invisible because they are unrecognized as legitimate citizen-subjects of the nation. This oscillation between two poles of deviant visibility renders them the site of enjoyment for the national gaze.

In *American Son*, the shameful citizenship of the Sullivans stands in marked contrast to the injured citizenship claimed by white subjects. The novel demonstrates how injury is most visible as damage done to white, propertied individuals, and least visible as the suffering of racial others. The reason for this racialized disproportion in the visibility of injury becomes apparent when we clarify the definition of injury. Min Song draws from the legal analysis of Carl Gutiérrez-Jones to elaborate on the connotations of injury:

> The concept of injury, as Carl Gutiérrez-Jones explains, is inextricably bound up with the law and with the state that provides the muscle to enforce the law: "like the verb form to injure, injury marks an act against 'jur,' against the law, rights, and accepted privilege" (2001, 24). Hence, this concept suggests the ways in which injury reifies a feeling of having been wronged within social, and bureaucratic, institutions that may or may not require some kind of mandated compensation. . . . [T]his articulation is . . . accompanied by questions of blame and recompense. Who caused the injury? In what ways might we enumerate a just compensation for the suffering caused by injury?[12]

If injury is an act against the law, then subjects must be recognizable as legitimate in order to have an injury acknowledged and redressed. The legitimacy conferred by property ownership, for example, means that damage done to one's property is recognizable as an injury against the owner's right to enjoy his property. However, violence done to less legitimate subjects—for example, police harassment of youth of color who are in the "wrong" part of town—is less recognizable as injury. Instead, it is simply considered enforcement of the law, one that preemptively protects property and whiteness from damage done by racial others. Injury and shame, then, are wielded to racialize whiteness as aligned with law and social morality and racial others as juridical objects that may be judged as outside social morality.

Walter Benjamin and other critics have pointed out how the violence of law enforcement not only aims at enforcing the content of law, but at preserving the very form of law. The violence of law and the state is transformed into law itself, while other forms of violence are criminalized and outlawed. In *American Son*, we see that violence against whiteness and property is criminalized in this way, while violence against racial others is implicitly sanctioned by law. Violence that protects whiteness and property is not seen as injury against the racially or economically subordinated; it is seen simply as law. Violence against whiteness and property, by contrast, is seen as criminal and degenerate. *American Son* reveals how violence committed by youths of color, often naturalized as lawless in its connotative senses (animalistic, savage, irrational), emerges from a condition of lawlessness in a more precisely institutional sense: exclusion from the protections of law; exclusion from having one's violations recognized and legitimated as injury.

The Lacanian insight that I would like to add to this analysis of violence and law is the understanding that jouissance, as well as violence, serves as a support and underside of law. Violence denotes force, ferocity, and aggression, but jouissance comprises an affective element of disgust and obscenity. And while violence is often brutal and cruel, it can often be understood through some kind of narration (for example, this person committed violence because violence was committed against him). Jouissance, however, cannot be narrativized, for it is a condition in which meaning and sense absolutely collapse. What is especially traumatic about jouissance is its enjoyment: the nauseating, disturbing satisfaction that one obtains from violence as pain *and* pleasure.

Animal Jouissance

The first line of *American Son* introduces us to Gabe's brother, Tomas, positing his most essential characteristic as his entrepreneurship, running a family business in which Gabe also participates: "Tomas is the son who helps pay the mortgage by selling attack dogs to rich people and celebrities" (15). Upon our entrance into the narrative, Tomas is immediately linked to the family business of marketing animal violence. We learn later that Tomas engages in a second mode of entrepreneurship as well—participating in an underground economy of stealing, circulating, and selling goods such as stereos, home fixtures, and so forth. We can see from Tomas's entrepreneurial activity that his role within the system of property and law is radically ambivalent. On the one hand, he engages in criminal behavior through selling stolen goods, and thus represents a threat to property and law. On the other hand, he trains and sells attack dogs to protect the very property system that maintains and generates wealth for the privileged few, at the expense of families like his. Tomas's ambivalence is the very ambivalence of racial jouissance, which both threatens and supports the national Symbolic order. This production of racial and animal jouissance in support of national law constitutes the Sullivan family business.

Significantly, it is Tomas's criminalized appearance as a Mexican gangster that makes his business of protecting property so lucrative. Who knows better how to protect against criminals than a criminal? Tomas understands that the value of his commodification is enhanced through making himself into a spectacle of racial criminality. In this way, the family business requires the hypervisible display of Tomas's body. His gangster tattoos give him the street authenticity that his clients look for, and Tomas deliberately displays them, wearing sleeveless and translucent white T-shirts (17, 45).

Tomas is thus not only the object but also the agent of racial hypervisibility. Let me continue quoting the introductory passages in *American Son,* in which Gabe presents Tomas as a hypervisible spectacle, while making his own presence recede from view:

> Tomas is the son who helps pay the mortgage by selling attack dogs to rich people and celebrities. He is the son who keeps our mother up late with worry. He is the son who causes her embarrassment by showing up at family parties with his muscles covered in gangster tattoos and his head shaved

down to stubble and his eyes bloodshot from pot. He is really half white, half Filipino but dresses like a Mexican, and it troubles our mother that he does this. She cannot understand why if he wants to be something he is not he does not at least try to look white. He is also the son who says that if any girlfriend criticized our mother or treated her wrong he would knock the bitch across the house.

I am the son who is quiet and no trouble, and I help our mother with chores around the house.

The client is some man from the movie business . . . who is coming over any minute so that Tomas can help him train the dog he bought to protect his home. This morning I have been helping my brother wash and train his dogs. (15)

The apparent good son–bad son dichotomy that is presented in Gabe's introduction—Gabe helps their mother, while Tomas makes her worry—is complicated when we consider the notion of family business. Tomas assumes the responsibility of helping to keep the family afloat economically. His gangster appearance embarrasses their mother in front of their extended family, and even more so in that he has chosen to embody the degraded persona of the Mexican. It is not so much the artifice of racial passing that she objects to, but what he passes as: Why not pass for white, which has a higher social status and value, and which allows for the safety of a normative visibility that is also an invisibility? By presenting himself as a criminalized Mexican, Tomas invites the gaze, scrutiny, and surveillance of the Other. While his own body is the primary object of the gaze, his mother is also scrutinized as the one responsible for his degradation. Ika is embarrassed because her son's appearance opens her up to judgment as a bad mother, a mother who did not raise her child to be respectable and upwardly mobile. In this sense, she feels that she has lost cultural capital within the network of her family. Tomas would seem to fail his mother in this sense of family business—maintaining the respectability of family reputation. It is clear, however, that Tomas understands his role in family business quite differently from his mother.

In fact, Tomas does briefly pass as white, so we know that his subsequent refusal to do so is a deliberate act (30). Lacking the economic resources to support and protect his family, Tomas assumes a Mexican gangster persona initially to signify the brute violence that is necessary to defend his family in their liminal neighborhood, *as well as* the entrepreneurship that will generate such resources.[13] To produce capital for family business in the economic sense, Tomas must be aware of how cultural capital is shaped beyond the Filipino family and how this cultural capital becomes economic capital. Tomas capitalizes on the unrecognizability of the U.S. Filipino and his white-Filipino race mixture by misdirecting the interpretation of his racial ambiguity, by embodying—counterintuitively—a degraded rather than elevated racial persona. This strategic performance of *mestizaje,* an apparent refusal to pass for white, demonstrates that Tomas understands that whiteness *in and of itself* is not necessarily a guarantee of upward mobility. As critical race scholars have shown, racial whiteness constitutes a valued form of property, recognized and protected by law. This property of whiteness can lead to the acquisition of other forms of property and capital, but such acquisition is far from universal.[14] We might say that for poor or working-class white subjects, the property of whiteness ideologically compensates or substitutes for such additional acquisition. In his immediate environment, Tomas perceives that the most immediate opportunities for generating capital take the form of racial commodification. If the unrecognizing gaze of the nation produces racial shame, as I have argued, then Tomas strategically solicits misrecognition to capitalize on racial shame. His ambiguously figured, mixed-race, brown body serves as a screen for the fantasy of the hegemonic gaze, and the fantasy that he produces is that of racial criminality and animalism: the illicit and brutal Mexican gangster. Thus, Tomas's Mexican appearance may not make sense within the logic of cultural capital within family networks, but it makes eminent sense within the logic of national and regional racial commodification. If Tomas's business is the marketing of animal violence, then he should "brand" himself as a metonym of such animalism with the persona of the lawless Mexican gangster.

Metonymically associated with his attack dogs and marked as an outlaw or criminal, Tomas is racialized as a brute, an animal. However, it is not a pure animalism that generates value so much as the interpenetration of animal jouissance with the rationality of capital and law. Tomas's business of protecting property brings together this rationality of law with the savagery of animal violence. Indeed, we can see how Tomas's dogs are valued precisely for their combination of rationality and brutality. Tomas raises the demand for and value of his dogs by marketing them as German in their lineage and training. The sardonic irony of Gabe's observation that even Jewish clients enjoy hearing about the dogs' German identities (20)

derives of course from the history of anti-Semitic persecution and geno-
cide in Nazi Germany, practices that were underwritten by the scientific
racism of eugenics and the rationalistic systemization of modern bureau-
cracy.[15] The signifier "German" is meant to index the efficiency and ruth-
lessness of the dogs' violence, unencumbered by sympathy, conscience,
or morality. The demand for such brutality is explicitly illustrated by the
increase in price that Tomas's pit bulls command after this breed becomes
known for killing children (21). The dogs represent a rational violence
even as they practice a vicious brutality. Moreover, the efficiency of such
rationality is linked to the notion of purity: the German pedigrees are
meant to convey a deliberate program of breeding for maximum effectiveness. The fantasy of their racial purity, resulting in the most ruthless, brutal,
and efficient violence, represents the culmination of modern rationality.
It is the instrumentalization of brutality in service of the law that is in such
high demand by the market. We can see here how surplus-enjoyment generates surplus-value, how the "abstraction" of profit is in fact structured by
brutality and violence. More broadly, we see in the novel how the impersonal "abstractions" of modernity—capital, law, citizenship, nation—are
supported and permeated by racial and imperial jouissance.

Tomas acts both in service and as threat to hegemonic law; following
Lacan, I consider this acting as an instrument of law to be the practice of
perversion.[16] Lacan conceives of law as undergirded by its obverse: obscene
enjoyment. While official law is represented as neutral and impartial, what
actually sustains law is the enjoyment of its enforcement as well as its
transgression. The animal jouissance of Tomas's attack dogs permits their
owners to enjoy this violence of law enforcement. Tomas also generates
enjoyment in the hegemonic gaze by producing shame through his sadism
and exhibitionism. One of the major aims of sadism, Erich Fromm explains,
is the pain and humiliation of the other: "to hurt actively, to humiliate, to
embarrass others, or to see them in embarrassing and humiliating positions."[17] Tomas's sadism is most obvious in his humiliation and abuse of
Gabe: toying with Gabe's desire to visit important clients; telling him that
he looks like a houseboy; beating him and cutting Gabe's bare chest with a
broken beer bottle (36–37, 18, 141). More obliquely but still powerfully,
Tomas sadistically embarrasses his mother through the hyperdisplay of
his racially degraded body. Linking Tomas with attack dogs, a gangster
appearance, and misogynistic violence, the novel's introduction associates
him with an aggressiveness that is brutal and exhibitionistic. Not only does

he display aggressiveness; the display itself is a practice of aggression. Exhibitionism imbues the body with the "to be looked at" quality that Laura Mulvey associates with the object of the gaze.[18] But while Mulvey assigns power to the subject of the gaze, the exhibitionist assumes power as the object of the gaze. Exhibitionism is a subcategory of perversion, of operating as the instrument of the Other. In exhibitionism, one solicits the gaze in order to conjure up enjoyment for the Other. Sadistically, the exhibitionist delights in compelling this jouissance and, moreover, in shaming the gaze by exposing its investment in jouissance and thus undoing the myth of its neutrality. Thus, Tomas's sadism is not only directed toward his family: his stance toward the hegemonic gaze is also sadistic. By so gleefully fulfilling the enjoyment of the gaze, Tomas not only unmasks its supposed neutrality but also takes delight in expressing his superior knowledge: "You pretend to be neutral, but I know you are driven by jouissance." Tomas's sadistic knowingness both serves and exceeds the purposes of national and racial hegemony.

CONSUMING AND ABSORBING SHAME

In chapter 1, we saw how the responsibility for managing and supporting migrant labor fell upon subjects in the private sphere, specifically the children of migrants and immigrants. Here I will explore a specific affective dimension of such management: the child's assumption of parental shame. In *American Son,* Asian American family business in its institutional dimension—the business of maintaining the family as a social structure—requires a filial absorption of the hegemonic, shaming gaze that falls upon the mother as a racialized and gendered subject. Significantly, the scenes and passages from the novel that most dramatize such shaming involve consumption. Twentieth-century formations of citizenship, as many commentators have observed, became increasingly entwined with consumerism, such that individual desire, choice, and rights were figured as consumer desire and choice.[19]

Consumer citizenship is a late twentieth-century form of the link between self-possession and liberal citizen-subjecthood. As I have mentioned, Filipinos have been racially construed as "incapable of self-government." At the turn of the twentieth century, they were considered not civilized enough, not rational enough, too close to nature, to be capable of self-government. In this way, they were seen as outside human law. At the turn of the twenty-first century, this exclusion from liberal subjecthood now uses the trope of criminality, of exclusion from the law as institution. As we will see, the Sullivans are excluded from the legitimacy of ownership and consumption that undergirds contemporary notions of citizenship. Instead, they are construed as illegitimate and indebted.

Early in the novel, Gabe tells us that he is embarrassed to be seen with his mother in public, describing the shamefulness of her incompetent consumption: "I do not like having her pick me up from school. She is short and dark and wears funny-looking purple glasses that are trendy on other people's mothers but which do not match her brown skin tone" (30). Ika's inappropriate display of commodities makes her and, by extension, Gabe hypervisible as objects of embarrassment, for these funny-looking glasses make an unseemly spectacle of her lack of taste and cultural capital. But this example also highlights how commodified fashion trends assume and normativize white consumers and white skin tone, so that brown skin tone becomes naturalized as the unfortunate and deviant accessory (the glasses *would* be trendy if not for her brown skin).

In "'A Nation of Thieves': Consumption, Commerce, and the Black Public Sphere," Regina Austin argues that the apparently mundane acts of buying and selling, when performed by black subjects, are rendered deviant. Black people are not recognized as legitimate consumers and potential owners of commodities; instead, they are apprehended and treated as potential thieves and troublemakers:

> Tales of the obstacles blacks encounter in trying to spend their money in white-owned shops and stores are legendary. Blacks are treated as if they were all potentially shoplifters, thieves or deadbeats. There can hardly be a black person in urban America who has not been either denied entry to a store, closely watched, snubbed, questioned about her or his ability to pay for an item or stopped and detained for shoplifting. Salespeople are slow to wait on blacks and rude when they do, or too quick to wait on blacks whom they practically shove out the door. . . . Any kind of ordinary face-to-face retail transaction can turn into a hassle for a black person.[20]

The racialized deviance of black consumption to which Austin refers corresponds to the deviant visibility of hypervisible surveillance on the one hand, and invisible disregard on the other. Hypervisibility and invisibility are both conditions of illegitimate consumerism, and as such they are not mutually exclusive but can shade into one another. As we see from Austin's examples, the exclusion of blacks from legitimate consumer citizenship results from the way that dispossession is naturalized as criminalization. That is, blacks are symbolically barred from legitimate ownership (including the liberal ideal of the self-possessed) and thus cannot legitimately consume. Black claims to consumption or ownership must be illegitimate, the result of stealing property or even the proprietors' time ("deadbeats" might hang around without buying; even buyers should not hang around but should leave as quickly as possible).

In the scene that I examine here, Ika is also positioned within the deviant visibility of the illegitimate consumer citizen. However, she is not criminalized in the same way as the black consumers in Austin's article. I will argue, rather, that she is rendered invisible because her proper position, as a brown immigrant woman, is as a laborer rather than a consumer citizen. Ika's invisibility is experienced as racial shame, but because this shame produces enjoyment, it also transforms into hypervisibility. For Gabe, the family business of filial responsibility means that he must absorb his mother's shame and become himself the hypervisible racial object of the gaze.

In this scene, Gabe and his mother walk down Third Street Promenade, a fashionable outdoor shopping district in Santa Monica, with heavy foot traffic. This mundane, everyday act of walking highlights how a regime of visibility organizes the negotiation of public space between subjects of different social status:

> The times I have been here with Tomas, people always step aside, even older men in suits with a girlfriend or secretary whom they reluctantly guide out of our way. But now my mother steps out of other people's paths, and I do too. We near a group of skinny college-student types. They look like engineers, nerdy, and I would not normally get out of their way. But even though the pale one in a yellow button-down shirt sees Mom, he acts as if he does not see her, and she actually has to squeeze beside a bench to let them pass. The biggest one clips her shoulder. I freeze. I glare at them, aware of the ice pick tucked behind my wallet, but they don't even notice me. (179)

In this narrative of competing claims to public space, we observe a number of complexities. Gabe himself might claim or not claim social space, depending on whether he is with the hypervisible Tomas or his invisible mother. We see how the power of such negotiation is not strictly determined by economic power. Tomas's racial hypervisibility, and specifically the way in which his embodiment is comprehended as lawless and criminal, means that he is feared as a potential agent of violence. Thus, even the economically privileged, such as businessmen, defer to Tomas's claim to space. Dismaying as it may be to have their masculine power abrogated, these businessmen exercise bourgeois codes of masculine responsibility by protectively moving their female companions out of harm's way, even as they register their dismay through their reluctance. While they know that law-enforcement officers and public opinion would side with them in the event of an altercation, the businessmen also position themselves as respectable and rational citizens who, presumably unlike Tomas, avoid anything that would disturb the public peace. Through his hypervisibility, in fact, Tomas has already disturbed the public peace.

If Tomas's racial hypervisibility claims a certain kind of everyday power to disturb the socially privileged, Ika's racial invisibility defers such power even to those who appear low in social rank. The example of nerdy engineers again highlights how economic privilege is not always equivalent to everyday social power. These engineering students will go on to earn high salaries, but their staid mode of dress, skinny body types, and pale skin tone (indexing their lack of outdoor activity, considered deviant in Southern California culture) register as low social status in everyday "street" interactions. Nevertheless, despite this devalued position, they refuse to see or acknowledge the racial immigrant woman, whom they physically displace without apology.

Gabe's mother then goes to a makeup counter, where she stands for several minutes. As she continues to linger, the salesclerk engages in a personal conversation with the pharmacist across the aisle, apparently ignoring this waiting customer. Remembering Tomas's past acts of intervening for his mother in public, Gabe assumes the filial responsibility of calling attention to his mother's plight. He interrupts the salesgirl's conversation and, to his own surprise, articulates his frustration in racial terms: "You shouldn't not serve somebody just because they look different" (182). Strikingly, this accusation of racism does not embarrass the salesclerk. Instead, it is the face of her colleague, the pharmacist, that reddens. Described by Gabe as "vaguely Hispanic" (181), the pharmacist sees what the salesclerk is blind to: that an apparently unremarkable everyday moment has become the site of racial humiliation.

When Gabe's mother first realizes that she is being overlooked, she "leans off the counter, checking to see if anyone has noticed her being ignored" (180). Ika is shamed by her nonrecognition by the clerk, but shame is not contained solely within this interpersonal circuit. Ika fears a deepening of her humiliation by the gaze of the Other, a gaze that is permeated with enjoyment. In what Gershen Kaufman called the "shame spiral," feeling shame makes one even further ashamed.[21] The initial experience of shame may result from the judgment of another, or even the self, that one is unworthy, resulting in the wish to hide. However, once the shamed person is aware of the gaze, there is no place to hide, for the gaze emanates from and penetrates everywhere. Gabe's mother may be invisible to the salesclerk, but this invisibility paradoxically makes her hypervisible to the Other. While we would like to believe that the gaze of the Other is impersonal and neutral, this gaze is in fact permeated with sadistic enjoyment. Such enjoyment feeds on this shame and this jouissance further shames the subject. Gabe notes, for example, that as he confronts the salesclerk, some bystanders linger out of curiosity to see if a scandalous scene will erupt (182). Why do these shoppers and pedestrians take time from their busy lives to watch an interaction among a teenager, a racial immigrant woman, and a salesclerk? Because they believe their spectatorship will result in a net gain of enjoyment. It does not matter to the crowd *who* ends up being shamed in this drama—Ika, Gabe, or the salesclerk—only that there is shame to feed the jouissance of their gaze.

Pressured by Gabe, the salesclerk finally acknowledges his mother. Ika, however, has become embarrassed by this sudden attention from the salesclerk as well as from the growing crowd. Ika is unable to attain the normative visibility of a legitimate consumer: her invisibility has become transformed into hypervisibility. As I mentioned in my discussion of Austin's article, both invisibility (disregard) and hypervisibility (surveillance) are structured by the illegitimate status ascribed to racial consumers, such that one condition of deviant visibility shades into the other. In order to deflect the gaze, Ika says, "Oh, no thank you . . . I'm just looking" (183). Contrary to conventional notions of looking as an assertion of power, this statement forfeits power. By saying that she is "just looking," Ika suggests that she may not have the economic power to buy, inadvertently confirming the salesclerk's judgment in ignoring her. Ika's statement that she is merely looking at the cosmetics—not asking for recognition as a consumer citizen—is the equivalent of the shamed subject averting her eyes from the bearer of the look.

The mother's deflection of the gaze means that Gabe now bears the brunt of the gaze. Gabe now becomes hypervisible as a troublemaker,

pathologized as paranoid, an overly sensitive racial subject who halluci-
nates racism where common sense apprehends nothing. Gabe is made
to look like a fool and, moreover, to bear the responsibility for having
solicited the gaze in the first place. Shame follows a circuitous route. First,
Gabe's mother is shamed by her nonrecognition as a legitimate consumer
citizen. Gabe attempts to counter-shame the clerk into recognizing his
mother. The salesclerk, however, does not recognize herself as shamewor-
thy. Instead, her Latina colleague, who comprehends the shameful affect
of nonrecognition, catches the contagion of shame. The mother's shame
is then compounded from feeling exposed to the sadistic gaze; she deflects
the gaze so that Gabe becomes its object instead. In the end, Gabe becomes the locus of racial shame, whose racial pathology the gaze can consume and enjoy.

When Gabe leaves the store, he finds his mother seeking the protections of invisibility. She is "just a few feet down from the storefront glass,
where she cannot be seen. . . . Mom has found the slender shadow of an
infant tree. She is always finding shade so her skin will not get darker"
(185). Why is darkening to be avoided? Because it both decreases and
increases her visibility. Darkening means that she is not recognized as a
legitimate citizen-subject. And, as we saw, the invisibility of nonrecognition is also the hypervisibility of shame. As Anne Cheng notes, "The values of racial visibility and invisibility can only emerge in relation to one
another even as such appearance of meaning almost always immediately
problematizes the signification against which it has defined itself. 'White
visibility,' for instance, relies on the invisibility and assumed normality of
whiteness, while 'black invisibility' acquires its shape precisely through its
very visibility as difference."[22] Recall that one of the engineering students
does see Gabe's mother and then acts as if he does not see her. In order for
these students and the salesclerk not to see Ika, they must first register
her racial difference in order to judge her as not worthy of being seen. To
modify Mulvey's phrase, Gabe's mother registers as "not-to-be-looked-at,"
but one must first look in order to un-look. This is how a racially marked
hypervisibility shades into invisibility, just as invisibility can also be rendered hypervisible to the enjoying gaze.

Indeed, we might consider this oscillation between lack and excess,
here in the field of visuality, to be a primary facilitator of racial jouissance.
Fantasy is structured by desire, which moves from object to object in its
endless search for satisfaction. In contrast, the mode of jouissance is that

of the drive, whose oscillating, pulsating circuit is its own satisfaction. As Žižek notes, for example, the ordinary act of shaking hands becomes obscene if one were meaninglessly to repeat such a squeezing of the other's hand.[23] Similarly, the hegemonic gaze derives enjoyment not only from the shames of racial invisibility and hypervisibility but from the very fluctuation between the two.

In this function as a kind of switchpoint between various visibilities, what does racial difference signify? The invisibility of Gabe's mother derives from her dissociation from the world of consumerism and commodities, her exclusion from consumer citizenship. Gabe recalls a similar incident, years ago, in which Ika felt humiliated and paralyzed by public nonrecognition. The Sullivan family is shopping at Fedco when a clerk skips over Ika's number. Afraid to call further attention to her nonrecognition—afraid to solicit the sadistic gaze whose enjoyment feeds upon her shame—Ika must rely on a young Tomas to take her number from her and get the attention of the salesclerk so she can buy her perfume. Ika's invisibility as a consumer citizen, and her invisibility in public space, indexes the invisibility of the racial immigrant woman as a figure of service labor.

In *The Ruptures of American Capital*, Grace Hong allows us to understand how the political economy of postindustrial capital shapes the disparate deviant visibilities of Ika and Tomas, the older brown immigrant woman and the younger brown male. Hong explicates an urban subway scene from Cherríe Moraga's introduction to the foundational anthology *This Bridge Called My Back*. The postindustrial shift in the U.S. economy, Hong says, helps us make sense of the gendered racialization of public space; for example, a young black male is spectacularly seized and arrested in a subway car, while women of color blend into the background. "This shift into service economies focused on racialized women as its labor force while displacing the industrial production that had previously prioritized racial male labor. In this context, women of color are not subject to scrutiny on the trains, as their presence is explained by their incorporation into a service economy, while the black boy on the train is positioned less as labor and more as the object of state violence and criminalization."[24] In visual terms, we might say that Ika is not-recognized as a legitimate consumer because she is labor, while Tomas is recognized as an illegitimate consumer because he is excluded from labor. Postindustrialization means that someone like Tomas cannot be seen as someone who earns a wage "honestly." Thus his consumption, even of public space, must be made hypervisible so that he can be scrutinized and regulated. Ika, meanwhile, is invisible because of her association with service work: what consumers demand is precisely the invisibility of service work, so that the office space, the hotel room, or the home magically becomes clean again. What the consumer demands from service work is the erasure of work itself. If the commodity dissimulates labor, as in Marx's formulation, then, paradoxically, service work functions as a commodity whose consumption must be disavowed. Let us recall that Tomas's business, the commodification of animal violence, also depends upon the commodification of himself as animalistic: his practices and performances of racial aggressiveness become naturalized through his brown body. Both Tomas and Ika, then, function as racial commodities, but while Tomas's commodification as racial criminal depends upon his hypervisibility, Ika's commodification as service worker must be made invisible.

We see in *American Son* how the deviant visibilities of race index the demands of capital and nation, converging in the form of U.S. global hegemony. Racialization oscillates between the invisibilities of service labor and the hypervisibilities of the commodity. Racial capitalism generates not only surplus-value but also a surplus-enjoyment that supports and reproduces the hegemonies of race, nation, and empire.

For Gabe and Tomas, the family business of filial responsibility means that they become the sites of shame for hegemonic enjoyment. Ika's invisibility becomes transformed into Tomas's and Gabe's hypervisibility. The infant tree that protects Gabe's mother from darkening stands, of course, for Tomas and Gabe. Tomas's apparent agency in his practice of racial exhibitionism, then, does not signify his freedom in the sense of choosing among equally available options. Tomas was thrust into the role of representing his mother in public at an early age, precociously exposed to the sadistic gaze of the Other. His response was to embrace the racial shame that he was asked to produce anyway. Experiencing himself as the instrument of the Other's jouissance, he assented to his role as the pervert. And because jouissance is by nature excessive, Tomas's hypervisible and hypercorporeal exposure to the Other's gaze now exceeds its original function of protecting his mother, so that it now exposes his mother all the more. Through the degraded corporeality of his tattoos, shaved head, and bloodshot eyes, Tomas exposes their family as the site of deviant domesticity and shameful citizenship. In debasing himself for the Other's enjoyment, Tomas has found a way to derive both surplus-value and surplus-enjoyment for himself.

The Fantasy of White Masculinity

Although Tomas is mostly represented as the agent rather than the object of sadistic shame, one surprising episode stages his humiliation by a movie producer—an incident that the otherwise-passive Gabe takes advantage of. Tomas condescendingly treats the producer's Latina wife as a maid, and she takes her revenge by insisting on her desire to buy Tomas's most beloved dog rather than the one he offers them. Tomas understands their refusal of the original dog, and their offer of an absurdly high price for his favorite, as the couple's display of their power to sever him from his only source of emotional tenderness. He refuses, but Gabe later capitalizes on this episode. He steals out of the house early one morning, sells the dog to the producer and his wife, takes Tomas's Oldsmobile, and continues to drive north. In leaving the familiar for the unknown, Gabe seems to exemplify the powerful myth of America as an exceptionalist space of new beginnings. One manifestation of this myth is that of the European migrant seeking to leave behind the constraints of the Old World for the opportunities of the New World. As Gabe is positioned at the westward end of the continent, his journey also evokes Frederick Jackson Turner's thesis of America as frontier. In this trope, the frontiersman finds rejuvenation in the wildness of the West, shedding the stultifying effects of a humiliating, feminized, and overcivilized urban lifestyle in the establishment East. Finally, Gabe's direction north alludes to the northward bid for freedom and escape from bondage in slave narratives, a journey fraught with the danger of being discovered. The setting of this episode over the Fourth of July weekend makes Gabe's quest for independence, emancipation, and enfranchisement even more pointed.

I read this long middle section titled "American Son" as a quest narrative in which Gabe attempts to escape the shame and jouissance of his family business. What he escapes into is the fantasy of white masculinity: he encounters a white father figure, Stone, a local tow-truck driver with whom he passes as white, and who subsequently treats him as a (white) son. This dynamic of quasi-kinship appears to give Gabe the normative recognition that would inscribe him as a universal, abstract subject, free from jouissance. One connotation of the book and section title "American Son" is the desire to be recognized as legitimate kin to the nation. In the end, however, we will see how the fantasy of white masculinity is in fact structured by a jouissance that feeds on racial others. This racial dynamic derives from the jouissance of imperial nationalism, which I discuss briefly in this section and elaborate on more fully in the next. This is the second connotation of "American Son": Gabe as the inheritor of the national "family business" of imperial jouissance.

Throughout his trip, Gabe is acutely sensitive to being looked at. He is afraid that someone will recognize and expose him as a racial outsider, a potential target for the hostilities of those who legitimately belong to these small towns. Gabe understands that his face and even Tomas's car are racial signifiers that could provoke violence (64). One does not have to act to be provocative; one merely has to appear as the racial other who is out of place, disturbing the hegemonic order by embodying visual excess.[25] When Stone does not give him or his car a second look, Gabe feels that he has escaped the hypervisibility of race. Stone seems to promise him the normative visibility that is associated with whiteness; indeed, we find that this normative visibility is precisely predicated on whiteness, since Stone confers this normative recognition only by mis-recognizing Gabe as white.

Although Stone's nonplussed reaction to the white Oldsmobile seems to be the product of small-town ignorance, Gabe feels that there is something strangely familiar about Stone. As it turns out, in the course of their conversation, Stone reveals that he is originally from San Bernardino County, east of Los Angeles. This information provides a foundation for their bonding, as both Stone and Gabe present themselves as refugees from Southern California. Stone pointedly abjects this region by repeatedly referring to Los Angeles, Riverside, San Pedro, and Venice as "shitholes" (82–83). Gabe then earns Stone's goodwill by agreeing that San Pedro is a "crappy place" (83). As Stone continues his tirade against Southern California, he makes clear the elements that make these cities shitholes: the "fucking Mexicans" and "mute Asians" that populate this region (84). To Stone, these racial others are excrementally abject, inspiring disgust and revulsion. And in his compulsion to repeat the word "shithole," we can see Stone's delight and enjoyment in reveling in this disgusting racial excrement.

Stone complains, "All those mute Asians won't even learn to speak English" (84). To not speak English is to be mute, to be outside of language altogether. If language is a primary characteristic that defines the human, then these speechless Asians are not human; they are animals in their speechlessness.[26] Sartre's description of shame applies to Gabe's response to Stone's statements: "Now shame . . . is shame of self; it is the *recognition* of the fact that I *am* indeed that object which the other is looking at and judging."[27] Recognizing himself as the target of abjection, Gabe immediately manifests the autonomic responses of shame, viscerally embodied in his humiliation: "My pulse beats in my neck and my temples and my fingertips. My eyes avoid the rearview mirror as a hot itchiness grows in my underarms and I want to take off my sweater. He must be blind" (84). Paralyzed, Gabe has no verbal response to Stone's statement. Indeed, a response is impossible. First, Gabe cannot believe that Stone does not recognize him as Asian: "He must be blind." Strangely, Gabe recognizes himself as the object at which Stone is looking, even if Stone does not. Second, Gabe does not want to disagree and thus lose the goodwill of the person he must rely on to reach a place of safety—yet agreement would constitute an absurdity, since he is Asian and does indeed speak English. Third, Gabe needs a moment to comprehend what has happened: that he has passed for white. His body recognizes that he is in danger, and this corporeal alarm makes him realize that he must be careful to avoid racial exposure. Gabe's escape from racial hypervisibility is precarious and can easily be undone. In all, Stone's statement has in fact rendered Gabe mute. That is, Stone's verbal act of abjection is not merely descriptive of Asian muteness; it also produces Asian muteness.[28]

What exactly does Asian muteness mean to Stone? Because Gabe does not say very much at this point in their conversation, Stone worries that Gabe has taken offense. Stone clarifies that he has nothing against Gabe as a "quiet guy," because Gabe's quietness means that he listens (85). However, the nonspeech of Asians is qualitatively distinct from the nonspeech of "regular" white guys. "It's just when those people come to this country and won't learn English, how can a person like that listen? No, it's a different thing" (85). For Stone, silence signifies differently depending upon racial formation. Although white silence indicates receptivity, Asian silence means refusal. The problem with Asian muteness, it turns out, is that it is really a sign of Asian deafness. In this odd logic, Asian muteness and deafness are neither states of nature nor states of being injured; rather, they are deliberate behaviors meant to injure whiteness. Stone's objection to Asians is their nonreciprocity, their refusal to participate in Symbolic exchange with him. Muteness and deafness are used to figure Asians as shameful in their innate lack, *and* as blameworthy in positioning themselves as outside the national Symbolic order—as excess. In refusing to join the national Symbolic network, Asians enjoy something that is inaccessible to Stone; they keep their jouissance to themselves. That is how

Asian muteness and deafness injure whiteness: by denying white subjects access to jouissance.

As Žižek elucidates, fantasies of the other's jouissance are themselves a mode of jouissance:

> What are fantasies about the Other's special, excessive enjoyment—about the black's superior sexual potency and appetite, about the Jew's or Japanese's special relationship toward money and work—if not precisely *so many ways, for us, to organize our own enjoyment?* Do we not find enjoyment precisely in fantasizing about the Other's enjoyment, in this ambivalent attitude toward it? Do we not obtain satisfaction by means of the very supposition that the Other enjoys in a way inaccessible to us? Does not the Other's enjoyment exert such a powerful fascination because in it we represent to ourselves our innermost relationship toward enjoyment? . . . [T]he fascinating image of the Other gives a body to our innermost split, to what is "in us more than ourselves" and thus prevents us from achieving full identity with ourselves. The hatred of the Other is the hatred of our own excess of enjoyment.[29]

For Stone, racially abject groups give body to his own inner antagonism. Stone dissimulates his own enjoyment by representing Asians and Mexicans as the site of such pleasurable disgust. Abjecting racial others as animalistic and excremental, Stone produces racial shame; he then consumes this racial shame for his enjoyment.

Gabe responds to Stone's racial epithets with an involuntary hyperembodiment: he becomes hot, itchy, and acutely aware of his beating pulse. These autonomic reactions are an "emergency response" to the hypervisibility of racial shame, signifying endangerment.[30] As the abject and thus a threat to the Symbolic order, Gabe fears that an agent of the Symbolic such as Stone could destroy him. It turns out, however, that Gabe is Stone's blind spot, for Stone does not recognize him as Asian. Once again, Gabe has escaped the hypervisibility of race with Stone. The two quickly form a bond as Gabe verbalizes his recognition and affirmation of Stone's abjection of racial others:

> It's just people like that that made me want to move up here, he says.
> I know what you mean.
> You do?

Yeah.

He thinks about this and nods. (85)

Comparing the territoriality of Mexicans to "pissing dogs," Gabe says that they act "like they're still roaming all the barrios killing each other down in Mexico." He continues, "Cambodians are the worst. It's like their war isn't over yet" (86). Gabe's use of simile to describe the violence of Mexicans and Cambodians (*"like* they're still . . . down in Mexico," *"like* their war isn't over yet") disavows the violence of American national space, and indeed the violence of American imperialism. The naturalization of racial subjects as uncivilized killers, lacking respect for human life, dissimulates the role of American imperialism and neocolonialism in instigating military and civilian conflict over resources and ideologies. The use of simile also mocks these racial subjects for their stupid confusion, implicitly asking, "Don't they know that they are in the United States, where we don't do such things?" Finally, let us look at the emotional and affective crux of these statements, in which describing others as provocative is itself a provocation. The main problem with Mexicans and Cambodians is their bringing of foreign jouissance into American domestic space. Without these foreigners, America would be a coherent, organic society, free from jouissance. But by penetrating American domestic space with their jouissance, these racial subjects "provoke" the jouissance of white hegemony.

We could interpret Gabe's comments as a strategic, camouflaging mimicry of whiteness in a bid for survival and safety. The narrative, however, does not indicate that Gabe thinks any differently from Stone. In this way, we might understand Stone as providing a vehicle for Gabe's own fantasy of racial passing, a fantasy of white masculinity as an escape from racial shame and racial jouissance.

Gabe's comments, by mirroring Stone's racial abjections, stimulate an animated response from Stone, who instigates an increasingly intimate reaction with Gabe:

You know, he says, getting excited, his eyes widening, I really know what you mean.

Suddenly he looks upon me with fatherly concern. An overwhelming warmth spread within me like an intake of hot sour breath. Blushing, I turn away.

He leans forward and fingers open his top shirt button, barely able to restrain himself. A gold chain connects to a pendant which rests against a nest of chest hair. He pulls it out.

Here, take a look at this, he says, handing it to me.

The warm, sweaty metal feels heavy in my fingers. It takes a moment of fumbling for the latch to snap open. There's a picture of a pretty blond girl inside.

He seems to be nervously studying me as if to see what I think of her.

Who's this? I finally say.

She was my daughter.

. . . I want to ask him what he means by "was," but I do not.

He unbuttons his shirt further, then peels back the damp fabric to reveal more of his chest. Matted chest hair clings to the shirt wool, then pops back. It seems weird that he would do this, and I look down.

Look here, he says.

There is a quarter-sized red scar on his chest, and suddenly he takes my hand in his sweaty palm and leads my finger to it. . . . His black chest hair feels thick against my fingertip, the skin warm. A pulse beats, though I do not know whether it is his or mine.

It's a bullet hole, he finally says. (86–87)

In a novel that barely narrates any nonviolent physical interaction between its human characters, this passage is quite surprising in its visceral intimacy and eroticism.[31]

Let me start with Stone's response to Gabe's mimicry of white complaint and racial abjection. Stone utters a cry of recognition ("I really know what you mean") that mimics Gabe's earlier statement of recognition ("I know what you mean"). Stone also displays signs of physical excitement, such as widening eyes. These widened eyes indicate the receptivity and openness, even vulnerability, of his look.

The mutual mimicry between Gabe and Stone indicates that they function for each other as mirrors, that their interaction is dualistic and Imaginary. At this point, their encounter is one of Imaginary whiteness. When Stone suddenly confers upon Gabe a look of fatherly care, Gabe responds with physical signs of shame: blushing, an overwhelming body heat, an aversion of the look. Why is Gabe ashamed? Most obviously, Stone's paternal look awakens Gabe's desire for such (white) paternal love and recognition, a desire that was suppressed because it was not reciprocated.

Gabe may be ashamed of having his nonreciprocated desire exposed to the gaze. However, I would like to venture a second explanation: that Gabe feels shame on behalf of Stone. Stone's look creates an intimacy between a white father and son. But Gabe knows that he is *not* the white son that Stone desires: Stone has betrayed his desire to someone who cannot reciprocate it. Gabe feels shame for Stone because Stone has revealed the vulnerability, and the blindness, of the white male look: a look that is not always equivalent to the hegemonic gaze, but one that seeks recognition from such a gaze.

Following this expression of fatherly care, Stone begins to undress and reveal his body to Gabe. He makes himself embodied and wants to be recognized as a body. Stone is "barely able to restrain himself," overcome with this desire. He starts not simply by unbuttoning his shirt, but by "finger[ing] open" his top button, as if it were a bodily opening. Stone "pull[s] out his gold chain and pendant as if it were a hidden body organ, and the pendant is suggestively described by Gabe as "warm," "sweaty," and "heavy in my fingers." Stone exposes an object that is normally hidden, offering something sacred to what he believes is the white male gaze. But Stone wants more than visual recognition; he hands the pendant to Gabe so that Gabe's witnessing is tactile as well as visual. Stone then continues to unbutton his shirt, further embarrassing Gabe, who "look[s] down" in shame at this inappropriate intimacy. Again, visuality gives way to tactility as Stone first asks Gabe to "look," but then takes Gabe's hand and leads his finger to the scar on his chest. Gabe feels the warmth of Stone's skin, the thickness of his chest hair, and the palpability of a pulse beating—but Gabe's inability to discern whether the pulse is his or Stone's insinuates the merging of their two bodies. Stone reveals his male vulnerability in the form of a wound, explaining that Gabe's finger is on/in a hole in his body, a bullet hole. In soliciting Gabe's touch on his scar, Stone reveals his desire to be embodied as a white male wound through this tactile recognition by another white male body.

Stone does not say what happened to his daughter or to his body. He believes that the intimate display of his secret locket and scar tell the whole story. Gabe is meant to understand implicitly why Stone embodies himself after their mutual abjection of racial others. Implicit, unnecessary to verbalize, is the embodiment of white masculinity as wounded by these racial others. Presumably it was "fucking Mexicans," whose innate violence Gabe confirms, that injured Stone and killed his daughter.

It is important to emphasize that this fantasy of white masculinity comes into being not through words—as I note, Stone's narrative is implicit—but primarily through Gabe's visual and *tactile* witness. Kaja Silverman has observed that sensation is overlooked as a component of identification because we have focused so much critical attention on tropes of visuality (the mirror stage, the screen, the gaze). Silverman cites Laplanche as an important touchstone in theorizing sensation, especially the importance of bodily openings, which "represent the points at which fantasy is introduced."[32] Touch not only communicates but produces desire. Stone's urgent embodiment not only consists of visual display; it also needs Gabe's touch for confirmation. Sight, the sense that is most associated with the human, is inadequate to the creation of their bond. Instead, it is the more intimate and animalistic sense of touch that seals their mutual recognition as white male subjects.[33]

Stone becomes embodied as a white male wound, injured by racial others. In this fantasy of wounded white masculinity, racial others are the agents and cause of his lack. White male lack is thus imagined as contingent, not innate: if it were not for these racial others, he would be whole and impenetrable, as his full name implies: Stone Garrett, or the stone garret. The cause of antagonism and division in his being is externalized and projected onto racial others, who he then abjects, expelling them from the Symbolic.

David Savran's work on post-1960s white masculinity provides a useful gloss for Stone's embodiment of white masculinity as a wound. In "The Sadomasochist in the Closet: White Masculinity and the Culture of Victimization," Savran discusses the emerging prevalence of hyperembodiment and injury in the late twentieth-century iconography of U.S. white masculinity, including cinematic characters played by Sylvester Stallone and Michael Douglas. Arguing that white masculinity found its privilege and power threatened by social movements of the 1960s and 1970s, as well as the worldwide recession of 1973–74, Savran finds that Freud's concept of reflexive sadomasochism explains its new iconography of injury and pain:

> Not only does reflexive sadomasochism provide the ideal mechanism to turn this new hero's pain into pleasure, but it also allows him to adjust to the exigencies of living in a (post)feminist and post-*Bakke* culture. It authorizes him to be both wild and domestic, to cultivate a "feminine" part of the self (or at least to endure his feminized flesh) and at the same time to subjugate

it violently, and to take on the roles simultaneously of casualty of feminism and affirmative action and of humanitarian. It allows him to play the part of victim and yet be a man.[34]

Self-mutilation, Savran continues, becomes "the purest and most absolute expression of virility."[35] Curiously and counterintuitively, the trope of the wound or injury produces white masculinity not as the site of penetration but instead as a self-enclosed, organic whole.

Rather, I see the insistent bifurcation of the male subject as a way (contradictorily) of preserving and even consolidating his imaginary coherence. . . . Reflexive sadomasochism, in particular, with its self-contained, narcissistic system of gratification, would seem particularly adept at reconstructing an independent, autonomous, masculine subject.[36]

We see in this interaction with Stone that white masculinity, in seeking recognition, wants to be embodied. If the visual field inscribes the quality called "to be looked at," then Stone's solicitation of tactile intimacy manifests his injured body as "to be touched." Critical race and gender theorists of citizenship have noted that white masculinity is traditionally posited as the disembodied, abstract universal, while racial, gendered, and sexual others are embodied, material, and particular.[37] How can we think, then, about Stone's urge for embodiment? I interpret this move toward embodiment as a drive toward jouissance and away from the dominant Symbolic of disembodied universal rationality. Indeed, the sadomasochistic pleasure-pain of recalling one's injury indexes such a drive toward jouissance. Recall Žižek's notion of hegemonic enjoyment being organized through fantasy of the other's jouissance. By imagining the racial other's enjoyment in injuring white masculinity, Stone organizes his own jouissance of an embodied injury.

Gabe catches a glimpse of this white male jouissance when he asks Stone how these northern small towns keep out racial "undesirables" (88). Again, Gabe's use of the term "undesirables" to reference racial others is both a performance of camouflaging mimicry and an indicator of his own fantasy that he himself is not undesirable but rather serves as the object of familial desire for Stone. Stone gets energized once again:

He shifts excitedly. You know how journalists keep coming up here to study reports of alien abductions?

Yeah.

Well, there's plenty of abductions, but it isn't aliens that do it.

I keep still. Menace fills the cab like steam in a shower. . . .

These locals are crazy, he says. They take troubles into their own hands. When undesirables come up, they tell them to get lost, and if they don't, that's their own peril. (88)

Stone uses the word "crazy" to refer to the jouissance of vigilante violence, an enforcement of a racialized territoriality and property system that engenders enjoyment through its lawlessness. The jouissance of white vigilante violence is meant to compensate for the racial jouissance referred to earlier in Mexican violence and Asian refusal to join in Symbolic exchange. Unlike such racial jouissance, however, the lawless violence of small-town vigilantism is implicitly sanctioned by law since there is no enforcement against it. This lawlessness is the obverse, even the foundation of law; it is an unwritten code that is accepted as necessary to social order while enabling the law to seem just. And this lawlessness is what makes these primarily white, small-town communities cohere. It is "not so much identification with the public or symbolic Law that regulates the community's 'normal' everyday life, but *rather identification with a specific form of transgression of the Law, of the Law's suspension* (in psychoanalytic terms, with a specific form of *enjoyment*)."[38] The freedom from crime that Gabe imagines these small towns offering is in fact predicated upon a criminality or lawlessness that is the flip side of the law. Gabe believes in and wishes for the modern conception of law as neutral, impersonal, and universal. What he finds is that the law offered by these small towns, and by Stone's kinship, is, to the contrary, permeated with enjoyment, an enjoyment produced by the consumption of racial others as the site of shame, abjection, and violence.

I described this lawlessness as an unwritten code and argue that this aspect of official disavowal is crucial. Even as everyone knows that the "locals are crazy" in their vigilantism, official journalistic accounts can only narrate the disappearances of people as an otherworldly mystery. In other words, alien abductions are comprehended within official discourse as a more reasonable explanation than white vigilante violence. Of course, there is a psychoanalytic logic to the ascription of agency to the inhuman in the case of vigilante violence, for jouissance is itself the inhuman core of the human. But what happens when this inhuman jouissance is in fact exposed?

We will see in the denouement to this section of *American Son* that the exposure of white jouissance to the gaze results in white shame, a departure from the pervasiveness of racial shame in the novel.

Toward the end of their journey together, Stone and Gabe take a break from driving and enjoy an idyllic moment of wordless communion as they sit in the sun. The paternal-filial bond is made explicit here in Gabe's comparison of Stone's eyes to those of his father's and Gabe's memory of a prelapsarian moment of communion among himself, Tomas, and their father (104, 105). After this idyllic moment, novelistic suspense builds as they near their destination. Stone mysteriously takes Gabe to a motel and appears to pay for the room himself. Does this interaction portend the fulfillment of the homoeroticism staged in earlier scenes? Does Stone have unwholesome intentions toward Gabe, as the motel owner seems to believe? No, we find out that Stone's intentions remain protectively paternal: he installs Gabe in a motel room because he has decided to reunite Gabe with his mother. Stone sees Gabe as a vulnerable young runaway and wants to return Gabe to what he thinks is the protective care of his mother.

Then a different suspense builds as Gabe and Stone meet up with Gabe's mother and his aunt Jessica. Jessica, the sister of Gabe's father, feels some responsibility for the family's welfare after her brother abandons them. In order to maintain his fiction of whiteness, upon which their father-son bond is predicated, Gabe tells Stone that his white aunt Jessica is his mother and that Ika is the family maid. Can this fiction be sustained? Stone practices what he believes to be socially appropriate behavior: he does not address Gabe's mother when Aunt Jessica is present, so that he can give his full attention to Gabe's "good mother" (92), the moral authority of the family. An increasingly bewildered Aunt Jessica finally explains that Ika, who Stone thinks is the Filipino maid, is indeed Gabe's mother. Stone is startled, then paralyzed by shame: "[H]is expression betrays the fact that this possibility had not occurred to him before. . . . He stares at me and I look down. . . . Suddenly his neck and cheeks turn red. . . . I can tell he wants to say that I told him Mom was our maid, but is too embarrassed" (126). In a turning of the tables, Stone is rendered mute.

Stone is embarrassed for a number of reasons. Most immediately, he has acted inappropriately in a social situation in front of a white person above his social standing, Aunt Jessica. Aunt Jessica carries herself as an authoritative and socially privileged person: she is of German descent, she owns a business, and she has been trained as a lawyer. Aunt Jessica is the socially powerful person whose stands in for the hegemonic gaze. By so obviously appearing racist, Stone realizes that he has committed a social transgression in front of a socially powerful person. Stone's speechlessness also results from the contagion of shame: he is shamed at Gabe's shame at his mother and at Gabe's shameful disavowal of his mother. But above all, Stone is paralyzed by the disintegration of his fantasy of a white masculinity, a fantasy that he now realizes was permeated by an animal-like intimacy with the animal-like racial other. The only other instances of wordless, physical intimacy narrated by the novel are those between Gabe and their dogs; in this way, the narrative posits a parallel between Stone and Gabe's dogs. The inhuman abject—precisely that element that must remain external in order for subjectivity to cohere—has intruded into Stone's fantasy of racial identity.

Stone's position is analogous to the keyhole scene that Sartre describes in *Being and Nothingness,* in which a man looking at an object through a keyhole suddenly realizes that he himself is being looked at. Not only is the subject of the gaze now the object of the gaze, but this subject is "caught looking," his voyeuristic desire exposed.[39] Gabe, who comments a number of times that Stone "must be blind" not to recognize him as Asian, unwittingly exposes Stone's visual castration—his white blindness. Stone is no longer the bearer of the look that coincides with the gaze. His blindness exposed, Stone is now the impotent, shameful object of the gaze.

While I have noted that Aunt Jessica is the bearer of the socially powerful gaze that shames Stone, I believe that Stone is even more unsettled by the transformation of Gabe's apparently normative white look into something that he does not even understand. Recall Tomkins's triggers of shame: "because one is suddenly looked at by one who is strange, or because one wishes to look at or commune with another person but suddenly cannot because he is strange, or one expected him to be familiar but he suddenly appears unfamiliar, or one started to smile but found that one was smiling at a stranger."[40] Stone solicited the recognition of white masculinity, in tactile as well as visual form. But this intimate interaction that he presumed to be familiar turned out to be strange.

What Stone believed to be the coherence and wholeness of white male identity—universal even in its particularity, abstract even in its embodiment—turns out to be penetrated by animal jouissance. This animalism, specifically in the form of animal knowledge, is exactly what unsettles Stone and what he cannot comprehend. Cary Wolfe, in *Animal Rites,* cites

Vicki Hearne's work on how certain areas of animal knowledge are opaque to human comprehension, for they are based more sensitively on smell, sound, and touch than human knowledge. In the example of a horse's sensitivity to the smallest movements of its human rider, for example, "The rider cannot escape knowing that the horse knows the rider in ways the rider cannot fathom."[41] Wolfe goes on to say, "The traditional humanist subject finds this prospect of the animal other's knowing us in ways *we* cannot know and master *simply unnerving*."[42] Where Stone thought he "knew" the racial other as the shameful abject, he now finds that he is known in a way that he does not comprehend. In being cut off from knowledge and the Symbolic, Stone feels himself abjected and shamed.

Believing that he occupies the position of the neutral, hegemonic gaze, Stone consumed the shame of the racial other in order to produce enjoyment for himself. In counterpoint to the construction of white humanity as rational and transcendent, racial alterity is construed as carnal and animalistically embodied. When Stone sees himself as permeated by animal jouissance, he feels shame at his incommensurability with the abstraction and neutrality of whiteness. Instead, his urgent need for embodiment and penetration becomes all too embodied. *American Son*'s interlude of Gabe's escape from enjoyment, signified by the fantasy of white masculinity as freedom from jouissance, turns out indeed to be only a fantasy.

Debt and Jouissances

Stone believes that he is paternalistically returning Gabe to the protective domesticity of his "good mother" (92). To unpack the tragedy of Stone's good intentions, which only lead to Gabe's entrapment and embeddedness in domestic violence and enjoyment, let us examine more closely this figure of the good mother. Ika does appear to align with the trope of the good parent as the immigrant parent who leaves her native country and sacrifices everything for the future of her children (166–68). Moreover, in relation to her delinquent son, she assumes the role of the innocent and long-suffering martyr mother, a role that derives from the colonial Catholic legacy of the Virgin Mary as maternal icon. As with the fantasy of the desiring and caring white father, however, this fantasy of the Filipina mother as sacrificial martyr also covers up enjoyment. Ika is generally presented in the narrative as a passive character, and it is this passivity that passes as innocence. But it is precisely by not intervening in Tomas's violently forged bond with Gabe that she profits from the crimes that they commit. She does not question where her new bed comes from, or her new brass bathroom sink, or the new couch, or the pearls and gold jewelry from Tomas. By turning a blind eye to such evidence of transgressions, she keeps herself morally pure. Indeed, by refraining from enjoyment, she puts all the more pressure on Tomas to enjoy. *The more she renounces enjoyment, the more he must enjoy for her.*[43] This is why Tomas recruits Gabe into the family business of lawless violence, so that Gabe can share his burden of jouissance. Part III of the novel, "A Dirty Penance," reveals how Gabe, under Tomas's sadistic tutelage, becomes initiated into the family business of jouissance. While Tomas has been the most spectacular embodiment of enjoyment throughout *American Son*, the novel ends climactically with Gabe's assumption of jouissance as he commits an act of violence so brutal that I borrow Deleuze and Guattari's phrase "becoming-animal" to designate its significance.

Gabe's apprenticeship in jouissance is facilitated by Tomas's construction of Gabe as an indebted and criminal subject. As the quasi-paternal figure and the perverse instrument of law in the domestic sphere, Tomas positions himself as the party that has been injured by Gabe's attempted escape. Gabe has transgressed domestic law by stealing Tomas's property—his car and his beloved dog. Gabe is thus constructed as the criminal who owes a debt to Tomas and must repay him by assisting him on his illicit "jobs." But Gabe can never fully repay Tomas. As the title "A Dirty Penance" signals, Gabe's debt to Tomas is moral as well as economic. No matter how much Gabe steals for Tomas, he can never fully repay his debt because his transgression is also a sin that can be forgiven only when Tomas chooses. Furthermore, the term "dirty" in "A Dirty Penance" intimates how Gabe's mode of compensation is permeated with obscene enjoyment. The narrative presents Tomas's judgment and sentence: "[S]ince I stole from him I should not mind stealing, and since my transgression was a crime, that is what I must do to pay him back. Each time we go out my stomach clutches. . . . I try not to vomit and make Tomas angry" (144). Gabe's jouissance is betrayed by his urge to vomit, a suffering that Tomas repeatedly solicits and heightens by making it also a cause for punishment. The law that structures Gabe's punishment is not neutral; it is muddied by a sadistic jouissance that both produces and penalizes Gabe as criminal. Gabe's work for Tomas is an indentured apprenticeship in crime and lawlessness, not only in their neutral senses of violating juridical law but also in the affective sense of jouissance.

This fraternal dynamic of indebtedness in fact capitalizes on more fundamental constructions of filial and familial indebtedness. Because he owes a debt of loyalty to his sacrificial mother, Gabe cannot explain his domestic predicaments to any other adults, for that would mean revealing his mother's failures (163, 168). Thus cut off from any avenues of escape or assistance, Gabe finds himself all the more inextricably bound to his brother. In addition, the entire Sullivan family is bound by their racial construction as inherently indebted and lawless in their being.

I turn here to the pivotal incident in which Gabe's mother is constructed as an illegitimate and therefore shameful consumer and owner, even criminal in her moral and economic debt. In this scene, the narrative contrasts differences in status and power as indicated by automobile type, one of the most conspicuous markers of social status in the Los Angeles area. Ika is picking up Gabe after school when she accidentally bumps her Toyota Tercel against the Land Cruiser in front of her. Compared to the powerful status symbol of the Land Cruiser, Ika's small, run-down Tercel marks her as degraded in value, lacking not only in economic capital but also in the cultural capital of knowing and displaying one's car as fashionable commodity. The "yoga mom," we will see, displays all the right commodities:

> The mother in the Land Cruiser gets out and walks over to Mom's car. She is blond and tall and thin and wears black yoga-class tights, and holds a Starbucks iced drink.
>
> . . . My mother looks bewildered and she clutches her elbow as the yoga mom continues to talk angrily down at her, one hand on her hip, her other still holding her Starbucks drink. By now the entire lawn of people has drifted over. . . .
>
> Mom is peering up at the yoga mom.
>
> I'm sorry, she says.
>
> The yoga mom's hand is on her slender hip, its bony shape visible beneath her dancer's stretch pants. That doesn't fix my dent, she says. She shakes her head and sighs. Do you realize this is a new car?
>
> Mom tilts her head, like a bedraggled little sparrow. I'm sorry.
>
> The yoga mom ignores her and turns to some random girl standing nearby. I mean, really, some people, she says. I was only a few feet away.
>
> . . . The yoga mom shakes her head. Well, then you'd better give me your license and insurance carrier.
>
> Mom touches her elbow. I don't have insurance, she says.

You don't have insurance.

No.

The yoga mom turns to the girl with the red backpack again. The girl seems embarrassed at being addressed, studying her bike's handlebars, but the yoga mom does not notice this. The *idiots* they let send their kids to school here, she says. People who can't afford insurance should ride the bus. (175–78)

Like the salesclerk at the makeup counter, the yoga mom is shameless even as bystanders are embarrassed by her behavior. Feeling injured and wishing to retaliate, the yoga mom sadistically shames Gabe's mother, creating a spectacle in which Gabe's mother is made into an object of public contempt and disdain. The visibility of Ika's racial difference, her status as an immigrant outsider, and her lower-class status as signaled by her incompetent consumption, all make her a safe target for the rage—and enjoyment—of the yoga mom. As she rants about how this accident inconveniences her, she makes an apparently irrelevant remark: "Can you understand? I'm going to have to bring this truck in, deal with the fucks at the dealership, rental cars. . . . I'm a busy woman, a *female* producer working in *sexist* Hollywood—I don't have time for this kind of shit!" (177, emphasis in original). The last statement, inflated as it is with a self-important narcissism, reveals the source of the yoga mom's rage and allows us to see why the "fucks at the dealership" are such a problem. Disrespected and humiliated—shamed—because of her gender subordination, she vents her rage not against the white men who hold power in her industry, but obliquely against less privileged men at the dealership, and directly against the brown immigrant woman who does not have the power to make her feel small, to retaliate against her, or to threaten her livelihood. She deflects the shame of her white femininity onto the poor immigrant woman of color. This shame takes the form of positioning Ika as an illegitimate consumer and owner. "The *idiots* they let send their kids to school here. . . . People who can't afford insurance should ride the bus" (178). Ika's inability to afford car insurance means that she does not deserve to own and drive a car. Moreover, Ika and her children are not legitimate consumers of education. They do not deserve education at this school and are present only through the generosity and permission of their "hosts." Ika and Gabe are thus indebted to the administrators and parents—the legitimate consumers, like the yoga mom—who "let" Gabe attend "their" school.

In this chapter, I have observed the various ways in which the deviant visibility of the Sullivan family indexes their exclusion from consumer citizenship. Ika, an older immigrant woman of color, is invisible as a consumer because she can only be comprehended as labor. Tomas, a young man of color who fashions himself as a hypervisible racial commodity, is a conspicuous object of consumption. In other words, the family's proper position is as objects, not subjects of consumption. What the encounter with the yoga mom highlights is the way in which consumption by racial subjects leads paradoxically not to ownership but to indebtedness. For any consumption by such racial subjects is constructed as enabled by the generosity and largesse of legitimate benefactors, racialized as white. By consuming, by making a claim to ownership, the Sullivans actually become indebted. Instead of becoming self-possessed subjects, they become dispossessed.

Bypassing the shame of gender, the yoga mom transforms shame into rage at damage done to her property, which is recognizable as injury. The cost of restoration can be quantified and compensation can be demanded. Her identity as a propertied subject thus serves as a conduit of recompense for the damages of gender. And it is Gabe's mother who must pay the price for these damages. Gabe's mother is vulnerable because the yoga mom can report her for disobeying the law by not carrying insurance. Thus positioned as illegitimate and indeed criminalized, Gabe's mother owes a moral debt to society as well as an economic debt to the yoga mom. The Sullivan family, as illegitimate consumers, are seen as "getting over" on the system, as illicitly acquiring not only property or value but also jouissance. This illicit quality of their relationship to the nation takes the form of indebted and criminal citizenship.[44]

As indebted and guilty subjects, Gabe and Ika bear what Saidiya Hartman calls "burdened individuality," a term that she uses to reference the racial constraints of the apparently free subject of liberalism. In describing the post-Emancipation period, Hartman shows that the free black person was seen as a newly responsible and potentially blameworthy individual. She notes that the guilt of conscience that was the hallmark of burdened black individuality bore an uncanny resemblance to the only form of agency ascribed to the enslaved: criminality. Moreover, emancipation was figured as a gift to freed blacks, who were thus obligated to their benefactors. This dynamic of debt and criminalization positioned blacks as bonded laborers. "Debt was at the center of a moral economy of submission and servitude and was instrumental in the production of peonage . . .

debt literally sanctioned bondage."[45] Just as Tomas impressed Gabe into servitude by making him the indebted and criminal subject, so the yoga mom constructs Ika as an indebted and criminal subject who must now pay off her debt through labor. Debt and criminalization sanction the extraction of surplus-value from the racial body, as well as the extraction of surplus-enjoyment from the racial other who has enjoyed too much in her "getting over."

The yoga mom proceeds to phone Gabe's home repeatedly to ask for the payment of $800, the estimate given by the dealership to repair the damage to her car. The intrusion of the yoga mom's demanding voice into Gabe's home highlights the insecurity of the domestic sphere for the Sullivan family. To Gabe and Tomas, the sum of $800 is outrageously expensive. First, as Gabe informs Tomas, "It was just a little scratch. . . . Her truck was so big the Tercel could barely do any damage" (197). Second, in Tomas's informal economy, repairs can be done for far lower amounts if one does not have to pay for brand-name service. Third, their mother, who cannot afford car insurance even with income from her two jobs, simply cannot meet this expense, and must take on a third job to pay off this debt. While Gabe and Tomas see the yoga mom as harassing and extorting money from a poor immigrant woman, the yoga mom sees herself as merely exercising her right to property. Not only is the law on her side; she represents the law through its enforcement. Like the vigilantes to which Stone refers, she takes the law into her own hands to ensure that the racial other does not get away with his or her presumptuous enjoyment. By positing the Sullivans as lawless, she renders them excess and obscene, shameful. Thus, like the vigilantes, the yoga mom derives her own form of sadistic enjoyment through enforcing the law; she gives body to the jouissance of law by enjoying the production and consumption of the Sullivans' racial shame.

Tomas acutely understands his mother as, once again, humiliated by her racial and gendered powerlessness, and he is enraged that his mother will not fight against the yoga mom. Tomas recognizes that Gabe, too, is infuriated by this humiliation of their mother, even when Gabe himself does not acknowledge the depth of his own fury. In the final phase of Gabe's apprenticeship in jouissance, Tomas awakens Gabe's rage in two ways. First, on a mysterious car ride, Tomas reveals that Gabe, as a child, used to shame their mother by running away and hiding during family gatherings. This revelation disintegrates Gabe's fantasy that he has been the good child, the one who does not shame their mother. He now feels shame and self-rage at having humiliated his mother. Second, when they arrive at their destination, which turns out to be the yoga mom's house, Tomas baits Ben, the yoga mom's son, into agreeing with racist comments against Ika. Tomas and Gabe ask Ben to walk with them toward their car so they can give him the payment.

> Listen. Sorry about the way our mom's so late with the money, he says.
> That's okay.
> Yeah, but it must be really annoying.
> Ben shrugs, walks with his head down.
> Sometimes she can be a real space cadet, Tomas says.
> Again, Ben does not say anything.
> Like the way she hit your mother's car. I mean they were only going a couple miles an hour. Tomas shakes his head. You know how clueless old oriental ladies like her can get.
> Yeah, Ben says, chuckling, happy to be included in a conversation with him.
> And the way she talks. Tomas shakes his head even more now. You ever talked to her, Ben?
> I know what you mean, he says eagerly.
> ...My brother looks at me now to make sure I've been listening. The hair on the back of my neck has pricked like needles and the air is motionless. (212–13)

As Tomas makes Ben into an agent of shaming their mother, Gabe feels his body tensing and everything becoming very still. This is the pivotal moment at which Gabe experiences jouissance not as its victim or object but as its conduit, for Ben is a very available outlet for Gabe's rage. Ben has been lured away from his house and is outnumbered by the two brothers. Tomas punches Ben repeatedly in the stomach and then hands a tire iron to Gabe; Gabe uses the tire iron to brutally beat Ben. This is the end of the novel. We are to understand this conclusion as Gabe's initiation into the enjoyment of lawlessness that has previously only been Tomas's burden to bear. Gabe narrates the ambivalence of enjoyment as he moves from apprentice to conductor of jouissance: "And though my stomach wrenches, I feel a rush not of anxiety but of confidence. In a scary way I realize I like it. Strangely, that only makes my stomach worse" (215). As I have noted, jouissance is not only enjoyment but a traumatic enjoyment, a satisfaction that is also a suffering. This is why enjoyment is a burden for Tomas, and why it provides him relief to have Gabe share in this family business.

As in chapter 1, this chapter highlights how the characters in Asian American novels are not only determined by sociopolitical hegemony but also activate structures and economies that counter hegemonic forces and ideologies. In my reading of *Bone*, Ona's status as sacrificial object points to a debt owed by the nation-state to its racial subjects. Here Tomas's and Gabe's brutality makes salient how hegemonic economies are not structured solely by capital but also by jouissance. While the Sullivan family is framed by the yoga mom as owing debts of capital and morality, Tomas reframes the terms of debt. Tomas says to Ben that they are here to "pay your mom," but since she is not home, they will pay him. From Tomas's perspective, they are indeed paying the yoga mom's family in kind. The yoga mom considers her property injured, in a legalistic judgment that demands compensation in the form of capital, extracted from Ika's labor. Tomas and Gabe, however, see the yoga mom as the instigator of psychic violence, invading their home and extracting money from their mother. The yoga mom's sadism extracts enjoyment from harassing their family; thus, to Tomas, the yoga mom is indebted to the Sullivans for her enjoyment. Her extraction of jouissance from them should then be repaid, in his formulation, in the jouissance that they derive from violence against her family. By reframing a debt of capital as a debt of jouissance, Tomas demonstrates an understanding of how capital, property, and law are permeated with racial jouissance.

As I have been arguing, the deviant visibility of the Sullivan family is part of a larger pattern of the "unrecognizability of Filipino and the Philippines in larger U.S. narratives."[46] Lack, as signified by tropes of invisibility and absence, is one way to figure this denial of U.S. empire. Other tropes, such as forgetting or hysterical blindness, might be appropriate as well, explicitly referencing the interested act of disavowal. However, I find Ann Laura Stoler's notion of "partial visibility" to be particularly resonant with *American Son*: "Some might argue that being an effective empire has long been contingent on partial visibility—sustaining the ability to remain an affective and unaccountable one."[47] I have found that the Sullivans' condition of shameful citizenship is characterized not solely by invisibility or hypervisibility, but rather by an oscillation between these poles of deviant visibility. The vacillating, pulsating visibilities of racial shame and racial jouissance are symptoms of empire's "unfinished business," evasive but no less powerfully felt and embodied.[48] Racial citizenship in *American Son* is a condition of traumatic incorporation; shamed by an illicit, indebted, criminal, and animal status, the Sullivan family members are both hypervisible and invisible as commodities and labor. Such deviant visibility and deviant citizenship are legacies and manifestations of U.S. empire and global hegemony.

After Gabe is initiated into the family business, Tomas puts his hand on his younger brother's shoulder in an act of recognition. Gabe's body experiences this touch as strange but familiar; after a moment, he recalls that their father used to touch them in the same way. This hand on Gabe's shoulder is a "ghost of a gesture" (103), a revenant of their American military father. Such an encounter with "tactile powers and their intangibilities," Stoler notes, is the very condition of haunting.[49] Bearing the imperial American patronym, the sons embody the legacies of empire and militarism, the violence of the American father and the shameful abjection of the Filipina mother.

The Sullivan family business of producing jouissance is a legacy and materialization of imperial national jouissance, as the family was borne of a history of U.S. state-sponsored militarism and violence. However, such militarism is not recognized as violence in ideologies of U.S. global hegemony; instead, it is figured as the spread of democracy and the rule of law. Juliet Flower MacCannell provides a psychoanalytic understanding of modern liberal institutions such as democracy and nation, terming this political modernity "the regime of the brother."[50] The modern ideal of democracy as postpatriarchal brotherhood is encapsulated in the inaugural and iconic phrase "liberté, egalité, fraternité." In this fraternity, the intergenerational rule of the father, in the form of monarchistic, religious, and feudal authority, is replaced by the same-generation governance of the brother. MacCannell uses Lacan's registers of Imaginary and Symbolic to interpret modern democracy, arguing that the "brothers" of democracy assume patriarchal authority at the level of the Imaginary, not the Symbolic. That is, they base their legitimacy on a likeness to the father, not on the actual Symbolic patriarchal function of prohibiting jouissance. Indeed, even as the brother embodies the authority of law, he also enjoys this embodiment of law. In MacCannell's keen insight, the terror of modernity lies in the narcissism of European male universalism. "It seems that what he 'enjoys' is the power to distort and center all familial relations on himself alone, warping the world into a fiction of fraternity, the dream of a universal, which becomes the nightmare lie of the family of man."[51] What is imperialism if not a form of democracy's jouissance—democracy's obscene transgressions against its own laws and principles? MacCannell's *The Regime of the Brother* focuses on the gendered suppression of the sister, but of course this regime is also racial and imperial, simultaneously incorporating and dispossessing "little brown brothers." The modernity of imperialist democracy thus is a family business in which law and its hegemonic gaze are not neutral but, rather, are permeated with enjoyment. The shameful citizenship of the Sullivans is but one locus of the imperial nation's family business of violent and brutal jouissance.

Let us consider one more practice of shameful citizenship: Tomas's hypervisible display of the Virgen de Guadalupe tattoo on his back, which in his environment is meant to evoke a street Mexican masculinity. Tomas's tattoo is especially suggestive in the light of my earlier association of Ika's assumed maternal innocence and purity with the Catholic icon of the Virgin Mary. I would like to suggest that Tomas's cross-racial passing as Mexican offers him a strategy of both refusing and revising his colonial inheritance. On one level, Tomas repudiates his abusive white U.S. military father as well as his victimized Filipina mother by identifying himself as neither. It is clear, however, that his feelings toward his parents are far more complex than simple rejection. For Gabe, Tomas has become an echo of the white father. And Tomas's most primal relationship is with his mother, who inspires in him an instinctive need to protect as well as a furious rage. Both these impulses derive from a sense of her vulnerability to violation, which in turn renders him exposed to danger as well.

This intense ambivalence toward the mother brings to mind another Mexican myth of maternity, La Malinche. La Malinche refers to Malintzin, the historical indigenous woman who consorted with the Spanish conqueror and thereby gave birth to the mestizo race. She is remembered and reviled as the site of imperial desire, violence, and enjoyment. We might understand Tomas's encrypting of the mother as La Virgen as a strategy of keeping her innocent and absorbing her shame as La Malinche, the colonial abject.[52] The significance of his tattoo, however, is multilayered: by engraving a proscribed and degraded cross-racial identification on his body, Tomas blasphemes against the very mother that he inscribes as sacred. And rather than erase his family legacy of imperial violence, this cross-racial identification as Mexican instead hypervisibly *manifests* the legacy of mestizaje that was born from imperial violence and enjoyment. I have shown earlier in the chapter how the paternal Symbolic function, linked to whiteness and imperialism, is sustained by an undercurrent of jouissance. Here we see how the fantasy of the pure native mother cannot escape these legacies of imperial enjoyment.

American Son interrogates and undoes the category of the domestic at several levels. As members of a U.S. colony in the early twentieth century, were Filipinos domestic or foreign?[53] Are the various figures of maids and domestic service workers, including Ika, interior or exterior to domestic space? Are Tomas's dogs domestic animals or savage beasts? Like his dogs, Tomas is valued and feared for straddling the line between savage and domesticated, lawless brute and law enforcer. Ika's domestic work means that her labor is at the heart of the American home, even as she herself is excluded from domestic respectability. And as a shameful secret of imperial jouissance, the Sullivan family is installed at the psychic heart of the nation, even as the hegemonic disavowal of this imperial enjoyment makes the heart of the nation alien to itself.

3 Romantic Citizenship

Immigrant-Nation Romance, the Antifetish, and Chang-rae Lee's Native Speaker

The opening of Chang-rae Lee's *Native Speaker* immediately introduces us to a domestic rupture: the Korean American narrator, Henry Park, tells us about the day that his wife left him. For Lelia, who is white, marriage to Henry had become unbearably alienating. Lelia's growing frustration over the years with what she perceived as her husband's emotional inscrutability is brought to crisis when he appears unable to mourn their dead son. Over the course of the novel, Henry takes on a final assignment in his job as a spy, while he simultaneously pursues reconciliation with Lelia. The eventual resolution of his marital breach converges, tellingly, with a misfortune that he must instigate in order to quit his work and return home to Lelia. This tragedy is the scandalous downfall of John Kwang, the Korean American politician Henry Park shadows for his last assignment. In this chapter, I examine why resolution in the domestic sphere coincides with spectacular failure in the public sphere. Does the former depend on the latter? Even more intriguingly, why does the libidinal energy of the novel seem far more concentrated on the promises and failures of the public sphere than the promises and failures of the private sphere, despite the narrative resolution offered by marital reconciliation?

Since its publication in 1995, *Native Speaker* has become one of the most commented-upon texts in the field of Asian American literary studies. How can we explain the qualities that have inspired so much commentary? Readers and critics find its interwoven concerns of ethnic identity, politics, and language compelling and resonant. Henry's work as a spy, for example, seems an appropriate metaphor for the Asian American as model minority: invisible, blending into the background, observing rather than being observed. A prominent, charismatic Korean American politician such as John Kwang allows us to imagine a more visible role for Asian Americans in public life. In addition, the highly literary language of the narrative provokes interpretive desire: What does this figure of speech mean? Why does the narrator make this particular allusion? While these readings focus on Symbolic and Imaginary dimensions of the *Native Speaker* (for example, the meaning of racial politics, the mirrored identities of the male characters), I want to focus on the foreclosed dimension of the Real, the element that threatens the Symbolic. This chapter, then, considers how jouissance disrupts the fantasies that undergird the realms of politics, language, and subjectivity. As psychoanalytic critics have noted, politics cannot be explained solely by reference to rational interests. We must also understand how political identifications and desires are structured as fantasies; in this case, the fantasy of romance between immigrant and nation. We will see that this fantasy of romance is subject to fantasmatic calculations of lack and excess.

Native Speaker stages a kind of contest between domestic romance and public romance, as represented by Henry's relationships with Lelia and with John Kwang, respectively. In the end, it is Lelia, not Kwang, who fulfills Henry's lifelong desire for recognition as an American subject. But curiously, it is Kwang, not Lelia, who is the more enthralling object of desire and romance in the novel. It is Kwang's charisma and aura that command our attention. It is Kwang's vision of a multiracial nation that compels our belief. And it is Kwang's appalling breakdown that devastates us. Especially traumatic is Henry's eventual complicity in this breakdown. What does it say about public romance that the narrative demands Henry's betrayal of this love? Henry himself remarks that every betrayal is a self-betrayal (314); in betraying Kwang and his immigrant constituents, Henry recognizes that he has failed in the realm of ethics. In response to such trauma and tumult in the public sphere, Henry and the narrative seek refuge in the apparent safety of the private realm. Domestic romance seems to provide the satisfactions of closure, reliability, and resolution that public romance does not. And yet this closure is not fully convincing to its readers, as evidenced by a long roster of critics who have grappled with the unsettled and unsettling meaning of John Kwang's derailed, visionary career.[1]

By investigating romantic citizenship in this chapter, especially in its modes of public and private desire, I hope to illuminate the psychic vicissitudes of U.S. nationalist feeling. First, I consider a long-standing version of national romance, that of American exceptionalism. Here I define

American exceptionalism broadly to mean the myth of America as a globally exceptional site of modernity, freedom, and choice. In this view, American subjects are free from the constraints, histories, and traditions that bind the people of other nations. This vision of freedom gives the United States a unique destiny in providing leadership to the rest of the world. I then go on to discuss a particular form of immigrant-nation romance that emerged in the late twentieth century: neoliberalism. By ostensibly liberating its subjects from the strictures of the state, neoliberalism promises even greater freedoms and bestows approval upon exemplary subjects such as the self-sufficient, hard-working immigrant entrepreneur. *Native Speaker* not only narrates, but also allegorizes, such neoliberal shifts from public to private. That is, by presenting the public sphere as failed and the private sphere as the key to self-actualization, the novel throws its own weight in with the momentous realignments of its historical period. Yet, as I suggest above in my reference to readers who remain unsettled, these realignments are not absolute. Even as the private sphere is presented as a refuge, the jouissance of public romance—the traumatic enjoyment that Henry experiences in his foray into a political romance between immigrant and nation—continues to haunt the romance of domestic intimacy, a more privatized version of immigrant-nation love.

By romance, I mean the idealization and elevation of the object of love. This object of romance is a specific embodiment of what Lacan calls the object *a*, the object of fantasy that promises the completion of self. Alienated from primal being by our entrance into language, we are produced as subjects of lack. We desire the object that we imagine will complete us and return us to a state of primal, full being. Romance is a particular staging of desire, an especially intense fantasy of passionate fulfillment. The affect of romance is one of euphoria and intoxication, for in imagining the merging of self and other, romance promises an ecstatic transcendence of self. The romance of America as the site of new beginnings offers a particular form of this self-transcendence: the death of the old self and the birth of a new self. We can see, then, that the immigrant is central to the romance of America, for the immigrant is perceived as someone who needs America to complete him, so that he can be part of the grand, national vision of rebirth and new beginnings.[2]

Throughout this book, I have attended to two dimensions of Asian American family business: the economic practices in which a number of family members participate, and the maintenance of the family as an institution in itself. I interpret family business in *Native Speaker* as the production of national fantasy, taking the form of romance between the ethnic-racial immigrant and the nation. Put otherwise, family business here is the construction and maintenance of an ethnic-racial romantic citizenship. We can understand the public mode of this romance through the representations of Henry's father and John Kwang, while the private mode of this romance takes the form of Henry's marriage to Lelia.

Over the course of several years, Henry's father comes to own and manage a number of corner grocery stores in Manhattan. As is typical of such ethnic small business, Henry also works in these stores. Knowing the story that "every native loves to hear" (49), Henry's father deliberately presents himself as a self-made immigrant entrepreneur, and thus as a "good immigrant." Lisa Park succinctly explains the difference between "good" and "bad" immigrant: the former contributes to the nation and serves as a positive model of self-reliance, while the latter burdens the nation and serves as a negative model of dependence.[3] As a good immigrant, Mr. Park is both subject and object of national romance. By believing in America's openness and meritocracy, he demonstrates love for the nation. So long as he confirms the nation's ideal self-image as benevolent and generous, he receives the nation's love in return.

While the Parks participate literally in an Asian American family business, Kwang takes the unusual step of making such family business figurative. Operating in the realm of electoral politics, Kwang represents and binds together ethnic-racial immigrant workers and entrepreneurs. By constructing a figurative family business out of literal family businesses, and aiming to represent them, Kwang's politics metaphorizes and metonymizes family business. Especially notable is Kwang's move from single-ethnic formation to multiethnic and multiracial formation: he embodies the national romance of transcending old ties and forging new identities. Like Mr. Park, Kwang openly displays his love of nation as a belief in America's openness. Similarly, in substantiating the unique multiracial destiny of America, he receives the love of his immigrant and nonimmigrant voters and supporters.

As I have noted, *Native Speaker* ultimately associates public romance with failure and domestic romance with fulfillment. Kwang's business of metonymizing immigrant family business is discarded by the narrative in favor of Henry's work in reforging a family with Lelia. The novel concludes with the fulfillment of the immigrant-nation romance figured through this interracial marriage between the "Anglican goddess," as Henry wryly and self-consciously calls Lelia (15) and the self-identified ethnic immigrant. And in the end, the privileged resolution of white-interracial domestic romance (the business of maintaining the family itself) also means the triumph of Lelia's form of family business in the economic sense. Lelia's speech therapy now incorporates Henry as an assistant. This work is a family business of linguistic and cultural assimilation, making the previously unknown and unincorporated racial alien into the knowable and legible national citizen. Lelia's family business of speech therapy becomes indistinguishable from the family business of their marriage, as both are modes of incorporating the racial and national other.

I begin my analysis by showing how John Kwang is the novel's premier object of romance, generating intense love and longing. I argue that the public romance between immigrant and nation is structured fetishistically. The fetish allows for the resolution of contradictory elements, in this case the understanding of the ethnic immigrant as both primordial and modern. Following my discussion of public romance, I examine two key blocks to romance in the novel, which I conceive as antifetishes: the migrant woman worker, as personified by the housekeeper Ahjuhma, and the underground money club that ends up destroying Kwang's political career. These two elements of the narrative are manifestations of jouissance that disrupt the fetishistic structure of national romance. Paradoxically, they embody the national and neoliberal ideal of the self-sufficient immigrant too well: they are so outside the Symbolic order that they are seen as enjoying this status and thus throwing the normative national subject off balance. As such, they must be exposed and regulated. Finally, I investigate white-interracial domestic romance as *Native Speaker*'s proposed solution to the traumas of the migrant woman worker and the money club. Because Henry's domestic romance is conflated with Lelia's speech therapy, I inquire into the ways that his marriage and his attention to the English language are privileged by the narrative as enabling romantic citizenship. Turning to a Foucauldian understanding of how governmentality permeates our intimate spheres, I note how domesticity and language pry open the ethnic-racial immigrant subject, rendering him legible to the hegemonic gaze. This transparency of the immigrant's "truth" is required for the romance between immigrant and nation.

PUBLIC ROMANCE

In *The Queen of America Goes to Washington City,* Lauren Berlant considers the tropes of desire and love in national discourses about the immigrant. Strikingly, the mutuality and reciprocity of this rhetoric of romance is subtly framed by a heterosexual paradigm in which the male initiates courtship and the female responds favorably if his intentions are judged to be genuine. Berlant notes that "immigrant discourse is a central technology for the reproduction of patriotic nationalism . . . because the immigrant is defined as *someone who desires America.*"[4] Berlant goes on to quote a passage from a 1985 special issue of *Time* magazine on immigration, which declares that Americanization "occurs when the immigrant learns his ultimate lesson: above all countries, America, if loved, returns love."[5] In this love affair, the masculine immigrant declares his romantic intentions and the feminine nation adjudicates the truth of these declarations, rewarding sincere love with reciprocity. In contrast to all other countries demanding patriotic love, what makes America exceptional is its return of love to its subjects in the forms of freedom, equal opportunity, and upward mobility. Sincerity begets sincerity: "above all countries," America is the site of authenticity, truth, and trust—but first, the immigrant must himself be the site of wholehearted belief.

For political theorist Bonnie Honig, the romance between immigrant and nation is theatricalized in periodic spectacles of immigrant naturalization rites. What is staged in these scenes, says Honig, is the choiceworthiness of America, as well as the consent to the nation that is so central to the myth of American exceptionalism.[6] The framework of modern heterosexual romance, with its figures of choice and consent, constructs the immigrant and the U.S. nation as exemplary sites of liberal modernity. It is this exemplarity of freedom that makes America exceptional and rationalizes its hegemonic position as a global leader.

Henry explicitly uses the term "romance" to describe his relationship with Kwang (139). Kwang's constituents and volunteers are, Henry notes, "a little in love with him" (132). In order to inspire their constituents and gain their support, politicians make themselves into objects of desire and fantasy, embodying themselves as the promise of a greater future. Specifically, the function of the politician is to mediate romance between his constituents and the nation.[7] At first glance, Kwang seems to be the *object* of romance. Henry, like his many other constituents, is drawn to his aura and charisma. But Kwang's allure also lies in his status as the *subject* of romance: by entering into the public sphere of politics, Kwang expresses his desire for and consent to the nation. The legitimacy of Kwang's status as an elected official signals a reciprocity in which the nation consents to him and, by proxy, to other ethnic and racial immigrants. In this way, Kwang serves as a conduit of immigrant-nation romance. The immigrant can project his desire for the nation and imagine this desire reciprocated. Meanwhile, the nation images itself as the object of immigrant desire and ardor. Kwang not only represents this reciprocity of immigrant-nation desire; he produces this reciprocity. In romance, the feeling of being desired awakens one's own desire, which in turn rouses the other's sense of being desired and desirous. Kwang's mediation between immigrant and nation serves to intensify the romance between the two parties.

Even before meeting Kwang, Henry sees and feels in the ubiquity of his name the adoration of his public:

> *They must have loved him.* Those first days I walked the streets of Flushing, I saw his name everywhere on stickers and posters, the red, white, and blue graphics plastered on the windows of every other shop and car along Kissena, Roosevelt, and Main. Downtown, near a subway entrance, sat a semipermanent wooden booth decorated with bunting and pennants and flags manned by neatly dressed youth volunteers in paper hats. They passed out flyers, pamphlets—A message from City Councilman John Kwang— buttons, ballpoint pens, keychains, lapel pins, every last piece of it stamped with his perfectly angled script, simply signed, John. (83; emphasis added)

Romance, as a mode of fantasy, transcends not only time but space. In fantasy, the object of desire can be projected without temporal or spatial limit. Similarly, in romance, one sees the beloved everywhere. Henry's colleague Jack uses language as a figure for this ubiquity, remarking that Kwang "is in the language now. The buildings and streets there are written with him. In this sense he exists" (169).

Kwang himself cannot literally be everywhere, but his official and campaign paraphernalia serves as substitute objects that promise his proximity to his subjects and thus generate further desire. We see how objects associated with Kwang acquire a sacred aura as well, as Henry describes pictures of Kwang on makeshift altars in mom-and-pop business stores: "John Kwang hung there with the first tilled bills of each denomination, a son's Ivy League diploma, a tattered letter of U.S. citizenship from the county clerk of Queens. You saw his face on the walls of restaurants, large-format color pictures of him standing arm in arm with the owners, the captured mood always joyous, celebratory" (83). The items that are enshrined and venerated by these immigrant entrepreneurs—including Kwang himself—are objects that facilitate and promise national belonging. These objects are taken as assurances that immigrant desire for the nation will be reciprocated with the nation's consent to incorporate them into its membership. The delight of association with Kwang is the euphoria of imagining a future of fulfillment and completion.

Following a long narrative interlude about an unrelated matter, Henry abruptly begins a subsequent chapter with a single sentence: "I went to him this way" (82). This sentence conveys a sense of captivation and compulsion, in which one is helplessly drawn by the allure of the beloved, whose naming is unnecessary because no one else exists. Henry later calls Kwang "arresting" (139). As Freud observes in *Group Psychology,* such a state of hypnotic paralysis describes both the state of being in love and the state of group cohesion.[8] Groups are constituted by a collective state of love for a charismatic leader. When Kwang unexpectedly visits his office, we see how he casts a spell on the workers:

> But everyone took notice of him. From the moment he stepped into the room, I thought each of us was suddenly oriented toward him. Janice and I were standing at the chalkboard.... I noticed that her posture had shifted in acknowledgment of the man approaching her back. She continued chalking times and places on the slate, but I saw that her eyes weren't following the motion of her hand. I thought she had it the way everyone else did, the way she was waiting for his touch on her arm or his voicing of her name. It made me think that she was a little in love with him, the same way Eduardo and the other people in the room were.... Somehow you felt for him a pin-ache of unneeded love on top of the respect and hope and plain like of him, that little bit of extra feeling that must separate even a good man and politician from a natural leader of the people. (131–32)

Henry notes how the energy of the room palpably shifts so that every single person directs her attention to Kwang. His presence awakens their desire for sensory contact and recognition. Moreover, Henry recognizes that Kwang's charisma derives from his ability to produce an excess of affect: the love one feels is "unneeded" and "extra." And the exquisiteness of this feeling lies in its almost imperceptible subtlety: it is a "pin-ache," a bare trace of pain that along with pleasure binds one to a love object, a tender feeling of vulnerability to desire. Kwang generates fantasy through this tinge of jouissance, an excess of the pain of desire that binds to the pleasure of fantasy.

In the sociohistorical context of the novel, Kwang's political charisma is not simply individual charm; it comprises something more. That "more," I argue, is the dream, fantasy, and romance of multiracial democracy. This is a fantasy that binds national subjects in a collective belief in American exceptionalism: the notion that the United States is the premier site of unlimited opportunity for all, no matter one's origins. Kwang serves as a collective object *a* because he promises to complete the incomplete project of American democracy, which has historically marginalized subjects like racial migrants and immigrants. What makes Kwang an exceptional ethnic figure is this cathexis of political desire on a multiracial level, rather than simply on the level of representing his ethnic (Korean) or even racial (Asian) community.

It is true, as many readers understand, that Henry is especially drawn to Kwang because of an ethnic Korean identification that facilitates paternal projection and filial desire. However, the fact that Kwang represents a *multiracial* constituency is key to his romanticization by Henry and others. If Kwang primarily represented Korean or Asian immigrants, he would not produce the same kind of magical effect. Only by widening the sphere of his influence to include those who are ethnically dissimilar does Kwang represent participation in modern democracy, beyond ethnic "clannishness." The public sphere, in Jürgen Habermas's definition, is the realm of political participation and debate.[9] Access to information and modes of communication are key elements of the public sphere because they facilitate rational deliberation by citizens of democracy. The public sphere is the product of modernity in the sense that it creates connections among people who are not related by family or acquainted by immediate locale. Thus, it is Kwang's modernity that is the site of romance—the modernity of emphasizing consent over descent; the modernity, as I have noted, of American exceptionalism—the notion that the United States is uniquely open in promising freedom and belonging to all its subjects.[10]

And yet, as Daniel Kim points out, Kwang is also presented as "undiluted" and "essentially Korean."[11] Kim argues that Kwang's appeal is his ability to universalize Koreanness, to use Korean cultural elements in a binding of multiracial community.[12] Kwang's simultaneous status as ethnic and universal reflects the ways in which his constituency is figured as both premodern and modern. I interpret this paradox of a premodern modernity, or an ethnic universal, through the concept of the fetish. The fetish structures romance by allowing for the fantasy of fullness through the disavowal of lack or loss.

In *Native Speaker,* immigrants are romanticized through a fetishization of their commodity objects, a metonymic process in which they themselves are figured as commodities. I refer to the fetish in its three major theoretical frameworks and connotations: primitivism, in which the fetish is an animated object or thing with magical powers; Marxism, in which it is a commodity object; and psychoanalysis, in which the fetish is an object of divided belief. In this last context, the fetish substitutes for a lack and thereby allows for a disavowal of this lack. Immigrant-nation romance is structured by fetish because the fetishistic disavowal allows for the concept of the ethnic as universal. In this logic of the fetish, the ethnic can become a universal national subject without losing ethnicity or origin.

While reconciling, Henry and Lelia take a trip to Staten Island and spend the night at a motel. Turning on the television, they come upon a local news story about the most recently murdered cab driver, one in a line of five or six in the past two months. Reflecting on the need of these workers to demand conditions of greater security and safety, Henry considers at first the impossibility that any one cab driver can represent or speak for the group: "They're too different from one another, they're recently arrived Latvians and Jamaicans, Pakistanis, Hmong." But he continues: "What they have in common are the trinkets from their homelands swaying from the rearview mirror, the string of beads, shells, the brass letters, the blurry snapshots of their small children, the night-worn eyes" (246). These items are fetish objects, imbued with a magical aura. Indeed, the televisual images of violence testify to the vulnerability of immigrants and their need for protection from a higher source (knowing they are considered too insignificant to warrant protection from the state): "They show the blood-soaked seat, the shattered windshield, a dashboard scent infuser tagged with a religious inscription in Spanish" (246). We understand now that the beads and family photographs are not only sentimental reminders of home; they are objects believed to embody and disseminate a life force, making one feel loved and protected. The blurriness of the family snapshots at first seems caused by a lack of access to newer photographic technologies. However, the subsequent reference to "night-worn eyes" demands a more subtle reading. Working long hours into the night is a way to provide for one's family, even as it separates one from family ("Your family was your life, though you rarely saw them," invokes Henry in his litany of the archetypal immigrant story [47]). We see the photographs through the "night-worn eyes" of the cab drivers; they have imbued the object with their subjective exhaustion and desire. While this passage begins with the initial assumption that these immigrant workers are too disparate to group together, we end up seeing how they are connected through common fetish objects. So, too, does Kwang serve as the most public and spectacular fetish object binding differently racialized and ethnic constituents, a protective talisman like the child's diploma or the letter of citizenship that promises the protection of belonging.

In one of the novel's many poetic passages, Henry describes Kwang's constituents, the working people of Queens, in a way that frames them and their commodities as both modern and premodern. He observes them from the 7 Train, on his way to Kwang's office for the first time.

> They were always loading and unloading the light trucks and cube vans of stapled wooden crates and burlap sacks, the bulging bags of produce like turnips or jicama as heavy on their sloping shoulders as the bodies of their children still asleep at home. They were of all kinds, these streaming and working and dealing, these various platoons of Koreans, Indians, Vietnamese, Haitians, Colombians, Nigerians, each offering to the marketplace their gross of kimchee, lichee, plantain, black bean, soy milk, coconut milk, ginger, grouper, ahi, yellow curry, cuchifrito, jalapeño, their everything, selling everything to each other and to themselves, every day of the year, and every minute.
> John Kwang's people. (82–83)

The poetics here are Whitmanian, sweeping the everyday into the epic in lyrical and cataloguing rhythms. Such epic lyricism performs the narrative's romanticization of immigrant workers such that the reader, too, is captivated by the hypnotic cadence and vision of this romance. References to immigrant commodities are pleasingly arranged in patterns of rhyme, rhythm, and repetition that are both ordered and syncopated: "kimchee, lichee, plantain, black bean, soy milk, coconut milk, ginger, grouper . . .

cuchifrito, jalapeno." Alliteration between words and phrases such as "always," "loading," "unloading," and "light"; "burlap sacks" and "bulging bags"; and "produce" and "still asleep" contribute to the musicality of Henry's description. The sonic pleasures of this passage capture Henry's sense of grandeur and euphoria at this immigrant tableau. As we see how immigrant life inspires such poetic beauty, we believe that the immigrant-nation romance is also a romance with the English language.

The term "always" figures the immigrants as timeless—that is, pre-modern: outside history, simply part of nature. They are "always loading and unloading"; their acts are repetitive, recursive, part of the cyclicality of nature. Indeed, they are elemental, "streaming" like rivers. However, even as this perpetual activity is characterized as premodern, it also fits into the modern neoliberal idea of an endless frequency of market transaction, taking place "every day of the year, and every minute." We see here how the apparent primordiality of immigrant workers actually facilitates their incorporation into the modern, neoliberal national economy.

The contrast between the first paragraph and the second is most striking and poetic. The shape of both paragraphs as well as their contrast renders the narrative tone prophetic, even biblical. The first paragraph consists of two anaphoric sentences, with its second sentence mostly a long, chant-like list. The second paragraph consists only of three words that are never-theless equivalent in meaning to the first long paragraph. These words comprise a subject phrase, with no verb: "John Kwang's people." The lack of a verb denotes a removal from time and history, with the unappended subject phrase signifying an ever-present presence. The brevity of the phrase stops the time of the narrative; it is an "arresting phrase" that creates a pause as if to pay homage, or to suggest a Benjaminian revolutionary possibility.[13] Finally, the content of the phrase removes us from the time of modernity, referring not to Kwang's constituents or his community, but to his people. This term renders Kwang's supporters premodern as if tribal, organically bound to a charismatic patriarch. The list of objects in the first paragraph functions doubly, embodying both a premodern chant and the modern accounting structure of itemization. So, too, "John Kwang's people" connotes two ideas at once: a primordial, organic whole made up of parts that are itemized in the first paragraph; and a modern commodity object that is equivalent to each of the objects in the first paragraph, and therefore also a part-object. We have here the structure of the Freudian fetish in which (modern) fragment and (primitive) whole coexist.

On another date of marital reconciliation, Henry and Lelia wander through New York City, rediscovering the delights offered by the cosmopolitan city as a way to rediscover their pleasure in each other's company. As they try to reignite their romance, we see how immigrant commodity objects also facilitate romance between the immigrant and the nation:

> What we *cherish* most are the specialty items from far away, what the people have brought with them or are bringing in now, to sell to the natives: Honduran back scratchers, Polish mothballs, Flip Flops from every nation in the Pacific Rim, Statuettes of Liberty (earrings and pendants), made in Mexico City. (282; emphasis added)

On one level, this cherishing by the "native" consumer is an instance of desire for the exotic other, the wish to consume ever-different objects that keeps the engines of capital running. But the inclusion of the national, if kitschy, icons of the "Statuettes of Liberty" earrings and pendant point us more specifically in the direction of national myth as the organizing source of pleasure.

In *The Sublime Object of Ideology*, Slavoj Žižek offers the notion of "commodity belief," which can help us make sense of consumer desire in this passage. In historical terms, we perceive traditional and feudal subjects as clearly caught in ideological and superstitious beliefs, Žižek notes. With the advent of modernity and capitalism, the subject presumably is freed from such superstition by rational thought. However, Žižek argues that we now operate under a regime in which belief is made "objective": objects (such as commodities) believe, in place of people believing. We believe that we are liberated from ideology because ideology is now materialized in commodity objects.[14] In Henry's narration, the global objects that metonymically stand for the immigrants that have brought them here serve the purpose of believing in American exceptionalism. These commodities are imbued with a faith in America as the privileged site of open possibility, worth the arduous journeys from far away. Animistically, they are the source of a life force that revitalizes American romance. Through metonym, immigrants are also made animistic: they are objects of nation that are imagined as magically coming to life by their belief in America.

In the above discussion, I use the term "modernity" to reference capitalism and liberalism, developments that loosened persons from more traditional bonds. If modernity represents severance from tradition, then the immigrant fetish becomes the projected site of cultural fullness and tradition. The fantasy of the immigrant as the embodiment of authentic culture enables us to disavow the deracinations of capitalist and liberal modernity, especially in its forms as national incorporation. While the immigrant as commodity fetish conforms to the logic of capitalist modernity, the immigrant as primitive fetish compensates for dissatisfaction with modernity by promising the fullness of tradition. In the romance of *Native Speaker*, the immigrant represents the primitive fetish, the commodity fetish, and the Freudian fetish that enables the fantasy of plenitude. Kwang serves as a specific fetish object, the object *a* that promises completion to the nation and the immigrant. To immigrants, he promises that their desire for the nation will be reciprocated. To the nation, he promises the revitalization of immigrant belief, immigrant plenitude, and the completion of American democracy.

The fetish represents the immigrant as both primordial and modern, as both whole and fragment. In this way, the myth and romance of American exceptionalism has it both ways: immigrants are accepted and incorporated on the basis of their consent, but any loss of their "descent" or origin is disavowed. Hence they are believed to remain whole, without undergoing any fragmentation or alienation. Like Kwang, they are both ethnic and universal. This is the very promise of the multiracial democracy that Kwang represents: that one can become a universal citizen of the nation while not losing ties to one's culture of origin. Recall that in chapter 1, I propose melancholic citizenship as a mechanism for keeping loss alive. In contrast, romantic citizenship compensates for loss by imagining the ethnic-racial immigrant as fetish.

Why must the immigrant be both whole and partial? He must be incomplete, the subject of lack, so that America can complete him. But he must also be whole in order to stand for his nation of origin, so that America can claim its exceptional status as a "nation of nations," the pinnacle of global preeminence. The very concept of American ethnicity—the very concept of America itself, as a nation of nations—is structured by fetish.

The fetish reconciles a gap between knowledge and belief; its formula is conventionally articulated as "I know very well *x*, but still I believe *y*." The function of the immigrant is to know that America is not, in its actuality, the site of perfect equality, and still to believe in America as the land of opportunity, the unique object that will complete him. As I have mentioned, the role of the nation is to adjudicate the sincerity of this belief, and to return love if it judges the immigrant's love to be true. In this alchemy, the truth of immigrant belief will result in the truth of American exceptionalism.

However, there are two major areas of *Native Speaker* that resolutely resist fetishization and romance. First, there is the figure of the migrant woman worker as personified by Ahjuhma. She cannot be fetishized because she does not position herself as the subject of lack. She is too full, which means that she is too full of jouissance. Similarly, Kwang's money club and its members cannot be fetishized because they are not positioned as subjects of lack. They are too full, too autonomous, figures of too much enjoyment. The migrant woman worker and the money club present the novel's major blocks and crises because they disable the nation's fetishistic romance with the immigrant.

THE MIGRANT WOMAN WORKER AS ANTIFETISH

In the specific dimension of her labor, the racialized migrant woman in *Native Speaker* is posited as an exception to the immigrant-nation romance. The migrant woman otherwise often plays a very different role in national fantasy: she ostensibly desires the United States as the site of freedom and emancipation from Third World constraints, most pointedly from the constraints of native patriarchies.[15] Such gendered figures provide support for the myth of American exceptionalism and for U.S. global hegemony. However, in *Native Speaker*, the most salient figures of migrant racial women are those that we know through their work. As workers, they are figures of constraint and bondage *within the U.S. nation,* and hence cannot support the myth of the United States as a site of female liberation.[16]

As some critics of the novel have remarked, Henry, the model-minority spy, is adept at reading and interpreting everyone around him except Ahjuhma.[17] She is the one person who remains opaque to him, and hence also to the reader. This opacity signals her deviant visibility. It is a visual blockage that renders her both invisible and hypervisible. Ahjuhma's invisibility is captured by her namelessness, which is evidenced in the long passages in which Henry refers to her generically as "the woman" (62–72; 77–81). I am particularly interested in the way that Ahjuhma's deviant visibility registers as an epistemological crisis within the framework of liberal subjecthood. She is an excess formation within liberal modernity, an apparent leftover of the feudal in her position of servitude and dependence.

As a problem of knowledge, Ahjuhma's invisibility shades into hyper-visibility or surplus. She is hypervisible in her deviant femininity. Her face and body elicit the horror of the sublime, rather than the pleasures of beauty and fantasy. As a live-in housekeeper, she is interior to domestic space, but the excessiveness of her interiority renders her deviant. Although domestic, she is also profoundly undomesticated as a figure of inhuman jouissance.

The story of how Ahjuhma came to live in Henry's home seems to be an archetypal story of a childhood fall from innocence. As in a fairy tale, Henry's mother dies of a mysterious illness, and a new woman must be brought in to run the household so that Henry's father can concentrate on his work as economic provider. Ahjuhma does not technically qualify as an evil stepmother, as Henry's father does not marry her and Ahjuhma has no legitimized claim to power in the domestic sphere. In fact, however, this nonlegitimacy lays bare the problem with evil stepmothers: they are often brought into households to assume the gendered labor of reproducing the household, but without the "natural" maternal care of a biological mother. Ahjuhma might be more accurately described as an indifferent domestic worker, and this indifference can be characterized on two levels: first, her lack of affect on the emotional level; and second, her genericization—she is only a function. Henry portrays his childhood home as pathological because of its lack of "natural" maternal care. When Lelia remarks that Ahjuhma practically raised Henry, Henry counters, "I don't know who raised me" (69). This response can be interpreted in two ways: "I don't know if anyone raised me" (Henry as orphan) or "I don't know the person who raised me" (she is a stranger). Both meanings are forlorn: Henry is alienated from his own home because Ahjuhma is so clearly a figure of work, not a figure of maternal care and affection. The entrance of Ahjuhma into Henry's life is represented as an invasion of instrumental labor into the sentimental sphere of home. Put another way, the problem of Ahjuhma is that she makes explicit the business of family business.

Ahjuhma's deviant visibility and obscenity is immediately apprehended in her embodiment as the antithesis of beauty and purity. Henry recalls his first associations of her with immobility, disease, and repulsive odor:

> A dim figure of a woman stood unmoving in the darkness . . . the stench of
> overripe kimchee shot up through the cardboard flaps and I nearly dropped
> the whole thing. . . . This woman, I could see, had deep pockmarks stippling

her high, fleshy cheeks, like scarring from a mistreated bout of chickenpox or smallpox. . . . Her ankles and wrists were thick as posts. (62)

As the antithesis of beauty, Ahjuhma is unseemly to look at. But her unattractiveness functions not so much to repel the gaze as to compel it, though one is transfixed by sublime horror rather than by aesthetic pleasure. The viewer is disgusted not just by the disfiguring marks of disease on her face but also by their status as bodily remnants of Third World backwardness (her disease was "mistreated" presumably because of primitive and nonscientific methods). The unfeminine thickness of her ankles and wrists links her to the working class, an association heightened by their comparison to wooden posts, that is, to rough and utilitarian things. The stark contrast between Ahjuhma's scarred face and the "smoothest mask" (62) of Henry's mother reveals how Ahjuhma is a grotesque and perverse substitute for his mother. Ahjuhma's deviant visibility indexes her status as the source of jouissance or traumatic enjoyment; her effect of sublime horror and obscenity traumatizes the viewer even as they compel the viewer's enjoyment.

Ahjuhma's deviant visibility makes her the perfect training ground for Henry's early forays into espionage. In espionage, one fixes the other as the object of surveillance and knowledge. Seeking an alternative to his parents' powerlessness as objects of the hegemonic gaze, Henry positions himself as subject of the gaze in his adolescent, inaugural act of surveillance. He and his friend tail Ahjuhma as she goes into town on her day off. Ahjuhma's act of leaving the house to venture into town would seem to be a move from private space to public space. However, for the live-in domestic worker, leaving the house is her only opportunity for privacy. Henry would not find transgressive pleasure in watching Ahjuhma within the home, for such watching is sanctioned by her status as an employee who must be supervised. Ahjuhma is already the object of surveillance within the home, available to the gaze and scrutiny of the masters of the house. Henry's only chance at transgressive voyeurism is to spy on her during her leisure time, her time away from the house.

The boys are gratified to discover and pronounce Ahjuhma to be "completely bizarre" (78). Their voyeuristic gaze is both unsettled and satisfied—traumatized and entertained—by apprehending the other as grotesque. What makes Ahjuhma a freakish spectacle to the boys is her deviant consumption. She eats a popsicle like a hot dog, taking three large bites. Flipping through the pages of a teen magazine, she "obviously look[s] only at the pictures" (78); her incomprehension of the text makes her interest in glossy pictures pornographic, and the magazine's niche marketing to American teen girls makes her interested gaze, as a middle-aged Asian woman, alien and pedophilic. In chapter 2, I discussed how Ika, the migrant woman worker, was judged to be an illegitimate consumer by a salesclerk who does not see her, and by the "yoga mom" who does not believe that Ika's son should be attending their school. Similarly, Ahjuhma is judged by Henry to be incompetent in the practices of consumer citizenship. When Ahjuhma wears the garish clothes that Henry's father buys for her, the narrative suggests her abject subordination in her inability to refuse his poor taste, or perhaps her cultural illiteracy at not realizing that the clothes are in poor taste. At Henry's high school graduation, for example, she wears an "iridescent dress" picked out by Henry's father, looking like a "huge trout" (79). Henry figures her not only as an animal, but an animal from the alien world of water.

In an explicit reference to Ahjuhma's inhuman status, the friend who calls her "completely bizarre" also pronounces her a "total alien" (78). It is Ahjuhma's deviant consumption, coupled with her near lack of social interaction, that renders her alien, inhuman, and incomprehensible:

> Her manner unnerved me. She never laughed. She spoke only when it mattered, when a thing needed to be done, or requested, or acknowledged. Otherwise the sole sounds I heard from her were the *sucking noises* she would make through the spaces between her teeth after meals and in the mornings.... She *smelled strongly of fried fish and sesame oil and garlic* ... my friends called her "Aunt Scallion," and made faces behind her back.
>
> Sometimes I thought she was some kind of *zombie*. (65; emphases added)

Henry calls her a zombie because she exhibits mechanical signs of life but is dead to the social world around her. Her refusal to laugh or speak for pleasure excludes her from normal human sociality. Ahjuhma uses language perfunctorily, and the only other sounds from her body are sucking noises, animalistic sounds that are incomprehensible as language. Henry's association of Ahjuhma with the odor of Korean cooking is an example of what Martin Manalansan calls the "smelly immigrant trope," a formation that renders the immigrant as violating boundaries between food and body, private and public, animal and human.[18] When Henry first encounters her, he cannot visually apprehend her ("a dim figure . . . in the darkness"), but instead is overpowered by "the stench of overripe kimchee." As Cary Wolfe notes, sight is the sense that is most associated with human faculty, while the sense of smell is especially associated with animals.[19] Ahjuhma is thus animalized in her primordiality.

I interpret the ascription of inhumanity to Ahjuhma as referring to her embodiment of jouissance. Consider Henry's use of the term "unnerves" in the passage above, describing Ahjuhma's effect on him. Wolfe uses this very term "unnerving" to describe the sensation of being known by the animal other without understanding or being able to incorporate this alien knowledge: "The traditional humanist subject finds this prospect of the animal other's knowing us in ways *we* cannot know and master *simply unnerving.*"[20] Henry, master of apprehending others, feels apprehended by her in ways he does not understand; through her faculties, he becomes an incomprehensible object to himself.

To be unnerved is to become frightened, yet to take fright is to become only nerve, to activate the "fight or flight" response of the sympathetic nervous system. Thus Henry himself loses the "higher" functions of the human and is reduced to an animalistic response. Ahjuhma's inhumanity also threatens Henry's humanity. Ahjuhma's ability to throw Henry off balance reveals her status as the object of jouissance, the piece of the Real that needs to be removed in order for one's Symbolic reality to achieve coherence. The reason that Ahjuhma haunts Henry is because she is too present, overly proximate; she exceeds his Symbolic framework. Her sounds and smells are the site of animalistic excess in the presumably human domestic sphere. As we will see, domesticity and language are the novel's privileged sites for the incorporation of the immigrant into the nation. In her disruption of the Symbolic and of proper domesticity, Ahjuhma exceeds the conditions for romance between immigrant and nation.

Ahjuhma is the one major character in the book who remains opaque, outside human connection, identification, or sympathy. Seen yet uncomprehended, she blocks knowledge. In this way, she occupies the position of the abject, that which is foreclosed from normative subjectivity.[21] Even more crucial than her exclusion from subjectivity, however, is her exclusion, as the abject, from objecthood. Ahjuhma cannot become the object of the fetish, romance, or fantasy. While she is literally aligned with the domestic sphere, she is undomesticated in the sense of dis-corporation from human culture or society. Ahjuhma is completely removed from any dynamic of desire, for desire is characterized by mobility and fluctuation. In his first encounter with Ahjuhma, Henry perceives her as "unmoving" and inert. This recalcitrance is an attribute of the Real, which, as Lacan posits, always returns to its place and cannot be positioned dialectically.

For normative subjects, Ahjuhma is a figure of jouissance, presumably enjoying her exclusion from the rules of the Symbolic order. For Lelia, as the consummate representative of the Symbolic order in her role as speech therapist and literary writer, such jouissance within her husband's household is unbearable. This is why Lelia commits the folly of trying to dialecticize Ahjuhma. She takes on the project of humanizing and individuating Ahjuhma by making her into a social other. Disturbed by Henry's indifferent and generic relationship with Ahjuhma and how this impersonality might spill over into their marriage, Lelia attempts to create a more human relationship with the domestic worker. She believes that her good intentions and good-faith efforts will render Ahjuhma comprehensible and legible, a fellow human being like them. Lelia's project of humanizing Ahjuhma may be understood as part of her larger aim of humanizing Henry. After all, Lelia believes that Ahjuhma "practically raised" Henry and therefore must be "just like one of the family" (69). And what would humanize Henry more than rehumanizing his family?

Ahjuhma, however, continually resists Lelia's overtures. Nevertheless, Lelia makes one last effort by trying to share the "feminine" domestic work of laundry:

One afternoon Lelia cornered the woman in the laundry room and tried to communicate with her while helping her fold a pile of clothes . . . not a word or a glance between them . . . the woman actually began nudging her in the side with the fleshy mound of her low-set shoulder, grunting and pushing her out of the room with short steps; Lelia began hockey-checking back with her elbows, trying to hold her positions, when by accident, she caught her hard on the ear and the woman let out a loud shrill whine that sent them both scampering from the room. Lelia ran out to where I was working inside the garage, tears streaming from her eyes; we hurried back to the house to find the woman back in the laundry room, carefully refolding the dry laundry. She backed away when she saw Lelia and cried madly in Korean, You cat! You nasty American cat!

I scolded her then, telling her she couldn't speak to my wife that way if she wanted to keep living in our house. The woman bit her lip; she bent her head and bowed severely before me in a way that perhaps no one could anymore and then trundled out of the room between us. I suddenly felt as if I'd committed a great wrong. (71–72)

Lelia believes that she and Ahjuhma share a universal female humanity that can be manifested by jointly performing "female" domestic work. Interestingly, however, the narrative works against Lelia's humanist wish by continuing to figure Ahjuhma as not quite human: grunting, emitting a shrill whine, trundling.

Although Ahjuhma is firmly positioned within the interior space of the house, she is also starkly regarded as most exterior to the belongings of home and family, as Henry's power to throw Ahjuhma out of the house reveals. Despite Ahjuhma's centrality and longevity in maintaining the Park household, she has no part in "our house." Henry is a child when Ahjuhma first enters the household, but he recognizes his right, perhaps even thinking of it as his duty, to scold her—to put her in her place as the immature rule-breaker who must be disciplined. Ahjuhma's severe bow in turn reveals Henry's absolute power over her livelihood and life, a stark hierarchy that Lelia so blithely tries to cover over. Ahjuhma's bow strikes Henry as anachronistic and premodern. Indeed, the bow reveals the quasi-feudal relations between Henry, who has a legitimate claim to the home as property through his family relations, and Ahjuhma, who evidences no alternative family relations, and hence no alternative to service work for the Park household. In *Native Speaker*, the migrant woman worker is a figure of constraint, not of consent. This constraint is naturalized by the narrative troping of Ahjuhma as inhuman. If Ahjuhma barely speaks or participates in social relations, how can she give consent? Recall, too, the paradox I referred to earlier, in which Henry cannot spy on Ahjuhma in the house because she is already denied privacy in the domestic sphere. Ahjuhma's relationship to the Parks is feudal in the sense that she is bonded to her masters in her home as well as her livelihood.

By insisting on her own opacity, Ahjuhma repudiates Lelia's fantasy of a knowable, universal humanity. She refuses to be incorporated into Lelia's liberal humanist regime of visibility, which privileges the fantasy of a mutual recognition that dissimulates severe power inequality. Ahjuhma is a figure of constraint; she is not legible as the subject that consents to the nation. The only agency she appears to exercise is that of refusal.[22] And significantly, what she refuses is the status of the liberal subject who consents to the fantasy of a same and equal humanity. Through this incident, we see that liberal subjecthood is not the ultimate aim for all persons; liberal subjecthood constitutes, in fact, an oppressive and dissimulating fantasy. Through her recalcitrant jouissance, Ahjuhma blocks the fantasy of liberal universal humanism that undergirds the romance of American democracy, citizenship, and exceptionalism.

THE MONEY CLUB AS ANTIFETISH

I turn here to another major block to the immigrant-nation romance in *Native Speaker:* the money club organized by Kwang's office. While Ahjuhma remains "stubbornly ethnic," the money club seems to cross ethnic and racial boundaries, for it is comprised of members of various ethnic communities. The problem that they both present, however, is that they are too full to be subjects of national romance. The subject of desire must be a subject who lacks, and who therefore needs the object—the nation—to complete him. Ahjuhma and the members of the money club, refusing to be subjects of lack, also refuse to be subjects in debt to the nation. They are so autonomous, so full of jouissance, that they block the fetish of immigrant-nation romance.

This is the denouement of the novel: Henry's boss, Dennis, asks Henry to submit the names of Kwang constituents who are part of an economic network in which members contribute money and request loans. Henry studies this network and does not find any irregularities—specifically, he finds no skimming of money from the campaign. He submits the information to Dennis, not knowing the identity of the client that wants this information. In the meantime, Kwang has begun to lose public support. He is unable to maintain a strong facade after his office is bombed, and the news media make a spectacle of him when he is found in a car crash with an underage (and undocumented) Korean "hospitality girl." Shortly thereafter, the evening news reports on "hard evidence" of Kwang's money club—presumably this evidence is the list that Henry submits to Dennis. Henry narrates, "The information, oddly, originates from the regional director of the Immigration and Naturalization Service" (329). What is odd to Henry is that he expects the money club to concern the IRS or financial regulators, not the INS.[23] The INS regional director comes on the air and declares that the illegal aliens whom they discovered through the documentation of the money club are already in the process of being deported. Made into a spectacle through his criminalization, his illicit sexuality, and his association with illegal aliens (via the hostess and the money club), Kwang is now the target of fervent, nativist public outrage. Mobs take to the streets and demand his ouster. What explains this primal fury? How is it that immigrant romance so swiftly pivots into the abjection of the immigrant as alien? And why does a network of economic capital become so easily conflated with illegal immigration?

The climax of the novel, the targeting of illegal immigrants for surveillance and deportation, blindsides Henry and the reader, because we have been led all along to believe that the target of surveillance, the site of scandal, must be money. From the beginning, we hear rumors about "street money" in Kwang's campaign (149). Henry's colleague Jack intimates that there may be irregularities in the money network that Henry oversees in his work for Kwang (291). Reporters chasing a scandal "[suggest] unceasingly how it must involve money, it must involve money" (295). So when the ultimate purpose of Henry's assigned surveillance turns out to be the identification and deportation of undocumented migrants, we are caught by surprise. However, I would argue that this apparent turn from money to migrants is a kind of feint; the target is indeed money, but this money is tainted by jouissance, and hence too diffuse and abstract to regulate. Therefore, the property of jouissance becomes transferred onto "illegal aliens," who can then be managed and deported.

Native Speaker is often read as a commentary on the forces that obstruct the political empowerment of racial communities through representation by elected officials like Kwang.[24] Certainly, Kwang's career is impeded by politicians like Mayor DeRoos who are threatened by his support among immigrant voters.[25] However, as I mentioned, I do not consider the money club an incidental component of the takedown of Kwang's political career. Where many critics see Kwang's campaign as the target of a threatened hegemony, and the money club as a means of taking him down, I propose that the money club itself is the target, and that Kwang himself, as a public figure, is collateral damage. Economic autonomy, in other words, is more of a danger to hegemony than political representation.

The problem of the money club in *Native Speaker* foregrounds the contradictions of the neoliberal nation-state. Neoliberalism and U.S. nationalism privilege self-managing and self-made subjects as ethical exemplars. The "good" immigrant is not overly dependent on the nation and its resources. But the immigrant entrepreneur who participates in the money club is *too* autonomous, *too* self-sufficient. While neoliberalism calls for autonomy from economic dependence on the state, the romance of American exceptionalism requires that the immigrant be *psychically* indebted to the nation. And though neoliberal ideology holds that capital indeed should be unregulated, the primal outrage against Kwang alerts us to the element of jouissance that permeates this particular nonregulation of capital.

Let us observe how political representation and the money club differ in the terms of their visibility. While Kwang's political career does bring previously marginalized peoples into the political process, his success confirms, rather than disrupts, the expectations of liberal democracy. His aim, to achieve the normative visibility of recognition by the Other, indexes the normativity of his political incorporation. The money club is an entirely different matter, as we see from its deviant visibility. As an underground economy, the money club was invisible to the larger public. Once exposed, it becomes hypervisible, eliciting severe scrutiny and surveillance. While Kwang's family business as politics is transparent to the hegemonic gaze, his family business as economics is opaque and disturbing to the Other's view. As I argue in the Introduction, this deviant visibility points to the phenomenon of jouissance, or traumatic enjoyment.

Modeled on the Korean *ggeh*, the money club is a credit-rotating association in which members regularly contribute money and are permitted to borrow a large sum at one point in the cycle.[26] Kwang's version of the money club is multiracial, open to any member of the immigrant communities that form Kwang's constituency. As with Kwang's political career, his ethnic exceptionalism is marked by such racial border-crossing. Henry's father plays his usual role as "traditional" foil to Kwang's modernity: "My father would have thought him crazy to run a *ggeh* with people other than just our own. Spanish people? Indians, Vietnamese? How could you trust them? Then even if you could, why would you?" (280). The candor of this passage punctures the liberal fantasy that all national subjects would naturally form a universal multiracial community, if only cultural ignorance could be overcome. Instead, this cultural ignorance or ethnocentrism is precisely a refusal of desire for such a community. Kwang's will to cross racial boundaries in the public sphere of politics marks him as a modern subject. But such border-crossing in the privatized realm of finance is threatening because it is not open to the regulation of the hegemonic gaze. This is why the capital of the money club becomes transfigured into illegal immigrants:

so as to once again particularize these subjects and monitor them under surveillance and regulation.

In its racial mixing, the money club is a form of financial miscegenation, a mode of enjoyment that is autonomous, unfetishizable, and inaccessible to the native, presumably white, national subject. At the level of plot, the public romance with Kwang is the element that must be dissolved in order for Henry to reconcile with Lelia in domestic romance. The jouissance of the money club, the underside of Kwang's political work, disrupts and dissolves this public romance. From another angle, we might say that racial border-crossing appears acceptable in its confirmation and support of liberal democracy. However, the flip side of this public racial border-crossing is its hidden underside as miscegenation in the privatized sector of finance, a universalization of capital that is scandalously inaccessible to the hegemonic Other of whiteness and the state. Miscegenation, then, must be displaced yet again to the private sphere of the white heteronormative family, so that its romance can be universalized into whiteness.

Recall that Mr. Park, Henry's father, exemplifies immigrant romance in his role as an immigrant entrepreneur. In his narration of the story that every native loves to hear, the crucial element of the money club must be disavowed. The money club is the element of jouissance that must be extracted in order for the fantasy of the immigrant romance to achieve coherence:

> Of course, in his personal lore he would have said that he started with $200 in his pocket and a wife and baby and just a few words of English. Knowing what every native loves to hear, he would have offered the classic immigrant story, casting himself as the heroic newcomer, self-sufficient, resourceful.
>
> The truth, though, is that my father got his first infusion of capital from a ggeh, a Korean "money club." (49–50)

Why must the money club be extracted from the story of the immigrant romance? Because this romance depends on the indebtedness of the immigrant to the generosity of the nation. Although immigrants are figured as "good" if they are self-sufficient and "bad" if they are *economically* dependent on the nation, the immigrant romance needs an element of *affective* or *psychic* indebtedness to the nation. The problem of the money club is that the immigrant becomes, paradoxically, *too* self-sufficient.

Neoliberal nationalism privileges the self-managing subject as ethical exemplar, and the ethnic immigrant entrepreneur is one such model figure of self-sufficiency. But the trauma of the money club exposes the contradictions of the neoliberal nation-state. The neoliberal state supposedly does not want to regulate the privatized realm of the market, but the imperial nation, with its myths and romances of American exceptionalism, requires that the immigrant be psychically indebted to the nation. The ostensible problem of the money club is that its circulation of capital is unregulated, but the primal nativist response indicates that the real problem is the unregulation of jouissance. The immigrant romance requires that the immigrant be seen as a subject of lack, desiring the nation as the object that completes him. The money club, however, positions him as overly self-sufficient, too full—too saturated with jouissance to have the hole or lack that the nation fills as his object of desire and romance.

To lay the groundwork for discussing the jouissance of the money club, I will detour into a discussion of blood and capital as mutually imbricated figures in the narrative. While capital is a modern system of abstraction, blood would seem to represent its opposite, a primordial materialization. We can see how these two elements already overlap and conflate, however, in the very structure of family business, which binds kinship and economics. In addition, the trope of inheritance ties together blood and capital: biological essence and property are transmitted not as separate entities but become each other through this transfer. Henry attributes his childhood frailty, for example, to "hav[ing] my mother's thin blood" (135)— actually having, within his body, as his property, the blood of his mother.

Recounting a tense discussion with Lelia about adoption, Henry makes his views plain that adoption is an inferior practice to the transmission of blood through biological reproduction:

> Adoption, I know, is a noble and mostly happy practice. No doubt an advancement for a culture. And yet for me, the prerogative is that you should still bestow your blood whenever able. You grow your own. For although your offerings of unconditional love and respect and devotion will make good of most any child, what you cannot give or else substitute is that tie unspoken and unseen, the belief in blood, that unbreakable connection telling your boy or girl that hers will never be a truly solitary life. (108)

For Henry, blood represents a primordial and inalienable connection, a fundamental and final bond. Blood relations stand for inalienable property, in which "your boy or girl" is "your own," "unbreakabl[y]." Biological family is the primal, premodern form that survives modernity's breaking of bonds and individualization into "solitary" lives. For Henry, the indissoluble link of blood means that one possesses one's kin, that one is possessed by one's kin, and that one cannot be dispossessed of this property. This primal property is to be differentiated from modern, capitalist forms of property, which are precisely alienable and transferable.

We also find a striking example of how property transmits and produces blood kinship in Henry's descriptions of their inherited residences. The father's house in Ardsley is the aspirational house for Henry and Lelia. They intend to move there when they are ready to have children again. In contrast to this ideal, heteronormative site for family-building, Henry says that the Manhattan loft in which they currently live is where things "went very wrong" (23) in their marriage after Mitt's death. Henry calls it a "surprisingly dysfunctional space" (24). Not coincidentally, Henry reveals, Lelia inherited this loft from her uncle Steve, who "lived alone and died of AIDS" (24). The novel sets Uncle Steve's death in the 1980s, when AIDS was associated with urban gay men and with the transmission of bodily fluids like blood. In a novel that is preoccupied with patriarchal figures, this inheritance decidedly queers patrilineal transmission. The route of this property transmission follows not the straight line of father to son, but the more crooked line of uncle to niece. Lelia inherits the loft because of her uncle's exclusion from the heteronormative, reproductive nuclear family, as well as her partial inheritance of her uncle's blood. This property that can be alienated and transferred from one party to another is shown to somehow transmit more primordial properties of nonnormative kinship.

Henry explicitly posits the money club as a form of capital accumulation and circulation that is alternative to the transmission of property within private families. "He was merely giving to them just the start, *like other people get an inheritance,* a hope chest of what they would work hard for in the rest of their lives" (334; emphasis added). The phrase that I highlight in this quote refers to the system of wealth that is passed on from generation to generation, a process of property inheritance and capital accumulation that becomes transformed into a sense of inherent entitlement, worth, and value. Melvin Oliver and Thomas Shapiro have shown how the historical production and transmission of wealth has been starkly racialized to the benefit of whites.[27] What is the significance of the money club as an alternative to private inheritance? The audacity of Kwang's money club appears at first to lie in the way that it moves inheritance from the private sphere to the public sphere. But our understanding of this transfer needs to be nuanced. Family inheritance is already regulated within the public sphere via the law and the state, while the problem of Kwang's money club is precisely its lack of regulation by the law and the state. What distinguishes the money club from traditional inheritance is not their spheres of operation, but a reverse relationship between kin and property. In traditional inheritance, kin relations facilitate the transfer of property; in the money club, the transfer of property creates kin relations. The former seems acceptable because kinship is already naturalized as a primordial form of property: "my" child has a right to "my" property. The latter, however, transforms the abstraction of alienable property into a primordial bond. The myth of a multiracial nation is that "primordial differences" are subsumed into universal citizenship; all subjects are rendered equivalent through abstraction. With the money club, the reverse occurs: abstraction becomes enjoyment that is excluded from the normative subject.

The transgression of Kwang's money club is the way that this alternate mode of transferring property and capital signifies *a mixing of blood,* and even more scandalously, a mixing of blood that is not open to the hegemonic gaze. The scandal is that Kwang's money club is not a single-ethnicity money club. Kwang has taken the ethnic Korean institution of the *ggeh,* the rotating-credit association, and opened it up to people of multiple ethnicities and races. A single-ethnic *ggeh* could be explained away as a traditional or clannish ethnic custom, as a sign of primitive superstition in not entering into the modernity of banking systems, as a form of underdeveloped premodernity. In contrast, the scandal of Kwang's money club is its multiracial mingling of money—a form of financial miscegenation that breaks down ethnic boundaries. In this multiracial network, the immigrant mixes with ethnic and racial others through the abstract form of money that nevertheless bears the trace of blood, both in its form as contribution (made from backbreaking, health-deteriorating labor) and as disbursement (to those seeking loans). In his role as facilitator of the money club, Henry demands an accounting of blood: "I want to know the blood you've lost, or that someone has stolen, or tricked from you, the blood you desperately want back from the world" (281).

Henry reminds us how the abstraction of money bears the trace of blood, a primordial substance. These immigrants have lost blood; they need to be repaid; they are owed a debt of blood. But can blood be repaid? Money can be repaid because it is an abstract, universal medium of exchange. But blood is primordial, particular; it is precisely not a universal medium of exchange because it is inalienable, cannot be dispossessed. In its material particularity, blood is in excess of the Symbolic; it embodies jouissance.

In a single-ethnic *ggeh,* money could be viewed as a kind of blood circulating through and binding a single ethnic body. Blood, in this troping, would stand for primordial connection, for ethnic tribalism or clannishness. The idea of a single-ethnic *ggeh* can be easily commodified, consumed, and comprehended as a quaint practice of ethnic premodernity. Once the money club is opened to different ethnicities and races, however, the circuit of this blood money takes the form of circulation among different bodies; it becomes abstracted as the exchange of equivalent modes (money), even as it retains primordial substance (blood). What is the difference between the culturalized commodity object, which can be consumed, and the abstraction of capital, which cannot be? The commodity object is a fetish not only in the Marxist sense but also in the psychoanalytic sense: it can be consumed as traditional culture. "Pure" economic capital cannot be consumed as traditional culture.

The problem of the money club is twofold. First, it produces abstraction and universality without whiteness.[28] Abstraction and universalism are modes that arose from European Enlightenment principles that have become vehicles for privileging white normativity; they are impossible to imagine without whiteness. Second, it produces jouissance that is inaccessible to whiteness. The money club is the embodiment of jouissance that disrupts the romance between immigrant and nation. If national romance fetishizes the immigrant as both premodern and modern, then the money club figures the migrant as excess, as *too* primitive and *too* modern. As I have argued, the commodity fetish helps to structure the fantasy of immigrant romance. It is precisely the concreteness of the commodity fetish that is absent from this formation of the money club because its mode is abstraction. As such, the money club cannot be subsumed into a comforting romance of multiracial democracy. Instead, it traumatizes this fantasy by revealing the excesses that are otherwise disavowed in immigrant romance.

The money club is too modern. If immigrant blood, in the form of labor, were to go into the making of a commodity object, that blood could be consumed as an organic, cultural authenticity. But instead, this blood is transformed into money; it takes the form not of organic authenticity but of abstraction. And this abstraction cannot be consumed. Through the money club, the immigrant has become too autonomous, not only in his economic agency but in embodying law itself.

Counterintuitively, the problem is that Kwang does *not* profit from the money club. As Henry meticulously ascertains, the redistribution of money is "clean" (291). There is no surplus profit, no upward redistribution of wealth. On one level, then, the money club is the site of lack according to neoliberal principles of generating maximum profit with minimal intervention. What is truly disturbing, however, is the way that the money club is the site of an *excessive* neoliberal practice. If Kwang skimmed money from this operation, profiting from the trust of his constituents, he would face public disapproval but would be easily comprehended as an archetypal corrupt politician. The fantasy of his ethnic constituents as premodern and naive subjects could be sustained, and Kwang could be perceived as a quasi-feudal lord demanding monetary tribute from his subordinates. But Kwang "gives" his immigrant constituents too much autonomy by not demanding a monetary tribute, as a feudal lord would. His money club formulates its members as not duped, knowing, and modern. Indeed, in their nonreliance on the state and their autonomy from state regulation, they embody neoliberalist principles, taken to its logical ends. Put another way, the *ggeh* is *excessively* neoliberal, and it is this excess that disturbs the national Symbolic, that demands regulation and expulsion in order to reconstitute the national Symbolic as a balanced, organic whole.

Moreover, by not profiting from the money club, we see all the more starkly that Kwang has set himself up as the law. The only thing that gives this microeconomy consistency is Kwang himself—the integrity, trust, and aspiration that he models for others—not any external law. Within the larger realm of electoral politics, Kwang may embody the law as an elected official, but he is also subject to the law and to the "rules of the game" in politics. As the fulcrum of this underground economy, however, Kwang is his own law. He is subject to nothing but himself. He and his constituents are not indebted to the nation; they are not subjects of lack that need the nation to complete them. And this excessive autonomy also means that they are too primitive, too tribal, in not being open to hegemonic signification and exchange.[29] In embodying the different excesses of the primitive and the modern, the money club traumatically disrupts the fetishistic structure of immigrant romance.

In the logic of the novel, the migrant woman worker and the money club operate as antifetishes: elements of jouissance that block the romance between nation and immigrant. In both cases, the immigrant is not positioned as the subject of lack and desire. She is too full, too autonomous. There is no commodity fetish to facilitate an apprehension of the immigrant as both ethnic and universal. In the case of the money club, we see an oscillation between excessive modernity and excessive primordiality. With the downfall of Kwang, public romance is shattered, and domestic romance ascends as the narrative resolution. From another angle, we might say that romantic citizenship demands that financial miscegenation be dissolved, so that miscegenation can take place within the sphere of white domesticity.

DOMESTIC ROMANCE

So far, I have explained how the immigrant-nation romance is structured by the fetish. I have looked at how the migrant woman worker and the money club block this romance through jouissance. In both instances, the migrant does not open up herself or himself to the hegemonic gaze, does not present the self as the transparent object of knowledge, and does not position the self as the subject of lack and desire. In other words, the migrant does not position the self as indebted to the nation, as having a hole that only the nation can fill as the ideal object of desire and fantasy. In the case of the money club, the migrant punctures national fantasy by too excessively following its rules and embodying neoliberal principles to an extreme.

In his public romance, Kwang seems to position himself in such a way as to enable the circuits of the immigrant-nation romance. In the end, however, he is exiled because he betrays this romance by facilitating the overfullness and overautonomy of the immigrant. The immigrant's courtship is judged to be insincere after all. He is deemed dishonorable, a cad, one who takes advantage of the overly beneficent, overly generous nation.

Thus it is up to Henry to redeem and confirm the immigrant-nation romance through the domestic romance of white heteronormativity. Henry does indeed present himself as the subject of lack and desire. Previously opaque to his wife, he is now willing to repair his marriage by becoming the transparent object of knowledge. He also understands himself as psychically indebted to his speech-therapist wife and to the nation for hailing and recognizing him. Why are domesticity and language the ideal sites of romance in the novel? Are they more fetishizable, and thus more accessible to the hegemonies of whiteness and the state than politics or economics?

Readers of *Native Speaker* have interpreted Kwang's downfall and Henry's reconciliation with Lelia in a number of ways. David Palumbo-Liu and Betsy Huang read *Native Speaker* as suggesting that the time is "not yet ripe" for the utopia of racial integration.[30] For James Kyung-Jin Lee, *Native Speaker* marks the contraction of the public sphere and the retreat into the private sphere.[31] I build upon Lee's argument here by inquiring into the significance of such a retreat. Daniel Kim, referencing Amy Kaplan's interpretation of American realist novels, argues that we should not read the novel's conclusion pessimistically, as novels do not give us political solutions so much as awaken political desires. Having said this, Kim also notes that *Native Speaker*'s resolutions reside more in culture than in politics.

The narrative frames the problem of Henry's marriage as a problem of intimacy. Both Henry and Lelia understand that *he* is the impediment to marital success, and that he needs to change if their marriage is to survive. Specifically, the obstacle to their marital happiness is represented as Henry's inheritance of a Confucian Korean culture in which duty and order are valued over the expression of emotional intimacy. The practices of family business (maintaining the institution of the family) for Henry's family of origin, in other words, are at odds with the practices and values of family business for Henry's conjugal family. As David Shumway observes in *Modern Love*, intimacy is the primary mode through which we understand marriage in contemporary American culture. Success in establishing intimacy distinguishes healthy from unhealthy marriages. If Henry cannot express emotional intimacy with Lelia, then he cannot express his consent to companionate marriage—the American norm of marriage that imagines equal partners openly communicating and sharing their feelings with each other. The marital resolution of the novel demands that Henry open up previously secret and opaque realms of affect to Lelia's gaze. Seen in the overall trajectory of narrative romance, Henry's exposure of his own intimate affect stages his choice of and consent to normative American culture—a prerequisite to the nation's consent to him as an appropriate citizen-subject.

Because Henry's experiences in the public sphere are so tumultuous, we are lulled into believing that the private sphere provides a safe and stable refuge from the public. Sämi Ludwig offers this kind of separate-spheres interpretation:

Real or authentic language can only be tested in the interaction between human beings, and best in the intimacy of a love relationship. This is a strategy of countering an alienating public discourse through private relationships . . . reality can only be changed and controlled on the personal level. . . . This is where in *Native Speaker,* Lelia, the wife and speech therapist, comes in. If the public discourse is dysfunctional, therapy can be provided in a private relationship. . . . Henry's professional failure is counteracted by the mending of his private marital situation. This second plot line is the one charged with much more potential for healing energy.[32]

For Ludwig, Lelia is indeed a therapist, offering healing to Henry in the domestic sphere through the exchange of "authentic language" "between human beings." It turns out, however, that the private sphere is not a realm of complete autonomy from the public sphere. Instead, the private sphere has become the site of subjectivation for the nation-state, for functions that are more conventionally understood as the province of the public sphere.

The novel ends with Henry and Lelia's home staged as a speech-therapy classroom. Let us carefully consider the brightly optimistic conclusion, in which Lelia writes her students' names "inside the sunburst-shaped badge. Everyone, she says, has been a good citizen" (349). Classroom citizenship is not simply a metaphor; schooling functions as an ideological state apparatus, a site where proper citizenship is indeed learned. And what does it mean that home and school are conflated in this scene? Significantly, Henry proceeds to use the collective pronoun "we" in naming the object of Lelia's interpellation; he sees himself as part of the "everyone" who is a "good citizen." What appears to be Henry's retreat into private domesticity is not an escape from the public sphere at all. In the neoliberal blurring of private and public, both spheres are explicit sites of subjectivation for the nation-state.

Henry's work for Glimmer and Company, which turns out to be contract work for the state, is part of a pattern of increasing privatization under neoliberalism. Privatization, in this sense, does not mean a reduction of state power; rather, privatization is a means for the state to achieve its objectives more effectively. Under neoliberalism, contract work has become more frequent and shorter in duration. The virtue of privatization, in neoliberal thinking, is that it is more efficient than government-run programs.

Why is privatized work deemed more efficient? Because it is not subject to regulation or accountability; it does not have to answer to demands for the public good. Henry performs the intimate labor of forming relationships with target subjects, and gaining their trust, in order to produce and record knowledge about them. Henry's espionage work is a technology of subjectivation; it is the work of biopower, or the production and regulation of bodies and subjects by the state, in Foucault's formulation. Building trust and relationships are necessary to the effectiveness of this productive surveillance. Henry serves as an informant, and perhaps more to the point, a native informant. His ethnicity allows him to more effectively infiltrate those "whole secret neighborhoods brown and yellow" (11), to penetrate previously invisible worlds and render them visible and knowable to the dominant gaze. It is important to note that the preceding phrase, "whole secret neighborhoods brown and yellow," is spoken by Lelia when she first meets Henry and tells him about the communities that she "penetrates" in doing her speech therapy. Henry's work in making himself more legible to Lelia is not separate from his imperatives in the workplace; rather, it is *continuous* with his espionage work in rendering racial and ethnic immigrant communities knowable to the hegemonic gaze.

If we recall Foucault's *History of Sexuality,* in which he articulates the concept of biopower, we can understand the trajectory of the novel, Henry's interpellation into national romance, via Foucault's repressive hypothesis. We believe, Foucault contends, that the truth of sexuality is repressed and needs to be liberated. What results from this belief is a prolific generation of discourse and knowledge production, the management of human bodies that he termed biopower. Transferring this model to the narrative of *Native Speaker,* we as readers believe that the truth of Henry's emotions is repressed and must be liberated for his marriage to be successful. In her patience and persistence as Henry's most constant interlocutor, Lelia serves as such an agent of freedom. A Foucauldian understanding of the novel reveals how Lelia's work of speech therapy, which becomes the family business of serving as patient interlocutors for immigrant children, is a form of biopower that is not only parallel to and continuous with Henry's previous work of subjectivation, but itself serves as Henry's own mode of subjectivation.

In her work as a speech therapist for immigrant children, Lelia performs the function of formation for the nation-state, transforming alien others into assimilable subjects of the nation. The forms that Lelia's work take on reveal the neoliberal objective of reducing government spending for social services by shifting responsibility to the private sector. As a freelance worker (or a contract worker, as Henry also turned out to be), Lelia constructs a speech studio in her home, where "[t]he public school has to farm [students] out to Lelia because it doesn't have enough staff" (233). Or she travels around the city, "bring[ing] her gear in two rolling plastic suitcases" because the schools "don't have speech facilities, or not enough of them" (348). We can understand the home of Henry and Lelia as the privatized site of a state apparatus. In his apparent retreat to the domestic realm, Henry continues the productive and privatized work of sorting citizens from noncitizens, but now including himself as the object of this work.

Indeed, we can understand the novel's turn from public romance to domestic romance as allegorizing and explaining the ascendance of neoliberalism in this period of the 1980s and 1990s. As we see in Henry and Lelia's careers, the work of managing and forming subjects on behalf of the nation-state increasingly became privatized during this period. The fact that it falls to Lelia, not to Kwang, to interpellate Henry as an American citizen demonstrates all the more keenly that the private sphere of domesticity, not the public sphere of politics, has become the proper site of subject formation. What *Native Speaker* suggests is the way that neoliberalism has harnessed the pleasures of the private, through fantasies and affects like romance, to enact this hegemonic shift into privatization.

As I have mentioned, Henry believes that the main problem of his marriage is his inability to express emotion genuinely. Instead, he *performs* emotion, a performance he understands as a masterful dissimulation of truth:

> On paper, by any known standard, I was an impeccable mate. I did everything well enough. I cooked well enough, cleaned enough, was romantic and sensitive and silly enough, I made love enough, was paternal, big brotherly, just a good friend enough, father-to-my-son enough, forlorn enough, and then even bull-headed and dull and macho enough, to make it all seem seamless. For ten years she hadn't realized the breadth of what I had accomplished with my exacting competence, the daily *work* I did, which unto itself became an unassailable body of cover. And the surest testament to the magnificent and horrifying level of my virtuosity was that neither had I. (161; emphasis in original)

By contrast, Henry views Lelia as authentic because he views her emotions as genuine, not performed; her appearance is identical to her emotional truth:

> She must be the worst actor on earth. And perhaps most I loved this about her, her helpless way, love it still, how she can't hide a single thing, that she looks hurt when she is hurt, seems happy when she is happy. That I know at every moment the precise place where she stands. (158)

For Henry, marital reconciliation means that he must meet Lelia's truth with his own; he must offer himself up as a transparent object of knowledge. Just as his work as a spy required him to serve as an informant, so too does this family business of saving their marriage necessitate his assumption of the role of native informant, transforming his previous inscrutability into an emotional truth that is recognizable to Lelia's gaze.[33] Consider that the novel begins with Lelia naming Henry an "emotional alien" (5) and ends with Lelia "speaking a dozen lovely and native languages, calling all the difficult names of who we are" (349). Although his naming still presents difficulty, he is no longer an alien, as Lelia is finally able to recognize him. Henry's naturalization from "alien" to "good citizen" is in the register of the emotional. In *Native Speaker,* emotional norms of expressiveness are understood as white American, and emotional pathologies such as suppression are understood as ethnic Korean.

Susan Koshy's concept of "sexual naturalization" helps us to understand how domestic romance, specifically in the form of interracial romance, is the institution that assimilates Henry into the national norm and language of emotional truth. Koshy explains the powerful appeal of interracial romance as a genre:

> Narratives of interracial desire came to be so influential because of their ability to address social questions precisely by seeming not to. They transformed political questions of difference that were the basis of social hierarchy by rendering them in the simulacrum of a "universal" language of the human heart. . . . In exploring the possibility of reciprocal interracial desire, these stories delineate the "anthropological minimum," or lowest common denominator, that is the precondition for romantic love. . . . [T]he anthropological minimum is postulated through qualities of mind and heart that enable romantic unions.[34]

Koshy's formulation helps us to see why and how readers like Ludwig interpret *Native Speaker*'s domestic sphere as not only separate from but also remedying the problems of the public sphere. Kwang's political career initially embodies the immigrant-nation romance, the hope of multiracial incorporation through the abstractions of universal national citizenship. Henry and the reader find themselves traumatized, however, when this romance runs up against the traumas of jouissance. The domestic sphere then becomes the haven for the immigrant-nation romance, the site where abstraction truly can take place through the "'universal' language of the human heart." Although the public sphere of politics is conventionally conceived of as the premier site of universalization and abstraction, *Native Speaker* posits domesticity and language as trumping politics in performing these functions.

I turn now to language as the site of romance between the nation and the immigrant. A conversation between two immigrant workers reminds Henry of his father's language: "Two workers, a Korean and a Hispanic, are sitting on crates and smoking cigarettes outside. . . . We listen to the earnest attempts of their talk, the bits of their stilted English. . . . I would give most anything to hear my father's talk again, the crash and bang and stop of his language, always hurtling by. I will listen for him forever in the streets of this city" (337). Henry finds this immigrant English poignant and heartbreaking: "And whenever I hear the strains of a different English, I will still shatter a little inside. . . . [T]hey speak to me, as John Kwang could always, not simply in new accents or notes but in the ancient untold music of a newcomer's heart, sonorous with longing and hope" (304). As with Henry's adolescent spying on Ahjuhma, the immigrant worker's moment of leisure becomes a moment of pleasurable voyeurism for the hegemonic gaze. This voyeurism is transgressive in the sense that one catches the other "off-guard," in a moment of truth outside the other's official persona. The Korean and Hispanic workers are likened to young children learning to speak; they eagerly try, but their attempts are still "stilted" by their lack of fluency. This earnestness is important because it demonstrates the sincerity of their belief in English as the medium of cross-racial communion. In the second quotation, the word "strains" connotes both musical phrasing and the effort of exertion. What "shatter[s]" Henry is this music of utmost exertion and belief; this is the bit of jouissance that supports the romance between immigrant and nation. We may think of this exchange between two racial immigrant workers as a counterpart to the cross-racial

exchange of the money club. Where capital was inaccessible to the hegemonic subject in the latter, and hence illicit, English is eminently accessible and hence a legitimate medium for national romance.

When Henry says, "I would give most anything," he speaks in the tone
of romance. His father's immigrant English is so precious, so treasured,
that it is worth more than any of Henry's possessions. Note that this
English is composed of "bits," or fetishistic part-objects. As in my previous
discussion of the fetishized immigrant, this immigrant English is new and
ancient, modern and primordial. Its timeless status indicates the atemporality of fantasy. And Henry's desire to listen "forever" also conveys the
atemporality of fantasy, the way that fantasy transcends secular time. The
romance of this language is sacred because of its status as untold. It is
kept in the heart: treasured, private, intimate. This is the secret kernel of
the immigrant, his intimate truth: the "longing and hope" he has for America. And it is America, among all other nations, that exceptionally inspires
this poignant yearning and faith. English is represented in *Native Speaker*
as the medium that makes the immigrant transparent and knowable, that
reveals the truth and sincerity of his belief in and desire for America. This
is why language is, in the end, the appropriate site of romance between
immigrant and nation.

Daniel Kim points to one of the novel's central incongruities, the "radical
disjuncture" between the immigrant vernacular English to which Henry
regularly refers and the refined language that he uses to describe it.[35] As
Kim observes, Henry uses highly literary tropes and diction to represent
this vernacular: "The central irony of Lee's immaculate prose style . . . is
that it seems so entirely evacuated of the immigrant sensibility it memori-
alizes. . . . His is the language that remains when every last trace of the
immigrant tongue has been scraped away."[36] Indeed, Kim calls Henry's
English "a kind of linguistic grave."[37]

We might say that indeed it is the death of immigrant languages that
enables their romantic depiction in the novel; no longer threatening in
their heteroglossia, they have become safe to aestheticize. Let us also note,
however, the jouissance of immigrant English. This accented and awkward
English does not flow smoothly, as denoted by its "crash and bang and stop"
(337). The capacity of this language to "shatter" Henry indicates this jouissance, the element that shatters the self. For Henry, violently assimilated
into the English language, English has become so standardized that *it* has
become dead. Even as the native is alienated *into* his native language (as

Lacanian theory has it), he is also alienated *from* it because it is so taken for granted. For immigrants, however, English is still new, taking the material form of new physiological and phenomenological practice, not abstraction. The letters of English, abstract to the native speaker, are still permeated with traumatic enjoyment for the immigrant, and it is this trace of jouissance that so affects Henry, that provides the support for his romance with immigrant English.

Let me conclude by noting a similar contradiction between narrative declaration and narrative practice. As we recall, Henry's "problem" is his emotional repression. His facility at his job, which requires the suppression of affect, is implicitly understood as related to his lifelong experience and indeed expertise at such restraint. For Glimmer and Company, Henry must produce writing of the most impersonal kind:

> I am to be a clean writer, of the most reasonable eye, and present the subject in question like some sentient machine of transcription. In the commentary, I won't employ anything that even smacks of theme or moral. I will know nothing of the crafts of argument or narrative or drama. Nothing of beauty or art. And I am to stay on my uncomplicated task of rendering a man's life and ambition and leave to the unseen experts the arcane of human interpretation. (203)

As with Daniel Kim's observation of the disjuncture between the vernacular and the literary, here we cannot help but pause over Henry's disavowal of theme, moral, craft, argument, narrative, drama, beauty, art, and human interpretation. For what is *Native Speaker* if not the most elegantly crafted, to say nothing of morally probing, example of all these literary elements? In direct contradiction to Henry's self-understanding as dysfunctionally repressed, he is in fact the most lyrical, sensitive, poetic, literate, introspective—the most emotionally authentic—narrator.[38] Romance lies in the style as well as the content of the narrative, in an intertwining of affect and language that the immigrant offers for the pleasure, and perhaps enjoyment, of the reader as national subject. *Native Speaker* not only represents but also practices romantic citizenship in offering the heart of the immigrant to the nation.

4 Perverse Citizenship

The Death Drive and Suki Kim's The Interpreter

I really wanted to write an American book. And to me, what America
is about, in some way, is killing your parents.

—SUKI KIM

Throughout *Inhuman Citizenship,* I have discussed Asian American narratives of family and home, inquiring into what they reveal about the psychic
lives of gendered racial citizenship and the U.S. nation-state. While these
texts do not strictly conform to conventions of the "domestic novel" as a
literary genre, I have chosen to center domesticity as a rubric of analysis,
reflecting on the relation between Asian American domesticity and nation-
state formations such as neoliberalism, imperialism, and exceptionalism. I
have thus loosely considered the other novels as narratives of domesticity.
In contrast, I would call Suki Kim's *The Interpreter* an antidomestic narrative.[1] The protagonist, Suzy Park, does not feel settled or secure in her
apartment; instead, she thinks of it as a temporary shelter from unknown
dangers. Not only does she relinquish her claim on family, but, as the epigraph suggests, but she is actually complicit in her parents' deaths. Indeed,
one of the most provocative elements of the novel is its last line, which
equates the orphaned status of Suzy and her sister with their embodiment of "American beaut[y]" (294). Finally, she contravenes the bonds of
marriage—that presumed foundation of domesticity—by seeking affairs
with married men. How can we explain Suzy's antidomesticity, in which
she not only avoids, but actively destroys, domestic feelings and connections? What might this antidomesticity reveal about gendered racial citizenship and U.S. nation-state formation? And how might murderous
impulses embody a beauty that is national as well as racial? In this chapter, I theorize Suzy's antidomesticity as a manifestation of the death drive.
Briefly, the death drive is the compulsion toward jouissance, toward a

146

senseless disordering of Symbolic reality. This death drive, it turns out, is a legacy of her family business, in which her parents served as instruments of the U.S. state. Drawing from Lacan's formulation of the pervert as the instrument of the Other, I show how Kim represents Korean American domesticity and citizenship as perverse—even perversely beautiful. In particular, I focus on how these perversions reveal the violence and jouissance that underlie dominant fantasies of the U.S. nation, especially the fantasy of America as an exceptionalist site of new beginnings.

Set in New York City, *The Interpreter* is structured as a detective narrative in which Suzy Park, as the unofficial investigator, seeks to identify the person or persons who killed her parents five years ago. As in a noir mystery, the protagonist discovers that she herself is implicated, however obliquely, in the crime. Suzy lives a hyperprivate existence. She does not have contact with her only surviving family member, her older sister, Grace, and she has very few social relationships outside of her affairs with married men. Suzy's parents disowned her ten years ago when she was twenty, for a disgraceful sexual transgression. Just as she was about to graduate from Columbia University, she instead turned her back on a respectable, middle-class future to become the mistress of Damian, a middle-aged white professor of Asian studies and the husband of her Japanese thesis adviser. She had lived with him for five years when she received word that her parents were killed in a shooting at their workplace, and she responded by promptly leaving Damian.

In the present, Suzy plays detective in her job as a court translator. She happens upon a witness who knew her parents, and she covertly interrogates him under the guise of translating for the prosecution. Following the traces of her parents and her sister, she eventually realizes that the murder of her parents is not the "original" crime. Rather, it is a clue to the "crimes" that founded Suzy's lifelong trauma (260). First, she discovers her parents' work as informants, which effectively positioned them as traitors within the Korean immigrant community. In exchange for citizenship and for payment, the Parks would inform the federal government about co-ethnic migrants who were undocumented or who otherwise broke the law, thereby laying the groundwork for the deportation of such migrants. Second, Suzy learns that as a child Grace was impressed into the role of translator for these deportation cases. In other words, Grace was pushed into the family business of deporting fellow migrants. As a minor and a child, Grace was in no position to maturely comprehend and willfully consent to this use of her bilingual language abilities. Not fully developed psychically, still dependent on her parents for survival, and legally bound to her family, Grace did not have the option of saying no to her parents' demand for her services.

As in noir mysteries, the point of the novel is not so much to answer the question "Who killed X?" as it is to use this question to open up the exploration of secret underworlds. Suzy encounters an ethnic demimonde of gangs, child trafficking, and a call-girl business en route to discovering the killer: DJ, Grace's ex-lover, and an undocumented gang member whose disappearance and reappearance indexes the jouissance that is ascribed to "illegal aliens." The question of his motive is what brings us to the true secret underworld of the novel: the Parks' family business of informing. In this chapter, I explore the legacy of this family business on Suzy and Grace. How might Suzy's antidomesticity be shaped by her parents' destruction of other homes and families? Even more troubling, what are we to make of the Parks' particular use of child labor in their family business, in which Grace is given the terrible responsibility of exercising state biopower in determining who is ejected from the nation?

I employ Lacan's paradigm of perversion to respond to these questions. The common understanding of perversion is that it refers to nonnormative sexual thoughts or acts, with the norm defined as genital heterosexuality. However, Lacan's definition of perversion is not concerned with the content of such thoughts and acts. Instead, perversion is understood as a particular configuration among the subject, the object, jouissance, and the Other. The pervert is one who "makes himself the instrument of the Other's jouissance."[2] Grace's parents have not only made themselves into instruments of the Other's jouissance, immersing themselves in the traumatic enjoyment of executing state power and deporting fellow migrants; they have also impressed their young daughter Grace into such jouissance and perversion. For Grace, the acts of interpretation and informing are the condition of her belonging to family and nation, the requirements of her perverse domesticity and citizenship.

This instrumentalization of the child is the primary trauma of the novel. Because she is so young, Grace is vulnerable and cannot give meaningful (uncoerced) consent to her use as an agent of the state. Unable to fully comprehend her own power, she becomes a vehicle of jouissance, a destroyer of human lives. Grace's coerced translation is a perverse variation of the primal scene of racial citizenship. In this primal scene, racial citizenship is bestowed in exchange for the violent repudiation and erasure of one's previous ethnic identifications. By definition, the primal scene is "premature," witnessed before the child has the capacity to make meaning from it, and therefore traumatizing. Grace, however, is not only witness, but participant. She is not only exposed to the scene of her origins as an American; she must actively bring about these origins by acting as the agent of such violence. Her trauma is a premature interpellation into perverse citizenship.

However, to understand the significance of the narrative structure, which focuses on Suzy rather than Grace, I turn to another Freudian paradigm, that of the masochistic fantasy. In his essay "A Child Is Being Beaten," Freud posits three stages of this fantasy: my father is beating a child; my father is beating me; a child is being beaten. The first scene is sadistic, in which the subject imagines her sibling being beaten. The second stage, in which the subject understands herself as the object of violence, is the tableau that is repressed. Although it may not have happened in reality, its imagining and repression result in the final scene. Here the spectator views a scene of violence, but it is not clear whether she identifies with the beater or the beaten. The hazy identity of the child in the third phase is likely due to a belief that such trauma is quite contingent: if my sibling can be beaten, why not me? The climactic revelation of the novel corresponds to Freud's first stage: my parents are traumatizing my sister. However, a curious feature of the novel in general is Suzy's very powerful identification with Grace. Grace was clearly constituted as the subject of the death drive, a process that I will analyze shortly. Suzy, too, is the subject of the death drive in her antidomestic compulsions, but we have no explanation for how this came to be except to speculate on her identification with Grace. But because Grace was made into an agent of power, identification with Grace must also entail an identification with the Other who beats the child. In this way, the subjective structure of the novel corresponds to Freud's final stage of the masochistic fantasy: a child is being beaten, but we do not know whether the subject identifies with the beater or the beaten. Thus, although Suzy seems to be excluded from the primal scene of her family's perverse citizenship, she nevertheless embodies this perversion as the antidomestic death drive.

Family business, in terms of the sheer amount of parental work required for family survival, meant that Suzy experienced domesticity as suspended and masochistic while she was growing up. We can also see that an antidomestic death drive is simply her legacy from her parents' and sister's family business of informing, which effectively destroyed homes and homemaking for fellow migrants. Finally, the family business of informing meant that the family was constantly on the run, repeatedly moving and starting over. This compulsive starting over, I argue, is a perverse version of the nationalist myth of America as the premier site for rebirth and starting over.

This notion of America as a unique location for beginning anew correlates with the American exceptionalist myth of Virgin Land. In this trope of sexual innocence lies the rationale of moral innocence. Donald Pease concisely articulates this myth: "The myth of Virgin Land enabled the American people to believe in their radical innocence because it permitted them to disavow knowledge of the historical fact that the national people took possession of their native land through the forcible dispossession of native peoples from their homeland. . . . At its core, the metaphor of Virgin Land was designed to fulfill Europe's wish to start life afresh by relinquishing history on behalf of the secular dream of the construction of a new Eden."[3] In this myth, American territory serves as a blank slate, a space of emptiness for immigrants to populate with their dreams of starting over. The violence of indigenous deaths and dispossession is erased. In addition, for successive waves of immigrants, interpellation into American national identity has meant the erasure of their previous ethnic and national identifications. The fantasy of America as a space that offers new beginnings—a fantasy that is inextricable from the notion of America as a site of "radical innocence"—relies on, but covers over, the destruction of the death drive.

I will show how perverse domesticity and citizenship, as represented in *The Interpreter*, reveal precisely this death drive. First, though, let me nuance this notion of the death drive. As a drive toward jouissance, the death drive connotes not only death as destruction and absence; it also connotes a strange surplus of life. I consider the disavowed lives and deaths, the unmourned losses and longings, of indigenous and immigrant peoples to be strange surpluses of life because they are not incorporable into the U.S. national Symbolic order. They are exactly what need to be extracted in order for national fantasy to cohere.

For Lacan, perversion is "an inverted effect of the phantasy."[4] His formula for fantasy is $\$ \diamond a$, the divided subject in relation to the fantasy object, the object *a*. He reverses this formula for perversion: $a \diamond \$$. Psychoanalytic critic Judith Feher-Gurewich elaborates on this inverse relationship between perversion and fantasy: "Perverts excel in exposing the fantasy of the other and the various social lies that such fantasy necessarily enforces."[5] I will show here how Suzy's perversions unveil the dominant fictions and fantasies of domesticity, nation, and citizenship.

I begin with an exploration of Suzy's antidomesticity as a manifestation of the death drive, explaining the distinction between drive and desire. I then consider how the conventional fantasy of domesticity is structured by desire and construed as wholesome and innocent. However, for Suzy, domesticity has been experienced, and claimed, as perverse and masochistic. Next, I discuss the dimensions of racial beauty as a potential signifier of domestic value, that is, value on the marriage market. In contrast to the wholesome innocence of "all-American" feminine beauty, Suzy and Grace's racial beauty perversely signals the death drive—but also, paradoxically, a rebirth. Suzy makes herself into a commodity fetish object, which strangely reanimates the specters of racial and ethnic migrant workers who have been rendered surplus.

I will also show how psychoanalysis allows us to understand *The Interpreter* as a narrative of racial and national trauma and enjoyment. Specifically, Kim's novel offers a theory of gendered racial citizenship as structured by perversion. Because the pervert is an instrument of the Other's jouissance or enjoyment, Symbolic fantasy does not cohere for her. Indeed, this jouissance upends Symbolic fantasy, unmasking its falsehoods, hypocrisies, and impossibilities. Suzy's perverse domesticity and beauty, I argue, expose the jouissant underside of U.S. national myths of innocence and starting over. In its tropes of perverse rebirth, *The Interpreter* suggests how U.S. nation-statehood is structured by the death drive, by tendencies toward death and destruction that produce race not as absence but as surplus: life that exceeds the Symbolic.

ANTIDOMESTIC DEATH DRIVE

In *The Interpreter*, perversion unveils dominant fantasies and fictions of the U.S. nation. In order to elaborate further upon the relationship between perversion and fantasy, we must first understand the distinctions between drive and desire. While the subject of fantasy stages desire, the perverse subject follows the drive. A striking feature of the narrative is its moments of disappearing desire: Suzy, for example, interprets the bitter taste of her cigarettes as the extinguishing of desire (34), and she "never longs for Mom's Nina Ricci perfume" (110). In my reading, the narrative provides a trajectory in which Suzy transforms from subject of desire to subject of drive. Indeed, her nondomestic and antidomestic trajectories seem to be the result of compulsions.

Given our ideological norms of social behavior and bonds, there is something intriguingly deviant about Suzy's hyperprivate, self-enclosed existence. She is utterly detached from her surroundings. The opening of the novel, for example, presents her as a stranger in her environment, someone who has not "bought into" the neighborhood that she visits for work (4). She fails to hear the salesclerk talking to her, as if she is enclosed in a bubble. A major element of this self-enclosed existence is her series of affairs with married men. She uses these affairs to ensure that she lives an isolated and secretive existence. If she takes on a bona fide lover, as she does with Damian, then the couple is shunned by friends and family who do not condone their immorality and lack of respectability. If they remain secret lovers, as she does with Michael, then she cannot be publicly acknowledged. Suzy does not register as a legitimate partner, as a participant in legitimate domesticity. She encrypts herself as a secret. This encryption, however, does not mean she has the security and safety of interiority that we often associate with domesticity. As the word "encryption" implies, Suzy's status is a kind of living death, an excess of the Symbolic—and this status is a danger to others.

Suzy is not merely excluded from normative domesticity; she acts as an agent of outright antidomesticity in her destruction of the sacrosanct bonds of marital trust. Traumatically enjoying such destruction, Suzy alarms and fascinates the reader. Domesticity, after all, is one of the primary grounding fantasies of subjectivity; a familial or marital break is often imagined as shattering one's very sense of self. At the same time, we are drawn to jouissance and to outlaw figures because they promise a primal being that we cannot achieve as subjects of the Symbolic. Dylan Evans explains how the compulsion toward jouissance takes the form of the drive: "The death drive is the name given to that constant desire in the subject to break through the pleasure principle towards the Thing and a certain excess jouissance; thus jouissance is 'the path toward death' (*S XVII* [Lacan, Seminar 17], 17)." Insofar as the drives are attempts to break through the pleasure principle in search of jouissance, every drive is a death drive.[6] While Evans equates drive in general with the death drive, I have chosen to specify "death drive" in this chapter because I want to suggest both the destructiveness of death and the strange status of living death as a surplus of life.

While both drive and desire circle around objects, they are distinguished by the affects produced by this circling. Desire is mobile and metonymic, moving from object to object. In desire, the object that we attain is never "it," the object that will give us satisfaction. In drive, however, the opposite is true. Not only do we attain "it," but we can never get away from it. The "it" in drive is jouissance, which obstinately sticks to us. Desire is the impossibility of attaining jouissance, while drive is the impossibility of getting rid of jouissance. In this way, the subject of desire is configured by lack, while the subject of drive is permeated by surplus.

The subject of desire constantly searches for the object that will complete her. In contrast, the subject of drive is self-sufficient and even self-affective. Affect follows an insular circuit through and is contained within the self. This is how we can understand Suzy's hyperprivate and self-enclosed existence. She is not the subject of desire seeking an object to complete her. Rather, she is the subject of drive, compelled to follow the circuit of jouissance that her family history has bestowed upon her.

How is the subject of drive constituted? Lacan's matheme for the drive is $\$\lozenge D$, or the subject in relation to demand. While desire is mobile and flexible, demand is rigid and repetitive. The object of desire can shift and change, but with demand there is no room for such displacement or interchangeability. The starkest case of demand in *The Interpreter* is that of Grace, who could not refuse what the Other asked of her.

As I have discussed previously, the child of immigrants is often impressed into the position of translator or interpreter. Because of her linguistic flexibility, the child embodies what is missing for both her immigrant parents and for the U.S. nation-state: her English completes her parents and her Korean completes the nation-state. In most cases, the parents and the state (or statelike institutions) represent different parties between which the child must negotiate: "Grace, since she was little, had to pore over a letter from the bank trying to make sense of words like 'APR' or 'Balance Transfers' or call Con Edison's 800 number for a payment extension. . . . There were always red-stamped notices in their mailbox. Once or twice a month, Grace skipped school to accompany Mom and Dad to the Department of Motor Vehicles or an insurance company or some other bureaucratic nightmare" (198–99). Grace is the parentalized child, the child who assumes parentlike responsibilities and enters a state of premature adulthood. Her own needs (for education, in this example) are subordinated to those of her parents, which are likely framed as requests to do what is "best for the family." In these everyday negotiations, Grace is faced with the demands of her parents, who must prove their good citizenship within the proper ideological state apparatuses. There is some semblance of triangulation as Grace mediates between her parents and the state, some breathing room. When Grace is appointed the role of translator in legal cases against other Korean migrants, however, her parents explicitly unite with the state in its repressive function, collapsing the triangle into a direct line of demand. In this instance, Grace has nowhere to turn. She can only become the object that plugs up the space of their now-compounded demand.

Suffocated by the congealing of these powerful, authoritative agents of demand—the family and the nation-state—Grace finds that there is no room for her desire, and she becomes the subject of drive.[7] When Suzy solves the case, she understands that Grace acts in accordance with the death drive by murdering their parents' murderer (DJ). But what about Suzy? How do we explain Suzy's transformation into the subject of drive? Grace acts as Suzy's double throughout the story, the elusive target that Suzy literally seeks on her quest, and the mirror image that Suzy seeks to compare herself to. As I hypothesized in my discussion of Freud's masochistic fantasy, I believe Suzy identifies with Grace as the object of trauma while also paradoxically identifying with the instigator of trauma. In deciding to abet Grace's murder, Suzy accedes to her status as embodiment of the death drive.

Slavoj Žižek reminds us of Lacan's notion of drive as *se faire*, the self-reflexive mode of making oneself *x*. This mode is neither active nor passive, but a curious amalgamation of both. For example, "Scopic drive is neither a voyeuristic tendency to see nor the exhibitionistic tendency to be seen by another, to expose oneself to another's eyes, but the 'middle voice,' the attitude of 'making oneself visible,' of deriving libidinal satisfaction from actively sustaining the scene of one's own passive submission."[8] As I discuss later, masochistic perversion also involves actively staging one's submission, choosing a master whose role is to deprive one of choice and will. Žižek reflects on how the act of choice in desire becomes *se faire choisir* in drive—that is, to make oneself chosen, as in predestination, in which one construes the self as chosen by God. Thus, he concludes, "The only—but crucial and highest—freedom I am granted in drive is the freedom to choose the inevitable, freely to embrace my Destiny, what will happen to me in any case."[9] As subjects of drive, Suzy and Grace understand freedom of choice not in its conventional liberal and American sense of unlimited opportunity. Rather, they conceive themselves as acceding to the inevitable destiny that has been bequeathed to them by their family business of perverse domesticity and citizenship. They accede to their position as agents of death drive, agents of jouissance.

As I have noted, the most spectacular manifestations of the antidomestic death drive in *The Interpreter* are Suzy's affairs with married men, her deliberate acts of destroying the fantasy of marriage as the site of fidelity and loyalty. Suzy remembers and reflects on her father's parting words to her as he disowned her: "Whore, hers was the life of a whore. Marriage was never an option, which might have been why she chose Damian" (134). Suzy's reflection on being interpellated as illicit references the dimension of drive: in making oneself chosen, one chooses what has been predestined. By choosing Damian as her illicit lover, Suzy chooses what has already been determined by her family business of antidomestic death drive: exclusion from, and destruction of, normative domesticity. Grace, too, after working as a call girl in her adolescence, wants to disqualify herself from any respectable marriage market. She explains her choice of attending Smith, a women's college, as an antidomestic, antimarriage gesture: "It had also been Grace who told Suzy that the only reason she applied to Smith College on early decision was that no decent Korean boy would want her now, because everyone knew Smith was for sluts and lesbians" (20). Accepting her exclusion from normative domesticity, Grace enjoys antidomesticity by assuming the gender outlaw status of an illicit, disreputable, perverse femininity.

DOMESTIC FANTASY, DOMESTIC PERVERSION

What is the dominant fantasy of domesticity that the Parks pervert? And what does this perversion reveal? Suzy imagines ideal domesticity in the form of what I call her "Montauk fantasy," a daydream that is reiterated a number of times in *The Interpreter*. This is a fantasy of family business in the sense of sustaining the family itself as an institution, such that parents and child have reached an optimal state of well-being. The overall feeling or affect of the fantasy is one of innocent, carefree leisure. Key to the fantasy is Suzy's imagining of her parents as subjects of desire and whimsy, in contrast to the way that her family has been, in actuality, grimly structured by drive. We can see this by contrasting the wholesome tableau of home and family that Suzy conjures up with the perverse versions that she has experienced and lived.

Montauk is one of the outermost towns on Long Island; its physical distance from Manhattan represents a distance from the hardships and turmoil of life in the urban core. On each anniversary of her parents' death, Suzy visits the Montauk shore, where Grace chose to scatter their parents' ashes. Although Suzy initially does not understand Grace's gesture, we find out later that Grace's choice of location recognizes and honors their parents' victims. A woman on whom their parents had informed committed suicide and was buried by her husband in Montauk. Sitting in the train on her annual pilgrimage, Suzy daydreams that she is traveling to visit her parents' new home in Montauk. As she is actually going to visit her parents' watery grave, this "new home" is precisely the one that was not possible in their earthly lives and can only be achievable in the fantasy world of the afterlife:

> She imagines their new home, a pastel oceanfront house they have just moved into. Dad's newest whim, the beach, the lighthouse, the moonlight, the edge of New York. "Oh, who would've ever thought," Mom would say, laughing, picking up Suzy at the train station in her brand-new Jeep. Mom behind the wheel in her Christian Dior sunglasses and a sky-blue tank top with tan lines showing through its straps despite the November rain, while Dad is out fishing for fluke, which he would then get the local fishermen to fillet for sushi later. Suzy would present them with a bag of Korean groceries, which her parents would delight in opening. Montauk is not Flushing, definitely not Woodside or Jackson Heights, no Oriental goods within miles. They would gloat over a jar of kim-chi, dried squid, salted Pollack eggs. They would laugh like children, and Suzy would squint from so much sun in their faces. (46)

In this fantasy, the parents are carefree, laughing, relieved of their burdens. In Sau-ling Wong's terms, they are not determined by Necessity, but they can "delight" in Extravagance.[10] Translated into Lacanian terms, they become subjects of desire, not subjects of demand. The metonymic and mobile nature of desire (moving from object to object) means that unpredictable whims can be indulged, that one can exclaim "who would've ever thought" because possibilities are open, not predetermined. Because possibilities are open, her parents are thus interpretable: meaning is not fixed or constrained.

The pastel colors of the house and Mrs. Park's tank top are signs of light-heartedness and innocence, while Mrs. Park's tan lines signify the leisure of sitting in the sun instead of working long hours indoors at a corner grocery store. These elements are central to Suzy's fantasy of her parents' relief from the demands of Necessity. Perhaps the most intriguing element of this fantasy is Suzy's role as filial daughter. In a reversal of the convention of the immigrant parents as agents of cultural transmission, here it is the parents who have "assimilated" to an upper-class, New York area, Waspish culture of leisure, and the daughter who fulfills her filial duty by becoming the agent of cultural preservation. In other words, it is the daughter's filial assumption of cultural preservation that unburdens the parents, that enables them to detach from demand and become subjects of desire. They can delight and gloat over their gifts of Korean food. Ethnicity becomes the marker of desire, not demand or constraint.

Note the prominence of commodities in this fantasy: the brand-new Jeep, the Christian Dior sunglasses, the sky-blue tank top. In *Consuming Citizenship*, Lisa Park finds that "second generation Asian Americans employ consumptive fantasies to imagine a 'normal' American family."[11] But this is a very specific fantasy of consumption: Park argues that second-generation Asian Americans conceive of commodity consumption as a way to pay off their debts to their parents. Thus, in Suzy's fantasies, commodities that signify upper-class Waspish culture are not the only important ones. Just as crucial, if not more so, are the commodities of Korean groceries that enable the fantasy of filiality, of paying off one's debt to one's parents for their sacrifices.[12] One of Suzy's vivid memories is her father's complaint that it was his hard work that fed the family; that "he slaved all day to put food on the table" (121). In her fantasy, Suzy takes on this position of feeding the family with food that is ethnically appropriate. This fantasy of sustaining the family is not only about physiological nourishment; it is also a fantasy of cultural continuity, a fantasy that disavows any cultural loss, disruption, or debt that might be demanded by migration to the United States. Commodities, then, do not signal assimilation and Americanization in a straightforward manner. The ethnic marking of commodities, as I argued in the last chapter, facilitates a fantasy that disavows loss. However, we will see later how the commodity fetish can also embody an eerie recuperation of such loss.

But first, why does Suzy want to imagine her parents as subjects of desire? If Suzy's parents are subjects of demand, they can only form Suzy and Grace as subjects of drive, as indicated in the formula $\$\diamond D$. But the parents are not the only Other here; the nation-state is the overwhelmingly more powerful form of the Other. Suzy's parents are not only subjects but also are objects of demand; they not only demand, but something is demanded of them. Suzy and Grace, then, are not only indebted to their parents; their parents themselves are indebted to the nation-state as Other. As racialized immigrants, they owe a debt of gratitude to the U.S. nation for its openness in "allowing" them in. This is why Suzy's fantasy of domesticity is at once a fantasy of fulfilled filial duty and a fantasy of consumer citizenship. Suzy wants not only to pay off her debt to her parents; she also wants to pay off her parents' debt to the Other. She can ensure her own citizenship only by ensuring her parents' citizenship.

The Montauk fantasy is a dream of ideal domesticity and consumer citizenship. It is a fantasy in which the parents are subjects of desire, not demand or drive. Ethnic commodities are fetishes in the sense that they cover over loss or lack. The point of the fantasy is to pay off parental and national debt, to become the whole, self-possessed liberal citizen-subject.

The Montauk fantasy of domesticity emerges a few more times in the novel. When Suzy muses on the possibility of visiting her friend Jen's house for Thanksgiving, she again becomes lulled by the dream of ideal domesticity: "the pastel house, Mom's brand-new Jeep, Dad's fishing rods, the bag of Korean goodies Suzy has brought from the city" (171). Later, while waiting for Maria Sutpen, the woman who now lives in her parents' last home, Suzy once more indulges in her reverie: "In her dream, she wanted to get them out of those immigrant neighborhoods. In her dream, she wanted to rewind their immigrant trekking. So she made up their pastel Montauk house. A shiny Jeep rather than the used Oldsmobile. Sunbathing and fishing instead of peeling-cutting-stocking fruit. TV before bed, like all other aging couples. *Nightline, Late Night,* the *Tonight Show.* Thanksgiving dinners. A game of Monopoly" (212).

In this iteration, Suzy explicitly recasts various marks of suffering into figures of wholesomeness and lightheartedness (for example, transforming the repetition of small-business labor into small-town leisure). In order to reposition her parents spatially from urban immigrant neighborhoods to Montauk, Suzy must imagine a temporal erasure and revision ("rewinding their immigrant trekking"). Indeed, temporality itself must become wholesome and normal. Suzy dreams of a life of retirement for her parents because such leisure, in the American Dream, is rightfully due to couples as a reward for their lives of hard work. Suzy would like to imagine her parents aging normatively, watching "TV before bed, like all other aging couples," rather than having their lives prematurely cut short. This premature mortality is one element of the Parks' perversion: a perverse temporality. Another magical transformation effected by this fantasy is the conversion of capital acquisition from perversion to innocence. Suzy imagines the consumption of property as an innocent board game of Monopoly, rather than the deadly serious trauma it has proven for her family.

Note, finally, the significance of Thanksgiving in these fantasy scenarios. Suzy's daydream of visiting Jen's house for Thanksgiving triggers the second iteration of the Montauk fantasy. The third iteration of the fantasy explicitly names "Thanksgiving dinners" as a key component of ideal domesticity. Thanksgiving is generally understood as a celebration of American national domesticity, in which family members gather with one another all across the country to commemorate a moment of national fellowship, providence, and plenitude. In *The Interpreter,* however, Thanksgiving is made into a ritual of perversity. Damian enjoys initiating—figuratively de-virginizing—Suzy into Thanksgiving as part of their corrupt domesticity (166)—a repetition of Suzy's literal de-virginizing by Damian over their first Thanksgiving together. Suzy's parents are then killed over Thanksgiving, so that it becomes an annual reminder of death. Finally, Thanksgiving marks the period between Suzy's and Grace's birthdays, a time during which they are the same age, suspended in time. In all, Thanksgiving, an icon of wholesome domesticity, becomes disturbingly perverted in *The Interpreter.* Of course, the very notion of Thanksgiving as an icon of wholesome and innocent nationhood covers over the violence done to indigenous peoples in the service of U.S. nation formation.

Suzy encounters the gap between the fantasy of domesticity and her own experience when she visits a police station in pursuit of her parent's murder case. Suzy projects normative domesticity onto the police officers, imagining that their "sweethearts must be waiting at home with a couple of toddlers" (172). One officer ogles her, but his partner Bill turns out to be shy, handsome, and nice. He is helpful and courteous, and she finds his voice soothing. Suzy recognizes how alien she finds men like him: "They remain out of her range, always. Something about them belongs to another world. Something about them suggests a home, a different kind of home from what she knows" (175). When Bill tells her to call him if she needs further help, the narrative voice notes: "She will never call him. It would not be fair to him" (176). If Bill, like his fellow officers, represents the fantasy of a healthy, wholesome domesticity, then Suzy recognizes herself as a threat to this fantasy. Indeed, as police officers embody the enforcement of law, Suzy represents the subversion of law, a break in the Symbolic order. Suzy's perverse domesticity can be seen most clearly in her experience and practices of suspension and alienation. We know from the narrative that the girls do not have a stable sense of home because their family moves every year. With Suzy's painful discovery about her family business, we realize that the parents move so frequently in an attempt to evade vengeful parties on whom they have informed—an attempt to elude the death sentence that finally finds them. I would like to consider this legacy of domestic transience in the light of Deleuze's insight that "waiting and suspense are essential characteristics of the masochistic experience."[13] While physical suspension is a possible practice of masochism, it is temporal suspense that is the crux of masochism:

> Formally speaking, masochism is a state of waiting; the masochist experiences waiting in its pure form. . . . The masochist waits for pleasure as something that is bound to be late, and expects pain as the condition that will finally ensure (both physically and morally) the advent of pleasure. He therefore postpones pleasure in expectation of the pain which will make gratification possible. The anxiety of the masochist divides into an indefinite awaiting of pleasure and an intense expectation of pain.[14]

If security and permanence are hallmarks of the fantasy of domesticity, we can see how Suzy has learned to postpone these pleasures of domesticity. Suzy's current apartment is described as bare, with hardly any furniture or decor. "The apartment resembles a temporary shelter. There is no sweetness here, no flowery sheets, no matching duvet covers, no framed childhood photos" (37). Through the simile of the shelter, Suzy's apartment is likened to a refugee camp or a transient resting place for the homeless. Because homemaking is gendered feminine, Suzy's domestic transience marks her femininity as deviant, as she does not practice any of the "sweetness" of decor associated with domestic femininity. We can see how conventional domestic femininity depends on liberalism's paradigm of possession, and how Suzy's transience indexes not only her dispossession from the regime of property, but from the regime of normative femininity.

Interestingly, Suzy experiences a certain satisfaction in nonpermanence. By staging fantasies of transience, she finds a masochistic pleasure in suspension. For example, she relishes lounging in the strange and luxurious surroundings of the Waldorf-Astoria hotel room after her dalliances with Michael, her current married lover (70). It is important to note that Suzy's moment of pleasure lies not in the sex act or in physical companionship, but in the suspended quality of time and space: not home, not work, no Michael, no one else. Suzy acts out the pleasures of transience and suspense in her work life as well, moving from job to job. The occupation in which she finds the most pleasure is the one that provides her with the fantasy of suspension. As a fact-checker at a literary magazine, Suzy sits at her desk reading copy. She enjoys pretending that she is reading magazines in a doctor's waiting room or in an airport lounge—both spaces of anticipation and suspense (13).

It is Damian who gives Suzy her most intense experiences of suspense, at the existential level of her lifetime as well as the mundane level of the everyday. When Damian invites Suzy to stay with him—after a chance encounter two months after she loses her virginity to him—Suzy finds a focus and shape for the pleasurable pain of anticipation: "She had been dying to see him. She could not think of anything other than wanting to see him. She had waited so long" (138–39). During their relationship, Suzy indulges in this masochistic suspense on the everyday level as well: "She sat patiently and waited for him all day" (283). As Deleuze conveys, pain is expected as the fulfillment of pleasure. The pain that Damian promises is the pain of disapproval, and ultimately severance, from her family— a pain of dispossession.[15] If domesticity signifies security and belonging, then suspense is its very opposite, the pleasure-pain of antidomestic jouissance to which Suzy is compulsively drawn.

Suzy's legacy of domesticity is one of masochistic suspense. This history of anticipation is narrated in a poignant passage describing her dreaming thoughts as she lingers outside the apartment of a man who may have clues to her parents' murders. In waiting for his return home—as she also later waits outside for Maria Sutpen outside her parents' last home—Suzy relives the main activity of her childhood: waiting for her family to return home.

The hand on her right shoulder is a gentle one. Must be Mom, or Dad finally home. She must have fallen asleep at the doorstep. She must have forgotten her key, and school must have let out early, and Grace must have sneaked out again. So she must have sat here and waited with her homework spread out, and still, when the homework was done, still no one came home, and she must have lain down for a while thinking she was hungry and it was getting darker and the draft from the hallway window sharper, and she was afraid that no one would remember her, that no one would find her here, and then sleep must have overtaken her, taken her breath away to an even darker place. . . .

But neither Mom nor Dad. Can't be, they've been shot. They will never come home again. (233–34)

The repeated term "must have" signals a return of the past. Suzy explains her suspense by saying that she "must have" fallen asleep while waiting for her family to let her inside the home. But there is another connotation of the term "must," and that is its association with demand. When Suzy waits for Maria Sutpen outside her parents' last home, she also remembers her childhood of waiting: "Still no Grace, no parents. So many afternoons, she had sat like this alone waiting for them. . . . Still no one came home. It would be hours before anyone came home. She was good at waiting. She was the obedient one" (211). This practice of submission to the Other's demand—and specifically the demand to wait—is the practice of masochism. There is no space for the recognition of Suzy's own needs as a child, such as the need for food, warmth, or protection. The fulfillment of any such needs belongs to the anticipated future, not to the experienced present. As I have discussed earlier, the drive takes the form of self-affection, or self-enclosure. Suzy's hyperprivate existence derives from her experience of domesticity as the realm of alienation. Her childhood state is described as one of utter isolation, left "all alone," abandoned by parents and sister (262). Suzy vividly remembers childhood domesticity as a waiting that felt endless.

Suzy's sense of suspended domesticity is due not only to the endless hours of waiting for her family members to let her into their home. It also results from the family being constantly on the run, leaving in the middle of the night to seek refuge in a generic motel, and finding new neighborhoods to settle in, where they can be anonymous. The reason for this of course is that the Park family business is the very opposite of innocent and wholesome: it is tainted by immorality and guilt. They are on the run because they have been marked for death by their co-ethnic community members, as they themselves have marked such co-ethnics for the symbolic death of deportation. This is why Suzy can only imagine her apartment as a temporary refuge, why she cannot indulge in the rituals of homemaking: because she believes herself to be still suspended, in hiding.

With the climactic revelation of the novel, we understand the social alienation of Suzy's hyperprivate life as deriving from her parents' social alienation, in which their isolation from their ethnic community effectively isolated them from human bonds in general. But we can comprehend the alienation of the Park family as the result not only of their family business of informing but also of their other forms of family business. Suzy links the relentlessness of her parents' work to the breakdown of their family: "With each job, with each endless hour they labored at dry cleaners, liquor stores, fruit-and-vegetable markets, nail salons, delis, truck-delivery service, car service, they seemed to have lost something of themselves, a sort of language with which they had communicated with each other and their daughters" (122). In Lacan's theory of the Symbolic, the subject is constituted by its alienation into language. Alienated from primordial being and enjoyment, the subject is construed as a subject of lack and therefore desire. Suzy's narration reveals the layered dimensions of this linguistic estrangement for immigrant families. If the universal subject is alienated into language, then the immigrant worker is further alienated *from* language, not only in the sense of having to speak a nonnative language, but also in the elemental dimension of language as creating intersubjective connection.

In this way, immigrant workers and families are not so much subjects of desire, as in Lacan's theory of alienation and lack, but subjects of demand. Responding to the demands of labor, they are abstracted into generic interchangeability, flexibly slotted into any one of a variety of service occupations.[16] Suzy's narration of her parents' occupations echoes that of Leila in *Bone* and Henry in *Native Speaker*, who also recite the various occupations and commodities of immigrants in list form.[17] The form of the list indicates the interchangeability, instability, and insecurity of this sector of service work. Suzy describes the constraints and dangers of these various forms of work: "None of the other jobs had panned out. Dry cleaning didn't bring in enough cash; fish markets smelled nasty; clothing repair was taxing to the eye; nail salons were toxic; liquor stores got robbed too often; car services were prone to accidents. Miraculously, they seemed to have saved enough to buy a store, which also meant that they came home even later" (143).

As Sau-ling Wong has demonstrated, the mobility that symbolizes freedom and choice in conventional American mythologies often connotes the opposite for Asian immigrant and Asian American subjects, for whom movement may be driven by demand and compulsion.[18] The list of Suzy's parents' occupations, for example, does not convey the freedom of unlimited opportunity. Rather, the Parks are driven by demand and constraint in their move from one form of work to another. The interchangeability of these occupations means, in fact, that movement is actually a form of fixation, a return to the same that characterizes drive and jouissance. We see, then, that Grace was not only the object of demand by her parents, but that her parents' demand of her derived from their own status as objects of demand. When these various forms of family business proved implausible, they turned to the family business of informing. This in fact was the "miracle" that provided the capital for them to buy their store, which in turn meant further alienation from their daughters because of the longer hours of self-employment. While the mythic immigrant narrative is one of choice and desire, we see in *The Interpreter* how immigrant life and labor are structured by drive—a drive to survive that turns out to be the same as the death drive, a living death.

The demands of immigrant labor produce deficits in language and in domesticity, but they also paradoxically produce a strange surplus of life in the form of jouissance and the death drive. Concomitant with the loss of "family language" discussed earlier is the figure of domestic space as itself truncated. "Who needs a family room? Her parents claimed. . . . How much living could one do when working seven days a week?" (141–42). Excluded from living, that is, from a life outside work, they comprehend this domestic space as unnecessary. After all, if they do not engage in the connective act of language with their family or with others, if language is not a site of intersubjective desire and recognition, then such a space of social interaction is indeed extraneous. This classification of a family room—we may also consider, suggestively, the "living room"—as extravagant stands for the notion that living, desire, and sociality outside labor is a luxury that they cannot afford, as in Leon's formulation in "life was work and death the dream."[19] Living without living, the Parks constitute the living dead, a paradoxical surplus of life. Unincorporable into the Symbolic, exceeding the Symbolic, they are life substance without the symbolization of life.

The premier way in which the Parks manifest this strange surplus of life is in their constant starting over. This compulsive starting over manifests in both forms of family business: in their economic means of survival—moving from job to job—and in their choice of shelter for the family, on the run from their community. Building on Sau-ling Wong's formulation of enforced versus voluntary mobility, we could say that the Parks are compelled to start over by drive, not desire. They signify the traumatic underside of the American national mythology of innocent new beginnings.

AMERICAN BEAUTIES

Let us recall Grace's deliberate act of decreasing her value on the marriage market, refusing normative domesticity by assuming a deviant and illicit femininity. Of course, deviant femininity can signify value in alternative ways, too. Here I investigate one manifestation of erotic feminine value: racial beauty. If white feminine beauty is portrayed in *The Interpreter* as wholesome and innocent, in what ways does racial beauty represent an alternative to or even perversion of this wholesomeness? How might we interpret these different beauties in relation to pleasure, enjoyment, and the death drive?

I turn here to the novel's conclusion, in which Suzy realizes, on her birthday, that Grace killed their parents' murderer by staging a boat accident in the very waters where she scattered her parents' ashes. As Grace chose Montauk for her parents' final resting place because one of her family's victims was buried there, Montauk and its waters become the site for symbolically uniting, in death, the Parks, their victims, and their murderer. Montauk also provides the setting for Suzy's fantasy of domesticity. Thus, *The Interpreter* quite clearly represents this domestic fantasy as veiling over, but also generated by, the death drive. In addition, however, Suzy's ritual of visiting Montauk on the anniversary of their parents' death coincides with the period of her and Grace's birthday, thus positing a connection to birth and life as well.

Suzy's solving of the murder case is belated, for Grace has already solved and avenged this family murder. Suzy's contribution is to abet Grace's crime by misdirecting the police detective in charge of the case. She tells Detective Lester that a group of Korean merchants sent the killer, names a witness, and then gets on a train to Montauk herself. Suzy relaxes and anticipates the next day, when she and Grace will be considered the same age: "The end of Suzy's birthday. One more day until Grace's. For now, they will remain the same. Two girls with no parents, such fine American beauties" (294). These are the last lines of the novel. Why does *The Interpreter* find its resolution in the achievement of beauty, similitude, and orphan status? How is beauty tied to national identification? Why does the resolution of their parents' murder through another murder enable Suzy and Grace to occupy the position of American beauties?

I will begin by analyzing Grace's murder of her parents' murderer, and Suzy's abetment of Grace. The two sisters effectively act as vigilantes, bypassing legal authorities and administering their own justice. How do we explain this? Let us return to Feher-Gurewich's explanation that the perverse staging of fantasy serves not to reinforce fantasy, but to unveil its troubling features: "Perverts excel in exposing the fantasy of the other and the various social lies that such fantasy necessarily enforces."[20] The pervert does not accept the law as given. Instead, she fashions her own law:

> [Perverts] defy whatever law presents itself to them, transgressing this law in the hope of finally discovering an order of reality stronger and more stable than the lies and deceptions that organized the psychic reality of their childhood. . . . [They] expose such deceptions, in order to impose a law thanks to which the Other can remain all-powerful. . . . [P]erverts are forced to create a law of their own making, a law that appears to them to represent an order superior to the one accepted by the common run of mortals.[21]

In noir detective stories, the protagonist often takes the law into his or her own hands because the police are inept. They may have access to evidence, but they do not know how to interpret these clues. As the police signify the law of normative domesticity in the novel, they do not have the same understanding of perversion that Suzy has. It is Suzy's interpretations that set her on the path to solving this murder. In the midst of a court translation, Suzy realizes that a witness knew her parents. In the guise of translating for the prosecutor, Suzy interrogates the man using her own questions, for her own purposes. Suzy is free to translate without having the faithfulness of her translation questioned because she herself is the certifier of such faithfulness. The terrible power granted by the state to the child translator, Grace, who was made into the instrument of the Other, becomes wielded by the adult translator, Suzy, for extrastate purposes. Though initially called into being to serve the Other, the pervert also subverts the Other by revealing its limitations and installing an alternative law. Racial feminine beauty, I argue, also has this power perversely to install alternatives to dominant notions of national innocence, death, and rebirth.

In *The Ethics of Psychoanalysis*, Lacan explains that the subject may access knowledge of death and the death drive through the signifier, through the recognition that one could disappear from the signifying chain in which he is constituted. The aesthetic is a key realm that leads one away from the self, "it being precisely the function of the beautiful to reveal to us the site of man's relationship to his own death, and to reveal it to us only in a blinding flash."[22] One manifestation of this elusive death-in-beauty is the femme fatale of the noir detective genre, the alluring woman who in the end promises only suffering and death. Grace occupies this position of the femme fatale in the novel, the object of pursuit by the detective (Suzy), who then discovers her own imbrication in the crime that she investigates. Grace's beauty is lethal. She is the girl with the boy-killer face (232). Quite aware that Grace's features are aesthetically finer to a discerning eye, Suzy is flattered when she is occasionally mistaken for Grace:

> Suzy was secretly happy, for she knew her sister was a beauty. They had similar features, but Grace had longer eyelashes, a finer complexion, sleeker cheekbones, poutier lips, and blacker, straighter hair. At first sight, there was no doubt that they were sisters, perhaps even twins to those who did not have an eye for beauty. But upon a closer inspection, it was clear that Grace had far superior features, *the sort of face a man might die for.* (58; emphasis added)

The eroticization of Grace's facial parts cohere into a transcendent aesthetic ideal, one for which a man would sacrifice his life. And indeed, a man did end up sacrificing his life for Grace, killing her parents out of love for her.[23]

Strikingly, Grace's beauty does not conform to the white-identified "all-American" beauty for which the girls strove as they grew up. Suzy describes their youthful desire for such beauty:

> Yet the one thing both Suzy and Grace so desperately wanted was to be American girls, full-fledged American darlings, more golden than the girl next door, even cheerier than the prom queen, definitely sweeter than all-American sweethearts. Far, far away from their parents' Korea, which stuck to them like an ugly tattoo. (122)

Normative beauty, which is also a national beauty, is associated with goldenness, cheeriness, and sweetness; with the sunny optimism of an America where anything is possible; and with the appealing simplicity of wholesome morality and domesticity. The suburban connotations of the "girl next door" archetype are made explicit when Suzy continues wryly, "The golden girl, the girl next door, the all-American sweetheart didn't get made in the gutters of Queens" (123). Suzy ironically notes that her borough, Queens, does not produce beauty queens; its ethnic, working-class neighborhoods can only produce waste material (gutters), not the purity of an all-American sweetheart. Suzy's metaphor of the ugly tattoo as Korea refers to the understanding of racial difference as indelibly engraved on their bodies, as marking an apparently unerasable difference from the ideal of pure white feminine beauty, as well as the unseemliness of such difference in the field of visuality. In this way, racial difference would seem to mean an exclusion from the American fantasy of starting over with a blank slate, for one is always already marked: nonblank, non-innocent, nonvirgin. I will argue, however, that there are indeed perverse ways of starting over, alternatives to dominant American fantasies of innocent rebirth.

Given the ideal of white American beauty, how can we explain the value of Grace's beauty, which departs from such an ideal? Sleeker cheekbones and poutier lips connote a more sophisticated and eroticized beauty than that of the all-American sweetheart, and the blackness and straightness of Grace's hair especially connote a beauty that embodies Asian racial difference. Susan Koshy points to the sexual capital of Asian women in America, who are produced as what she calls the "sexual model minority."[24] Koshy explains that various historical factors such as the model minoritization of Asians and the way that U.S. feminism put into crisis traditional white domestic norms have led to an increased value of Asian and Asian American women as domestic and sexual partners. Leslie Bow and Anne Cheng have also pointed to the valued hyperfemininity of Asian American women, whose beauty is often construed as neutralizing or compensating for the "lack" of racial difference.[25] And as Cheng explains in her interpretation of Nancy Kwan's performance in the film *Flower Drum Song* (1961), the effect of this beauty cannot be understood simply as aesthetic pleasure. What is compelling, rather, is an uncontainable enjoyment that disturbs and traumatizes. As a mode of enjoyment, this racial beauty is perverse, and we can see such perversity in the deviant temporality of this beauty. *The Interpreter* presents Suzy as subject to a grotesque and gendered version of what Lisa Park calls premature adulthood and prolonged childhood: premature aging and prolonged youthful beauty.[26]

Suzy's college roommate, Jen, symbolizes the all-American beauty from which Suzy is excluded: "She has always been the image of what Suzy was not, what Suzy could never be—the ultimate emblem of the American dream" (160). Suzy notices one day that Jen has reached the prime of her life, attaining a fully mature beauty that evades Suzy:

> She's gotten older, Suzy notices for the first time, but in just the right way. Her blond hair is pulled back in a simple ponytail; the light mauve lipstick complements her creamy glow. Looking at Jen bundled in a knee-length camel coat, Suzy can see a woman reaching her prime in her thirties. Jen has never looked more radiant, Suzy thinks. So confident, so knowing, so perfectly compassionate. The same does not apply to Suzy herself, of course. Linear age eludes her. With her parents' sudden death, Suzy skipped her youth completely. (157)

The appropriate maturing of Jen's beauty contrasts with Suzy's accelerated aging. With her parents' untimely death, Suzy too is pulled out of normative time. Suzy's scandalous affair with Damian also prematurely aged her. Interpellated as a whore and an orphan by her parents when she is twenty, she thinks of herself as washed up at twenty-nine. Most intriguing in this narration of mature beauty is Suzy's description of Jen as "perfectly compassionate." This compassion marks Jen as an eminently moral subject, in contrast to Suzy's amorality, corruption, and perversion.

Suzy remembers a scene in which she is exempted from normative time by an artist, an expert in aesthetics: "Asian girls don't age, do they?" a painter for whom she had posed once told her, moving into her face a bit too closely. He was wrong. He implied that being Asian was a different destiny. He thought it bought her time" (139).

In this economy of beauty and aging, the painter postulates Asian femininity as an asset, indeed as currency, "buying" time. Asian women are seen as maintaining signs of youth for longer periods of time (fewer wrinkles, more supple skin). Suzy disputes the notion that Asian racial difference "buys her time" by slowing down the decrease in feminine value that accompanies aging. For Suzy, the traumas of her life have led to the opposite: a sped-up aging that hastens the decrease in her value by any measure of the marriage market.

But what if we took the painter's words literally? He doesn't refer to the mere slowdown of the aging process. He refers to not aging at all, to maintaining an eternal youth and thus eternal life. His remark figures Asian women as outside the normative time of mortality, outside the order accepted by "the common run of mortal," an exceptional province that Feher-Gurewich dubs the realm of the pervert. The painter's words figure Asian women as vampiric in their apparent gift of eternal youth.[27] But Suzy nuances this formulation in positing that exposure to traumatic forces (the sun, for vampires; family trauma, for Suzy) causes rapid aging. The prolonged youth of racial beauty is a form of suspended temporality, while its rapid aging manifests accelerated temporality. What the novel's conclusion marks is the return of Suzy from accelerated time to suspended time: "For now, they will remain the same" (294). In this trajectory, Suzy deliberately assumes the temporal suspension of masochistic perversion. This temporal suspension allows her to assume a relationship of sameness to Grace.

The novel's resolution of similitude evokes the Imaginary dynamic of mirror imagery. Throughout *The Interpreter,* Suzy's experiences with mirrors have been awkward and not satisfactory.[28] In contrast, Suzy is mesmerized by Grace because Grace's face is the main reflective surface in which she apprehends herself. We can thus understand Grace as Suzy's double, which psychoanalysis considers as "that mirror image in which the object is included."[29] Let us keep in mind that the subject only comes into Symbolic existence through the subtraction of the object. In other words, the double is an impossible figure of surplus: "The double is the same as me— *plus the object a,* that invisible part of being added to my image. . . . The double is always the figure of *jouissance:* on the one hand, he is somebody who enjoys at the subject's expense. He commits acts that one wouldn't dare to commit. . . . On the other hand, he is not simply someone who enjoys, but essentially a figure that commands the *jouissance*."[30] Grace is Suzy's mirror image, with the surplus enjoyment she embodies as an agent of a state-sanctioned death drive. As the Other with the object *a,* Grace embodies a fullness of being, a surplus that is not beholden to Symbolic law. And Grace's role in the novel is to command Suzy's own enjoyment, to draw Suzy into fully assuming the lawless enjoyment of the death drive.

Lacan's argument that beauty can reveal one's relationship to death is based on his notion that beauty actually serves as a barrier to the truth of the death drive, which "is not pretty to look at."[31] It is by interpreting, perhaps penetrating, the "splendor" of beauty that one may approach the destructiveness of the drive.[32] The trauma of the death drive lies, however, not only in its destructiveness. Surprisingly, it also lies in its capacity to generate what has never been before. The death drive, says Lacan, "challeng[es] everything that exists. But it is also a will to create from zero, a will to begin again," a "will to make a fresh start."[33] I would like to link the traumatic renewal of the death drive to Deleuze's provocative point that rebirth is the most significant rite of masochism. Most strikingly, Deleuze figures this masochistic rebirth as parthenogenetic, an asexual reproduction that counters heteronormativity.[34]

For Deleuze, masochism is to be distinguished from the Freudian paradigm of Oedipal law and desire, for masochism disavows and suspends patriarchal law. The Oedipal subject represses his incestuous desire for his mother and his homicidal impulse toward his father because of the prohibitions of patriarchal law. In contrast, the masochistic subject appears to submit to patriarchal law, but this submission masks a subversion of the law. The masochist submits to the punishment of law in the service of idealizing the mother-figure, who tortures him in order to expel the spirit of the father within him. With the father expelled, the subject undergoes a parthenogenetic rebirth, so that he becomes a replica of the mother. Who or what is the father that is excised in *The Interpreter*? It is the paternal state and its laws for common mortals. At the moment in which Suzy decides to abet Grace, the narrative apparently merges the voices of the two sisters: "Fuck KK boys. Fuck grocers who hated her parents. Fuck INS. Fuck the Bronx DA. And most of all, fuck Detective Lester" (293). As embodiments of the death drive, Grace and Suzy are compelled to annihilate these surrogates of the law in the service of creating an order superior to that accepted by these mortals.

Let us return now to the question of racial beauty, in which Grace's beauty is distinguished from the white, all-American ideal. The proverbial golden girl who embodies a wholesome and optimistic American spirit represents this ideal. It is precisely because the golden girl embodies the Symbolic order so perfectly that she is dead: clichéd, static, a signifier of pleasure but not enjoyment. In its stead, the Asian feminine beauty that concludes *The Interpreter* more readily plays the role of a beauty that allows the death drive to emerge, a beauty that kills but also reanimates, producing a surplus of life in death. If ideal white beauty is a signifier of the nation ("all-American"), the effect of racial beauty is not signification or meaning but senseless jouissance. This is why Suzy and Grace straddle the line between law and lawless enjoyment, perversely acting as instruments of the Other's jouissance.

Suzy remembers a rare moment of intimacy between the two sisters. On their way home from church as young adults, "Grace turned to Suzy and said in a clear, bright voice, 'One day, if you find yourself alone, will you remember that I am too? Because you and I, we're like twins" (211). Grace invokes a curious condition of being together in aloneness, a condition that cannot be understood in terms of simple merging or autonomy, for it is a paradoxical union in solitude. The figure of identical twins connotes the pathos of this condition: the union of a primordial oneness that then splits into two ones that remain forever separate. While others have speculated about whether Grace and Suzy are twins (57–58), it is Grace's sanction of this twin identity that permits Suzy to understand her quest as leading to the masochistic rite of parthenogenetic rebirth, in which Grace and Suzy are "the same." In a perverse rebirth, Suzy assumes her position of similitude to Grace, as embodiment of the death drive. Just as rebirth may be practiced through the perversion of masochism, so too can it be practiced through the perversion of fetishism. We will see, surprisingly, how objectification serves as a mode of perverse rebirth.

OBJECTIFICATION AND PERVERSE REBIRTH

Following his definition of perversion as the inverse of fantasy, Lacan continues, "It is the subject who determines himself as the object, in his encounter with the division of subjectivity."[35] The pervert is the antithesis of the subject of fantasy because she eschews subjectivity as such. The subject of fantasy, divided by the Symbolic order, believes that the object will complete him. In contrast, the pervert avoids this very division *by occupying the place of the object.* As an object, Suzy embodies a strange surplus of life: she is inert, yet human and alive, unincorporable into the Symbolic order. This strange surplus of life, I will show, is the disavowed surplus of the myth of American rebirth.

In this section, I consider Suzy's perverse practices of self-objectification. The objectification of women and people of color is conventionally considered as a mode of dehumanization and subordination, an exclusion from universal, normative subjectivity. I argue, however, that we may interpret acts and modes of self-objectification as critiques of liberal, universal humanist subjecthood. In making herself into the object of property, Suzy refuses the hegemonic injunction of aspiring toward liberal subjecthood, which is defined as the subject of property, will, and agency. Domesticity and citizenship are modes of property and possession: one lays claim and is claimed by one's home, family, communities, and nation. By making herself the object rather than the subject of possession, Suzy also transforms herself into the object of possession in an otherworldly sense. She becomes possessed by the specters of the dispossessed, those who are rendered surplus by national fantasy.

As the subject of drive, Suzy relates to Damian through the unyielding certainty of demand: "It had to be Damian. It could only be Damian. No one would have claimed her with such absolute disregard" (161). What is being disregarded in this claim? Certainly, social norms and social approval are being disregarded in this affair between an older, married, white professor of Asian studies and a younger Asian American female student. Damian's position as a married man is only one element of the illicitness of this affair. His occupation as a powerful, professional Orientalist and Suzy's subordinate status as a young Korean American student lay bare the power inequalities and racial fetishism that give their relationship its transgressive, erotic charge. The affair is perverse in the sense of disregarding the laws of social norms and proprieties. But most crucial to Suzy's masochistic perversion is Damian's disregard for Suzy herself, for her will and desires. Recognizing in Damian's absolute disregard his status as the Master who is subject to no law but his own, Suzy masochistically submits herself to his claim. By disowning her will and desire, Suzy disclaims liberal subjecthood and claims, instead, a masochistically perverse objectification.

As a mistress to married men, Suzy's position outside social morality as illegitimate and illicit is also a state of dispossession. Suzy has no legitimate claim to her lover, for he has already been claimed by a legal spouse. Moreover, by running off with Damian, Suzy ensures that she is dispossessed of any claim on her family when her parents disown her. The grammatical construction of such disowning is misleading: because the parents are the subjects of this clause, they appear to be the subjects of loss, actively giving up their ownership of kin. In fact, however, the actual subject of loss and relinquishment is the daughter, who is now barred from making any legitimate claim on family, domestic belonging, or respectability.

The fantasy of domesticity, which for Suzy exists *only* in fantasy, is predicated on the notion of legitimate claim to property in and possession of one's home and family. The norm of liberal subjectivity that undergirds national citizenship is similarly based on a presumption of property and possession in one's self. Suzy spectacularly refuses both domesticity and liberal subjecthood through her perverse practices of masochism and fetishism. Specifically, she refuses to become the *subject* of property, instead making herself into the *object* of property and possession. In other words, Suzy's dispossession means not only that she is excluded from possessing but also that she herself becomes possessed. In Suzy's masochistic fantasy of being claimed by Damian with absolute disregard, what was being disregarded was Suzy's will itself. She could make no claim; she could only be claimed. And in Suzy's subsequent affair with Michael, she fashions herself as a commodity fetish, an object adorned with the many other commodity fetishes that Michael purchases for her so that she can deliberately accede to her position as a "kept woman" (29).

The *Interpreter* represents Suzy's erotic life as formed mainly through her affairs with Damian and Michael. However, Suzy recalls an originary moment that "*marked her as the other woman*" (54; emphasis in original). In her first year of college, she finds herself alone in her dorm room with the boyfriend of her roommate. Trying to escape the awkward silence, Suzy is about to leave when "she felt his hands on her shoulders. He said nothing at all. . . . He slowly turned her around and kissed her without hesitation, not the sweet and soft kind, but the forceful probing of a tongue that was confident and mechanical" (54). Until she meets Damian, Suzy experiences only repulsion or disappointment when she kisses other boys. "It was as if nothing quite erased the initial shock of being kissed by someone who was not hers, a kiss that was stolen, claimed from her flippantly, a kiss so abrasively illicit that she seemed to deserve it, as though she was not worth much to begin with. It stuck with her, the shame, the smell" (54). The sense of punishment ("she seemed to deserve it") and diminishment of being ("not worth much") in this passage, as well as its prolonged breathlessness, convey the awakening of masochistic pleasure. This masochistic pleasure, a pleasure in suffering, is generated by the jouissance or illicit nature of this encounter, which is referred to in Suzy's phrase, "a kiss that was stolen." Who is the agent of stealing and who is being stolen from? Although the passage ascribes agency to the boyfriend in his flippant claim of the kiss, it also narrates the erotic experience as belonging to Suzy. The errant boyfriend acts in claiming the kiss, but from Suzy's perspective he is an instrument of enjoyment. Both Suzy and the boyfriend benefit from stealing jouissance from the Other, in transgressing social law; both have stolen something to which they have no claim.

Suzy's berating of herself in the passage above reveals how the masochist embodies law in order to undo it. Transgression of law must be punished, and the masochist is the agent of law in punishing herself. However, the masochistic experiences pleasure not only in her crime but also in the very punishment for her transgression. This is how masochism facilitates lawless enjoyment. According to Deleuze, "The law now ordains what it was once intended to forbid, guilt absolves instead of leading to atonement, and punishment makes permissible what it was intended to chastise."[36] Perhaps the most radical practice of suspension in masochism is that of suspending the law.

While Suzy wants to be claimed and owned, she does not want to own. What she specifically eschews is the legitimacy or lawfulness of ownership. She thinks of Damian and Michael as men "who will never be hers" (67). For Feher-Gurewich, jouissance refers "to the right to enjoy the use of a thing, as opposed to owning it. The jouissance of the Other, therefore, refers to the subject's experience of being for the Other an object of enjoyment, of use or abuse, in contrast to being the object of the Other's desire."[37] Feher-Gurewich explicitly aligns ownership with desire, and we can subsequently see that enjoyment aligns with drive. Suzy's affairs are not relationships of legitimate claim or desire; rather, they are structured by an antidomestic death drive and produce transgressive enjoyment. Suzy eschews ownership because it produces pleasure but not enjoyment. And Suzy's family business teaches that belonging, whether to kin or nation, must always involve traumatic enjoyment.

It is no accident that Suzy's name makes a nervous lawyer think of the infamous fictional "Suzie Wong," as Suzy plays the role of the eroticized racial fetish in her encounters with Damian and other white men (10). Suzy fashions herself as a commodity fetish object in her affair with Michael. She wears and adorns herself with Michael's many luxurious commodity gifts: "The black cashmere coat that costs double her rent, and the pinstriped pants [that] are sleek enough for any Hollywood starlet" (3–4). "An array of silk shirts and cashmere sweaters" in her bedroom certifies her, she thinks, as "a bona fide mistress" (28). Clad in items that she perceives as the property of her benefactor, Suzy believes herself a similar object of property, a kept woman.

Dutifully performing the rituals of an appreciative lover, Michael understands the importance of marking and celebrating Suzy's birthday. "Of course he would remember. He would probably send her a dozen long-stemmed roses, boxed. He would make reservations at the Rainbow Room. He would slide across the table a blue Tiffany case in which there would be a set of sparkling diamond earrings. He would do everything so that she would feel the weight of a mistress" (114). What is this weight of a mistress? Most obviously, it refers to the extravagant gifts as a burden, in the sense that the mistress feels indebted and obligated to her benefactor. In addition, these gifts are intended to provide a substance and presence that compensates for Michael's lack, his unavailability outside their dalliances. Michael intends them to function as remainders and reminders of his presence, so that Suzy can miss him when he is absent. But in fact, Suzy "never thinks about [him] when he is not around, which he never is" (67). Michael has mistaken Suzy for the subject of desire, when in fact desire is quite absent for Suzy.

Ultimately, I would argue that the weight of a mistress, generated by the weight of the commodities given to her, is meant to compensate not only for Michael's unavailability because of his marriage. Even more dramatically, this weight is a desperate defense against Michael's more general anxieties about disappearing. To understand this anxiety more fully, consider Michael's most recent gift package: "every possible Chanel beauty product wrapped in the newest Prada" (200). As the novel tells us early on, "Michael wants Suzy in the latest fashion. He wants the latest of everything" (28). Michael's shifting fixations on the most recently released products in their every incarnation reveal his status as the obsessive subject of capitalist desire, for whom newness and variety generate a ravenous need to own. Because desire is never satisfied by its current object, it must continue to seek new objects.

In addition to serving as the obsessive subject of capitalist desire, Michael also functions as the obsessive subject of capitalist production. His occupation is vaguely suggested to be some kind of agent for transnational capital in the field of digital technology. Set at the turn of the twenty-first century, an era of belief in the limitless expansion of finance capital, the novel frequently depicts Michael's travels to Europe and his compulsive phone calls to Suzy. His frenetic reports on his transactions and negotiations act out his obsessiveness: "those Brits just ate it up, man. They fucking love the whole crap. They've got it all mixed up. They think Java's some coffee from the Caribbean, and HTML a code name for the newest hip-hop nation. They're sure I'm their Bill Gates, and I told them, 'Bill and me, we're like brothers'" (21). Michael's transatlantic phone calls are virtual monologues, in which he gives nonstop accounts of his daily activities and barely asks after Suzy. The obsessive can only prove his existence through constant activity; to stop acting or talking would call his existence into question. Indeed, "Michael always volunteers his exact whereabouts to Suzy, as though he is afraid of disappearing between the airport runways somewhere in the world" (79). Michael represents the obsessive status of capitalism, frenetically seeking out more and more, relentlessly mobile, and anxious about its evaporation (which, indeed, we did spectacularly witness in the financial crisis that started in 2008). In *The Interpreter*, the Korean immigrant population forms a body of spectral labor, appearing and disappearing according to the needs and demands of the nation and capital. The Park family is of course a primary agent of this disappearance, as well as a prime example of this disappearance and spectralization. Michael represents the counterpart to this spectral labor: the spectralization of capital, which is intangible and transient, always on the verge of evaporating. In making Suzy into a commodity fetish embodying the weight of a mistress, Michael hopes to compensate for his own uncertain, tenuous existence.

In Marx's famous formulation, the commodity fetish alchemically transforms the relationship between men into a relationship between things. What does this mean for Suzy? By making herself into a commodity fetish, Suzy puts herself into relation with objects and things that do not qualify as human. If Michael represents abstract capital as the profits that were extracted from laborers such as Suzy's family and community, then we might think of this labor as fantastically transformed into Michael and the commodities that he buys for Suzy. By receiving, wearing, and identifying herself with these commodity objects, Suzy becomes magically inhabited by, or possessed by, her family and community. By disclaiming the legitimacy of ownership and liberal subjecthood, Suzy is dispossessed but also possessed, making herself into the site of lawless enjoyment in the form of living death. She is possessed by specters—inhabited by racial migrant work and workers as the living dead.

Recall that the psychoanalytic definition of the fetish is an object that stands for an absence, thereby allowing for the disavowal of that absence. Suzy's presence in a narrative that keeps everyone else at a distance is almost claustrophobically intimate. She is a kind of fetish for the reader, a pervasive presence that stands in for all the absences that haunt the narrative: her sister Grace, her parents, the other Korean immigrants and migrants who lost their lives and loved ones to the traumas of state deportation. But the extravagant hyperbole of Suzy's self-fetishization reveals precisely her possession by these spectral others. Suzy refuses the self-possession of liberal citizenship, embodying instead the dispossession and possession of perverse citizenship. Suzy's self-objectification is a strange form of rebirth, the reanimation of those who were destroyed by the death drive of the U.S. nation-state. This strange excess of life that Suzy embodies is the disavowed surplus of national fantasy, and the overflow of a capitalism that is otherwise imagined as impersonal accumulation.

The novel ends with the silence of the drive, in which Grace's watery burial of her lover's body also buries the traumatic narrative of her family. This silence, as in *Bone*, is not a silence of absence or lack, but one of surplus. Discussing the *se faire* aspect of the drive, the mode of making oneself seen or heard, Joan Copjec says: "What is made audible—or visible—is the void as such, contentless and nonsensical . . . in exposing itself, it does not seek to communicate itself."[38]

We can see the irony of Grace's and Suzy's positions as interpreters, given that interpretation is superfluous in drive. In a commentary on Lacan, Jacques-Alain Miller explains how drive differs from desire, contrasting the equivocations of desire, which takes into account others' desires and prohibitions, with the blind insistence of drive:

> The drive couldn't care less about prohibition; it knows nothing of prohibition and certainly doesn't dream of transgressing it. The drive follows its own bent and always obtains satisfaction. Desire weighs itself down with considerations like, "they want me to go, so I won't" or "I'm not supposed to go that way, so that's the way I want to go, but perhaps at the last second I won't be able to do it anyway.". . . [T]he drive is an activity which always comes off. It leads to sure success, whereas desire leads to a sure unconscious formation, namely, a bungled action or slip: "I missed my turn," "I forgot my keys," etc. That is desire. The drive, on the contrary, always has its keys in hand.[39]

Desire is eminently interpretable because it codes its concerns with prohibition and transgression. Desire is contingent. It depends on other factors in unpredictable ways. Drive, however, is indifferent and has no need for a code. As Miller says elsewhere, when there is nothing left to interpret, we are in the realm of the drive.[40] At the novel's conclusion, Suzy questions her own practice of interpretation: "What the hell's an interpreter if she can't even interpret her own sister?" (293). Grace's master stroke is to bury the whole violent narrative of her family in the waters of Montauk; we are left at the end only with a silence permeated by jouissance—a silence that is surplus.

Characteristic of the noir genre is what Copjec calls the "lonely room," emblematic of spaces that are uninhabited. Suzy's apartment is an example of such an uninhabited space, as is the apartment of the witness that Suzy stakes out, as are most of Suzy's childhood homes. Such domestic spaces are spaces of alienation: "Who needs a family room? . . . How much living could one do when working seven days a week?" (141–42). These lonely rooms are sites of the death drive. Copjec contrasts the lonely room of noir detective fiction to the "locked room" of classic detective fiction. The locked room is a space of mystery because its contents must be explained and interpreted. In contrast, "What noir presents to us are spaces that have been emptied of desire . . . nothing more can be gotten out of them. *They are no longer interpretable* . . . they will never yield anything new and cannot, therefore, hide anything."[41]

Is Grace, with Suzy's abetting, hiding something by burying DJ in the water? Are Grace and Suzy hiding their own secret guilt in the death of their parents, their death wish for their parents? On the contrary, Grace's and Suzy's implication in their parents' murder—and the murder of their murderer—is but a logical extension of their being impressed into the family business of "disappearing" others. As subjects of drive, the sisters have been emptied of desire. Their family business was to excise others who exceeded the law, and Grace merely continues this family business. The sisters are not hiding their secret guilt; they are simply executing their family business of disappearance. There is nothing to hide, nothing to interpret, no secret kernel of guilt or desire—only the act of "*swim[ming] through [the] waters*" of the death drive.[42]

Coda

Each chapter of *Inhuman Citizenship* ends with an allusion to a heart or a secret kernel. In chapter 1, I call for an embedding of Ona's heart in our own, so that we may participate in *Bone*'s project of animating what is otherwise left behind. Chapter 2 considers how imperial jouissance bequeaths to the Filipino family the secret and alien heart of the nation. To be deemed worthy of citizenship and love, the immigrant in chapter 3 must offer his heart to the nation. Finally, as if to undo all the foregoing work of imagination and interpretation, chapter 4 culminates in a dissipation, in which the secret kernel of the Park family is dissolved.

We may wish for endings to provide closure, but we wish even more for an afterlife, a continuing resonance. With these four figures—the reanimating heart, the alien heart, the sacrificial heart, and the dissolving heart—I hope to suggest both the reverberations of the racial inhuman and the void of jouissance. In this coda, my intention is to echo these four chapters by considering how racial jouissance itself recurs, rebounds, and spreads.

In *The Melancholy of Race*, Anne Cheng recalls that whenever she mentioned in conversation that she was writing about the film *Flower Drum Song*, her interlocutor, regardless of race, ethnicity, or gender, would invariably burst into his or her rendition of the musical number "I Enjoy Being a Girl."[1] How might we think about the infectiousness of this song, whose referent is the exuberant performance by the Asian American actress Nancy Kwan? Why is the automatic response to hearing about the film not intellectual or narrative discourse, but rather the reembodiment of a showstopping spectacle and recital? Put another way, what does it mean that these various conversation partners were de-individualized in their momentary possession by a fictional Asian American woman, the character of Linda Low?[2] And why is it enjoyment—an enjoyment of femininity that is explicitly cited in the song title—that is so infectious?

At first glance, Linda Low appears to perfectly embody the fantasy of early 1960s, Cold War national femininity. The abundance of postwar American prosperity means that she has the resources and the leisure time to alternate easily between several fashionable outfits and hairdos. She coyly and directly solicits men's attention through flirtation and entertainment. She even takes part in a tableau of space-age futuristic domesticity, pressing a button to automatically make orange juice and toast for her imagined husband. What I want to highlight, however, is the way that femininity in *Flower Drum Song* forms yet another vector of the racial inhuman and traumatic enjoyment that emerge from family business.[3]

Femininity is represented as consummate artifice in the musical number's song lyrics, costuming, and performance. Linda sings with delight of a "brand new hairdo," "my eyelashes all in curls," and talking on the telephone with "a pound and a half of cream upon my face." As she takes a break from singing, she replicates into three mirror images, so that she can watch herself simultaneously don a frilly dress, a ball gown, and a bikini in her mirrors, each with their appropriately formal or fun hairstyles. This production of serious femininity recalls other lines in the film that link racial femininity to the production of machines: "Right off the assembly line! Not a scratch on her! They don't make 'em that way over here anymore."[4]

Linda declares herself "strictly a female female." This strong adherence to gender norms again posits femininity as artifice. Paradoxically, however, such bondage to femininity also appears to unleash enjoyment. The lyrics to "I Enjoy Being a Girl" express feminine pleasures as extravagances that can barely be contained: swiveling and swerving her hips, flipping over flowers from a "fella," "drooling" with delight over dresses made of lace. Cheng argues that Linda's performance "exceeds the boundaries . . . of a *proper* joy." Rather, Linda's joy is "uncontainable."[5] Her enjoyment spreads to her spectators and listeners, who cannot suppress their desire to sing. What can we make of this irrepressibility and uncontainability of traumatic enjoyment?

The distinction between affect and emotion helps to explain the infectiousness of jouissance. Both affect and emotion refer to states of feeling, but affect is generally conceived of as more inchoate, less formed, not clearly legible or narratable. Because of this formlessness, affect is also less attached to particular subjects.[6] Emotion, by contrast, is felt as belonging to an individual or defining an individual at a particular moment. Although jouissance may invoke emotions such as rage or shame, its condition is one of unintelligibility and senselessness, and so its intensity should be thought of as affective in nature. And this intensity is what spills over and permeates others.

Sara Ahmed's notion of "affective economies" also allows us to think about affect as something that is produced through circulation, rather than something that properly belongs to and is contained by an individual subject.[7] Indeed, for Ahmed, "affect does not reside positively in the sign or commodity, but is produced only as an effect of its circulation. . . . '[T]he subject' is simply one nodal point in the economy, rather than its origin and destination."[8] Although Linda Low may appear to be the origin and source of jouissance, I would say instead that she has assumed this condition—the better to spread, like a virus, the affect of jouissance. I interpret her embodiment of the national symptom of enjoyment as an ethical act of assuming and transmitting responsibility for the national unconscious. While I have used metaphors such as infection, transmission, and virus to refer to the spread of jouissance, I do not mean that jouissance is a disease that must be cured. Instead, I intend one final trope of inhuman citizenship in invoking the Asian American protagonist as a virus.

By paying attention to the circulation and transmission of traumatic enjoyment, I have demonstrated how Asian American domestic narratives may be read as narratives not only of subject formation but also of subject antiformation. Jasbir Puar, noting how we have "exhausted the modern subject," has observed the limitations of thinking primarily in terms of the "disciplinary subject and its identitarian interpellation."[9] *Inhuman Citizenship* is one response to a similar call by Kandice Chuh for reconceiving Asian American studies as a "subjectless discourse."[10] As I mentioned earlier, the end of analysis, for Lacan, is subjective destitution. Throughout this book, then, I have shown how the affects of jouissance devastatingly bring subjectivity into crisis, and in this desubjectification they confound human status.

Asian American family business, which depends on the affective labor of the child of immigrants, operates in ways that both serve and threaten the fantasies of the U.S. imperial nation-state, especially the myths of exceptionalism and neoliberalism. What supports and disrupts national romance is a racialized jouissance, or traumatic enjoyment. The nation traumatically enjoys the various forms that the racial inhuman takes: the living dead, the animal, the antifetish, the death drive. In contrast to the hegemonic belief that racial subjects should counter racist dehumanization by assimilating into normative humanity, the second-generation protagonists of these novels assume the role of the racial inhuman. In this way, they do not identify with the dominant subject of national fantasy, but rather with the nation's symptom, its traumatic Thing. Lacan refers to such counterintuitive identification as "traversing the fantasy": dissolving the fundamental fantasy through a confrontation with traumatic enjoyment. In surfacing and embodying national forms of jouissance, these Asian American protagonists assume responsibility for the national unconscious. I therefore interpret these Asian American narratives as ethical acts of confronting the alien at the core of the nation, and indeed at the core of the human. As many critics have pointed out, the process of Americanization is a traumatic disturbance for many of its subjects, objects, and abjects. It is no simple act of inclusion or exclusion; it is instead a harsh rendering into the extimate—the external intimate. What I call "inhuman citizenship" refers to this traumatic incorporation and ex-corporation by the imperial nation-state, as well as the acts of embodiment, circulation, and transmission of its symptoms of jouissance.

Acknowledgments

I have always enjoyed the acknowledgments section of books, which takes us behind the scenes and reveals how the apparent solitude of writing is actually part of a network of circulating ideas and affect. It gives me the greatest pleasure here to convey my appreciation to those who have imprinted the shaping and reshaping of this book. For providing me with a sense of community in my first years of working in critical race studies and Asian American literature, I thank my colleagues and mentors at the University of California, Berkeley: Norma Alarcón, Mark Chiang, Jeannie Chiu, David L. Eng, Candace Fujikane, Elaine H. Kim, Susan Schweik, Karen Su, Theresa Tensuan, Sau-ling C. Wong, and the late Barbara Christian. For their support and scholarly example, I thank Alexandra Chassin, Anne Fleche, Frances Restuccia, Alan Richardson, Kalpana Seshadri, and Christopher Wilson at Boston College; Lena Choe, Tim Dean, Stephanie Foote, Lisa Lampert, Martin Manalansan IV, William Maxwell, H. Adlai Murdoch, Robert Parker, and Zohreh Sullivan at the University of Illinois, Urbana-Champaign; and Victor Bascara, Jeff Chang, Grace Kyungwon Hong, Lisa Lowe, Viet Nguyen, and Min Hyoung Song in the fields of Asian American, critical race, and cultural studies.

Terry Beers, Phyllis Brown, Michelle Burnham, Bridget Cooks, Perlita Dicochea, Diane Dreher, Judith Dunbar, Marilyn Edelstein, Eileen Razzari Elrod, Janet Flammang, Linda Garber, John Hawley, James Lai, Sharmila Lodhia, Pauline Nguyen, Roseanne Giannini Quinn, and Juan Velasco warmly welcomed me into the community at Santa Clara University. For their comments on various parts of the manuscript, I thank Phyllis, Bridget, Marilyn, Linda, John, James, Sharmila, Roseanne, and Juan, as well as Rick Baldoz, Susan Lurie, Jerry Miller, and Megan Williams. James, Laura Ellingson, and Laura Nichols were my sounding board for this project during my sabbatical. During the final stages of writing, Anitra Grisales helped me to clarify many points with her editorial suggestions. For her rigorous readings of these chapters from their earliest days to the present, and for providing such an inspiring example of a scholarly life, as well as an ethical one, I especially thank Michelle Burnham.

I appreciate the feedback that I received when I presented early versions of my book chapters. Thank you to Beth Lew and David Palumbo-Liu for inviting me to the Asian Americas workshop at Stanford University; and to Rhacel Salazar Parrreñas for organizing our megasession on neoliberalism for an Association for Asian American Studies conference. Rhacel's incredible productivity should be intimidating, but her passion for scholarship is, instead, infectious.

Christine So mentored me through the book-writing process and has been a wonderful accomplice in academia. Kimberly Chun, gifted writer and inquiring mind, consistently expressed her interest in this book through its many stages. Jiyoung Kim, though she lives across the continent, has been a constant and everyday companion as I write on the computer. I thank her for countless moments of hilarity and wisdom.

I have been blessed with the most talented, demanding, and generous writing partners. Celine Parreñas Shimizu taught me to appreciate the beauty, creativity, and intensity of writing and of life. Stephen H. Sohn has been unbelievably patient and meticulous in reading through my many drafts. To Celine and Steve, my very profound gratitude; their presence is embedded in these pages.

Santa Clara University supported this book project through a Paul Locatelli, S.J., grant, a Thomas Terry grant, and a grant from the Provost's office.

At the University of Minnesota Press, I thank Adam Brunner, Richard Morrison, Erin Warholm-Wohlenhaus, and my two anonymous reviewers, whose thoughtful comments helped me to improve the book tremendously. Adam's faith in this project in its earliest stages gave me encouragement during a crucial time. Thank you to Cherene Holland for her careful copyediting.

For their sustaining support and love, I thank my parents, Victor Fong-Shou Chang and Mary Mei-Lee Chu Chang; and my brother's family,

David, Marisol, Trinity, Ian, and Michael Chang. Susan Brunson has generously cared for our family when we most needed it. Thelonious Coltrane Brunson-Chang came along just in time to make the revision process joyful. Finally, this book is dedicated to Russell Brunson, whose abiding faith, love, and good humor are among the many gifts with which his presence has graced my life.

Notes

INTRODUCTION

1. The "Flash Gordon" comic strip was illustrated by Alex Raymond and first published in 1934. Hagedorn recognizes Ming's association with the "yellow peril" discourse of twentieth-century American culture in her various iterations of Orientalist fantasy later in the poem.

2. See chapter 2 of Chen, *Double Agency*, 35–59, for an interesting reconsideration of Fu Manchu as racial stereotype.

3. For histories of the Asian American movement in the 1960s and 1970s, see Maeda, *Chains of Babylon*, and Wei, *The Asian American Movement*.

4. Hagedorn, "Ming the Merciless," 169.

5. See Eve Oishi for a discussion of "bad Asians." Briefly, bad Asians eschew respectability by behaving badly, against conventional morality. Celine Parreñas Shimizu is also concerned with the "bad subjectivity" of Asian Americans, especially Asian American women, who are sexualized. Oishi, "Bad Asians," 221–22; Shimizu, *The Hypersexuality of Race*.

6. Donald Pease provides a number of overviews of American exceptionalism, including post–Cold War American exceptionalism. Pease, "Exceptionalism"; *The New American Exceptionalism*; and "Rethinking 'American Studies after U.S. Exceptionalism.'"

7. Castronovo, *Necro Citizenship*; Holland, *Raising the Dead*; Roach, *Cities of the Dead*; Eng and Kazanjian, *Loss*; Petersen, *Kindred Specters*; Brogan, *Cultural Haunting*; Jacques Derrida, *Specters of Marx*.

8. Kingston, *The Woman Warrior*, 172–82.

9. Wong, *Reading Asian American Literature*, 89.

10. Ibid., 181–82.

11. Lane, *The Psychoanalysis of Race*, 5.

12. Viego, *Dead Subjects*, 4.

13. Evans, *Dictionary of Lacanian Psychoanalysis*, 91–92.

14. Homer, *Jacques Lacan*, 62–63.

15. Dean, *Beyond Sexuality*, 917–18.

16. The title of the welfare reform act of 1996, the Personal Responsibility and Work Opportunity Reconciliation Act, emphasizes how privatization was framed as a moral as well as economic concern.

17. Cacho, "The Violence of Value."

18. For overviews of posthumanist scholarship, see Cary Wolfe's introductions to *What Is Humanism?* and *Zoontologies*, xi–xxxiv and ix–xxiii, respectively. A good deal of this posthumanist theory explicitly emerges from and engages with the discipline of philosophy. There is a vast body of scholarship on inhuman figures such as vampires, ghosts, and monsters in world literature. The past decade has seen tremendous growth in the field of animal studies; one recent manifestation of this in literary studies is the cluster on animal studies in a March 2009 edition of *PMLA*. In Winter 2008, the journal *MELUS* published a special issue imagining the nexus of the "Alien/Asian." As racialized populations across the globe are rendered surplus to global capital and its Symbolic regimes, I hope that this study will contribute to a new understanding of ethical responses to such brutal and rational violence.

19. Gilroy, *Postcolonial Melancholia*, 1–26.

20. Cheah, *Inhuman Conditions*, 6.

21. Some examples of these supernatural beings include the black voodoo priestess and the "Magical Negro" in American cinema. A recent version of the black voodoo priestess is the character Tia Dalma in *Pirates of the Caribbean: Dead Man's Chest* (2006) and *Pirates of the Caribbean: At World's End* (2007). Tia Dalma, played by the black British actress Naomie Harris, is revealed to be the goddess Calypso, who grows into a giant and then explodes into a multitude of crabs. The Magical Negro is an archetypal mystical character who helps the white protagonist to redeem himself or herself. Recent cinematic incarnations of the Magical Negro include Michael Clarke Duncan's character in *The Green Mile* (1999) and Will Smith's character in *The Legend of Bagger Vance* (2000). See Hicks, "Hoodoo Economics," for an extended discussion of magical black men in the films *Unbreakable* (2000), *The Green Mile*, and *Family Man* (2000).

22. Gilroy, *Postcolonial Melancholia*, 4.

23. Žižek, *How to Read Lacan*, 47; emphasis added.

24. Ibid., 46.

25. Lee, *Urban Triage*, xiv.

26. A speech by President Ronald Reagan in 1984 provides an example of how moralistic "family values" became equated with economic production under neoliberalism. Praising Asian Americans for their belief in "the responsibility of parents and schools to be teachers of tolerance, hard work, fiscal responsibility, cooperation, and love," Reagan also remarked, "It's no wonder that the medium incomes of Asian and Pacific-American families are much higher than the total American average." Cited in Takaki, *Strangers from a Different Shore*, 475.

27. Anderson, *Imagined Communities*; Brown, *Domestic Individualism*; George, *Burning Down the House*; George, "Domesticity"; McHugh, *American Domesticity*; Tate, *Domestic Allegories of Political Desire*.

28. Berlant, "Citizenship," 37.

29. Stoler, *Haunted by Empire*, 13–14; emphasis in original.

30. Gordon, *Ghostly Matters*, 17.

31. Freud, "The Uncanny," 221, 226.

32. Bhabha, *The Location of Culture*, 9–19.

33. Freud, "The Uncanny," 224; emphasis in original.

34. Bhabha, *The Location of Culture*, 9.

35. Cho, *Haunting the Korean Diaspora*, 14.

36. Lowe, *Immigrant Acts*, 16.

37. Kaplan, "Manifest Domesticity," 602.

38. J.-A. Miller, "*Extimité*," 74–87.

39. Asian American studies scholars such as Peter Kwong have pointed to a bifurcation of Asian American populations into working-class and middle- or upper-middle-class strata. This bifurcation is due to the way in which U.S. immigration policies recruit Asian immigrants as both labor and capital, different kinds of resources for the nation-state. I have chosen to focus on working-class narratives of family business because they illustrate most starkly why the labor of children is necessary for family survival. Professional Asian immigrants have greater human capital from which to draw, including their education, facility with the English language, and professional skills. For these reasons, they are less reliant economically on the labor of their children.

40. Carr, "At the Thresholds of the Human," 134–35.

41. For scholarship on ethnic and Asian American small businesses, see Light and Bonacich, *Immigrant Entrepreneurs*; Ronald Takaki, *Strangers from a Different Shore*; and Sucheng Chan, *Asian Americans: An Interpretive History*.

42. See erin Khuĕ Ninh's *Ingratitude* for a breathtaking analysis of how thoroughly the Asian immigrant family is imbricated in American capitalism, and the attendant costs that are wrought especially from the daughter. While Ninh and I worked on our projects in parallel, I would like to acknowledge the productive resonances between my attention to Asian American family business and Ninh's study of how "Asian American intimate relations reveal themselves to be profoundly ordered by a capitalist logic and ethos, their violence arranged around the production of the disciplined and profitable docile body" (6).

43. Lye, *America's Asia*, 2.

44. Ninh, "The Cautionary Tale."

45. Lasch, *Haven in a Heartless World*.

46. L. Park, *Consuming Citizenship*, 66.

47. Ibid., 65.

48. Ibid., 69–70.

49. See Berlant, *The Queen of America Goes to Washington City*, 25–53, for her theory of "infantile citizenship."

50. Chakrabarty, *Provincializing Europe*, 4.

51. Lacan, *Écrits: A Selection*, 49.

52. Lacan, "Proposition du 9 octobre 1967 sur le psychoanalyst de l'École," 23.

53. Lowe, *Immigrant Acts*, 8–9; emphases in original.

54. Lowe clarifies that naming her central trope of "immigrant acts" does not discount the population of native-born Asian Americans, "It is rather to observe that the life conditions, choices, and expressions of Asian Americans have been significantly determined by the U.S. state through the apparatus of immigration laws and policies, through the enfranchisements denied or extended to immigrant individuals and communities, and through the processes of naturalization and citizenship. It is to underscore that . . . immigration has been a crucial *locus* through which U.S. interests have recruited and regulated both labor and capital from Asia." Ibid., 7.

55. Marianne Hirsch is perhaps the best-known critic on postmemory, in which subjects "remember" events that happened to earlier generations and may have preceded their births. For analyses of postmemory in Asian American cultural production, see Chu, "Science Fiction and Postmemory Han in Korean American Literature"; Eng, *The Feeling of Kinship*, 166–98; and Mimura, *Ghostlife of Third Cinema*, 93–103.

56. See Sara Ahmed, *The Promise of Happiness*, on the "affect alien."

1. Melancholic Citizenship

1. For analyses that use the paradigm of melancholia to investigate race, nation, and colonialism, see Cheng, *The Melancholy of Race;* Eng and Kazanjian, *Loss;* Khanna, *Dark Continents;* Gilroy, *Postcolonial Melancholia;* Muñoz, *Disidentifications;* Parikh, "Blue Hawaii"; and See, *The Decolonized Eye.*

2. For a history of neoliberalism, see Harvey, *A Brief History of Neoliberalism.*

3. Interestingly, there are few historical markers in Ng's novel. The most topical reference is to a newspaper with headlines about San Francisco politicians Joseph Alioto and Dianne Feinstein, who served as mayor and supervisor in the 1970s.

4. Reddy, "Asian Diasporas, Neoliberalism, and Family," discusses the intersections of neoliberal discourse, paradigms of family, and asylum cases.

5. Chang's "Chinese Suicide" uses Edelman's argument to interpret Ona's death as a "queer death that generates, rather than evacuates, political possibilities" (105).

6. Gordon, *Ghostly Matters.*

7. Although these men lived a "bachelor" lifestyle, many of them were married and had wives in China who could not immigrate to the United States.

8. For scholarship on *Eat a Bowl of Tea*, see Eng, *Racial Castration;* Kain, "Refracted Identity(ies) in Louis Chu's *Eat a Bowl of Tea*"; Ling, *Narrating Nationalisms;* and Hsiao, "Facing the Incurable."

9. Leila's twice-removed status as affiliative rather than filiative grandchild—she is the stepdaughter of Grandpa Leong's "paper," or fictive, son—instantiates one of the

main concerns of the book: the meaningfulness of family as socially constructed rather than based solely on biological lineage.

10. Renan, "What Is a Nation?" 8–22; cited in Khanna, *Dark Continents*, 12. Renan remarks, "Forgetting . . . is a crucial factor in the creation of a nation. . . . The essence of a nation is that all individuals have many things in common and also that they have forgotten many things . . . every French citizen has to have forgotten the massacre of Saint Bartholomew." Renan, "What Is a Nation?" 11.

11. See also Anne Cheng's reading of Maxine Hong Kingston's *The Woman Warrior*. Cheng, *The Melancholy of Race*, 83–91. Cheng considers Kingston's text in the light of Abraham and Torok's theories of transgenerational secrets and argues that "*[t]he mother is the mourner in the text, and the daughter the melancholic repeater of her grief*" (87; emphasis in original).

12. In the latter half of the nineteenth century, the percentage of Chinese females ranged from 3.6 percent (1890) to 7.2 percent (1870) of the Chinese population (Chan, "Exclusion of Chinese Women," 94). Asian American studies scholars tend to see the Chinese Exclusion Act of 1882 as a landmark because it was the first law to exclude immigration on the basis of race. However, Sucheng Chan points out that the exclusionary Page Law preceded the Exclusion Act by seven years (it was passed in 1875). Ostensibly a law to exclude Chinese prostitutes, it was enforced so broadly as to exclude almost all Chinese females. See Chan for a discussion of how exclusion laws against Chinese women were enforced, and Kang, *Compositional Subjects*, for a cogent analysis of how Asian women were thus constructed in U.S. hegemonic discourse.

13. In her discussion of the War Brides Act of 1945, Chan notes: "During the 1950s, women made up 50 to 90 percent of the Chinese entries during particular years. Their presence pushed the skewed sex ratio of the Chinese-ancestry population closer to normalcy—it became 1.3:1 by 1960" (Chan, *Asian Americans*, 140).

14. M. Jacqui Alexander, "Erotic Autonomy as a Politics of Decolonization"; David Eng, *Racial Castration*, 4–15; Gayatri Gopinath, "Nostalgia, Desire, Diaspora"; Anne McClintock, *Imperial Leather*, 352–89.

15. I am indebted to Nayan Shah's *Contagious Divides* for this analysis of non-normative domesticity as racial danger. See especially chapter 3, "Perversity, Contamination, and the Dangers of Queer Domesticity," 77–104.

16. Colleen Lye quotes from an 1862 text, *Chinese Immigration and the Physiological Causes of the Decay of a Nation,* as an early example of "yellow peril" discourse pathologizing Asian immigrants as germlike contagions. Lye, *America's Asia*, 55.

17. Ting, "Bachelor Society," 278. Similarly, David Eng remarks of *Eat a Bowl of Tea*, "In Chu's novel, the drama of reproducing the nuclear family comes to be the sine qua non of Chinese American assimilation into national body." Eng, *Racial Castration*, 180.

18. Lowe, *Immigrant Acts*, 122–23.

19. Thomas W. Kim discusses how these family explanations mystify the cause-effect relationship in *Bone*. Kim, "'For a paper son, paper is blood,'" 52.

20. Lowe, *Immigrant Acts*, 126.

21. Ibid., 123.

22. Benjamin, *Illuminations*, 257.

23. Lowe, *Immigrant Acts*, 126.

24. At a conference presentation, Ng referred to this withholding voice of the narrator, giving an example from the first page of the novel: "Too much happened on Salmon Alley. We don't talk about it" (3). Vivian Chin points out that, unlike the "Chinatown tour guide" type of narrator (and, I would add, unlike the mediating "Americanized daughter" narrator that Sau-ling Wong describes in "'Sugar Sisterhood': The Amy Tan Phenomenon" [197]), Leila does not overly explain Chinatown customs. The example that Chin gives is Leila getting angry at Nina for inappropriately wearing red, but not explaining to the reader that red is a color of celebration in Chinese cultures. Chin, "Finding the Right Gesture," 373. On the Chinese American narrator as Chinatown guide, see Wong, "Autobiography as Guided Chinatown Tour?"

25. See King-kok Cheung's *Articulate Silences* for a nuanced interpretation of silences in texts by Hisaye Yamamoto, Maxine Hong Kingston, and Joy Kogawa.

26. In 1906, an earthquake in San Francisco caused a fire that destroyed municipal records. Chinese men could then register as citizens and register children (real or fictive) that had been born to them in China. "Paper sons" purchased the birth certificates and identities of these newly registered children. Chinese migrants were often detained on Angel Island for interrogation to verify their identities, so these would-be migrants had to memorize the details of their fictive lives (for example, extended family makeup, village layout, etc.) Some would-be migrants were deported. Jennifer Ting points out that the phenomenon of paper sons was an alternative form of reproduction for these Chinese immigrant men, while Tina Chen interprets this practice as a strategy of impersonation. Ting, "Bachelor Society," 277; Chen, *Double Agency*, 21–26.

27. Brostrom, "Interview with Fae Myenne Ng," 88.

28. Patterson, *Slavery and Social Death*.

29. Sharon Holland discusses how the "peripheral existence or marginal space" to which the racialized subject is relegated "describes a living death." Holland, *Raising the Dead*, 17.

30. Freud, "Mourning and Melancholia," 164.

31. Abraham and Torok, *The Shell and the Kernel, Volume 1*, 181; emphasis in original.

32. Similarly, Leila disapproves when Nina tells Mah and Leon about her abortion because Nina has transgressed the unspoken family rule to keep certain matters secret.

33. My colleague Michelle Burnham has noted to me the felicitous resonance of "Luc" with "luck," as in Leon's "luck-red tie." For Leon, Luc embodies a talisman of luck, a vehicle of good fortune.

34. Barthes posits the one who waits as feminine: "Woman is faithful (she waits) . . . [a] man who waits and who suffers from his waiting is miraculously feminized." *A Lover's Discourse: Fragments*, 13–14. Leon and Luc's partnership in the laundry

business continues a long history of Chinese men working in feminized niches such as laundry work, restaurant work, domestic work, and other service work. As David Eng remarks, "The nation-state's sustained economic exploitation, coupled with its political disenfranchisement, of the Asian American male immigrant is modulated precisely through a technology of gendering not adjunct but centrally linked to processes of Asian American racial formation. . . . [T]he exploitation of immigrant labor is mobilized not only through the racialization of that labor but through its sexualizing." Eng, *Racial Castration*, 17.

35. As the subject of lack, Leon is feminized in this failed romance with the United States. Seduced and betrayed by the nation-state, he inhabits the position of the fallen woman. In this way, he and Mah occupy similar positions.

36. Leila narrates her memories of her and Ona sewing piecework as children (129–30; 178–79). See Lowe, *Immigrant Acts*, 120–27 and 168–73, on "the vulnerability of the immigrant home to capitalist penetration" (168–69) in *Bone*. For a discussion of the global restructuring of labor on the basis of race and gender, see Mitter, *Common Fate, Common Bond*.

37. Kang, *Compositional Subjects*, 181.

38. See Castronovo, *Necro Citizenship*, for a discussion of death as a trope of freedom in American literature and culture.

39. The examples of suicidal threats and symbolic suicide come from Goellnicht, "Of Bones and Suicide": An interviewee in Nee and Nee's *Longtime Californ': A Documentary Study of an American Chinatown* describes racial anxieties over the presence of Chinese in the United States and interprets exclusion laws as intending to "make us die out altogether" (25). Elaine Kim, *Asian American Literature*, points out that Chinatown is represented as a place of death and decay in Frank Chin's writing (180–89).

40. Chakrabarty, "The Time of History and the Times of Gods," 35.

41. Wynter, "On Disenchanting Discourse," 435–46.

42. Benjamin, *Illuminations*, 262.

43. See Ninh, *Ingratitude*, for a trenchant analysis of how daughters are figured as the primary agents responsible for paying back immigrant parental sacrifice.

44. For Thomas W. Kim, this "improper[ ]" citation of Jesus by the Leongs subverts notions of either Buddhism or Christianity as the one true faith. Kim, "'For a paper son, paper is blood,'" 51. I interpret the Leongs' ecumenical pantheon of gods as an instance of innovative "counting," or ascription of value.

2. Shameful Citizenship

1. Stoler, *Haunted by Empire*, 23.

2. Bascara, *Model Minority Imperialism*, 135.

3. Said, *Culture and Imperialism*, 9.

4. Lewis, "Introduction," 107.

5. Sedgwick, *Touching Feeling*, 36.

6. Sedgwick and Frank, *Shame and Its Sisters*, 135.

7. See, for example, Ahmed, *The Cultural Politics of Emotion,* 105.

8. See Min Song's *Strange Future* for a discussion of immigrants and racial others as "the strange."

9. Isaac, *American Tropics,* xviii.

10. Ibid., xvi.

11. Kaplan, "Left Alone with America"; Campomanes, "Afterword"; Bascara, *Model Minority Imperialism;* Isaac, *American Tropics;* See, *The Decolonized Eye.*

12. Song, *Strange Future,* 115.

13. Selena Whang explains how masculinity of color signifies a more explicit violence than white masculinity: "In a white masculinity, the nexus of power-aggression-violence can be neatly introjected into civility, seduction, refinement and culture. . . . For a degraded masculinity, identity has already felt the effects of masculine sexual sadism. Therefore, pain marks its relation to power-aggression-violence. Masculinity of color, in spasm, fumbles any kind of introjection. Instead, a degraded masculinity reveals in its halting, clumsy way, the sheer force of sexual sadism and the death drive, both as a receiver and a perpetrator." Whang, "The White Heterosexual Couple," 127.

14. Cheryl Harris's article "Whiteness as Property" is a touchstone for this discussion.

15. Hannah Arendt's *The Human Condition* is a touchstone for our understanding of how modernity institutionalizes terror and violence.

16. The common understanding of "law" is that it refers to the rules that govern a particular society. In Lacanian psychoanalysis, law refers to the Symbolic order, to the very foundation of sociality.

17. Fromm, *Escape from Freedom,* 144.

18. Mulvey, "Visual Pleasure and Narrative Cinema," 19.

19. Grewal, *Transnational America;* Hong, *The Ruptures of American Capital;* Miller, *Cultural Citizenship.*

20. Austin, "A Nation of Thieves," 230.

21. Kaufman, "The Meaning of Shame," 568–74.

22. Cheng, "Passing, Natural Selection, and Love's Failure," 533.

23. Žižek, *The Plague of Fantasies,* 72.

24. Hong, *The Ruptures of American Capital,* xi.

25. This logic is similar to the notion that a woman's appearance can provoke rape, or that discovery of one's erotic object as same-sex can lead to murder. In these frameworks, the appearance of the racial, gendered, or sexual other disturbs one into violence.

26. For a discussion of the animal, the human, and language, see Wolfe, *Animal Rites,* 44–94.

27. Sartre, *Being and Nothingness,* 350; emphasis in original.

28. Interestingly, Asian American critics have also expressed frustration with Asian American "muteness." The introduction to the 1974 Asian American literary anthology

Aiiieeeee! figures Asian American "muteness" (lack of voice) as castration (lack of phallic power).

29. Žižek, "Enjoy Your Nation as Yourself!," 597; emphasis in original.

30. Lewis, "Introduction," 16–17.

31. Gabe most often experiences physical intimacy as physical closeness with their dogs. For a discussion on human-canine intimacy, see Kuzniar, *Melancholia's Dog,* 107–35.

32. Silverman, *The Threshold of the Visible World,* 14.

33. Cary Wolfe reads Freud's *Civilization and Its Discontents* as theorizing this association between sight and human civilization. According to Freud, walking upright led to a shift from smell to sight as the primary sense of stimulation. The distance from objects of contemplation then led to a sense of the aesthetic. Wolfe, *Animal Rites,* 2.

34. Savran, "The Sadomasochist in the Closet," 140–41.

35. Ibid., 141.

36. Ibid., 144.

37. Pateman, The Sexual Contract"; Young, "Polity and Group Difference"; Fraser, "Rethinking the Public Sphere."

38. Žižek, *The Metastases of Enjoyment,* 55; emphasis in original.

39. Sartre, *Being and Nothingness,* 347–54.

40. Sedgwick and Frank, *Shame and Its Sisters,* 135.

41. Hearne *Adam's Task* (109), quoted in Wolfe, *Animal Rites,* 4.

42. Ibid.; emphasis in original.

43. Žižek notes that the foremost commandment of the Lacanian superego is "Enjoy!" Žižek, *For They Know Not What They Do,* 9–10.

44. Although I interpret Tomas's pressing of Gabe into indebted servitude as an allegory for the general construction of the Sullivans as indebted subjects, as illustrated in the incident with the yoga mom, a telling difference is Tomas's avowal of deriving sadistic enjoyment from this relationship, while the yoga mom positions herself as a neutral, impartial enforcer of law. As a socially privileged subject, the yoga mom disavows the jouissance that she derives from placing socially subordinate subjects in bondage to her.

45. Hartman, *Scenes of Subjection,* 131.

46. Isaac, *American Tropics,* xvi.

47. Stoler, *Haunted by Empire,* 9.

48. See, *The Decolonized Eye,* xxxi.

49. Stoler, *Haunted by Empire,* 1.

50. MacCannell, *The Regime of the Brother,* 3.

51. Ibid., 16–17.

52. Intriguingly, Gabe's narration also projects onto Latina characters a fantasy of ideal, nurturing maternity. First, the Mexican wife of a movie producer displays maternal identification with their dog Buster, and regards Gabe kindly (46–47). Second, Gabe feels sad at seeing a Mexican woman alone at a pizza parlor and is relieved when

her children join her (157–58). Third, the Latina pharmacist at the mall who recognizes Gabe's plight "sounds like somebody's mother. It's strange I should know this, but somehow I feel certain" (184). These Latina characters seem to promise Gabe a benevolent parental regard that is free of jouissance and shame. In contrast to the substantial narrative of Stone as a fantasy of white fatherhood, these are very ephemeral moments in the novel. This disproportion might be explained by the absence of the white father creating a psychic void that needs to be filled, and the presence of the native mother demanding a psychic attention that can only fleetingly be detached.

53. The contradictory status of the Philippines, Puerto Rico, and other U.S. colonies was captured by the description of such territories as "foreign to the United States in a domestic sense" in a 1901 U.S. Supreme Court ruling. Sarita See and Allan Isaac suggest how national ambivalence about colonization resulted in the linguistic disarray of "convoluted legal phrases" and "disappearing clauses." See *The Decolonized Eye*, xii; Isaac, *American Tropics*, 23–47.

3. Romantic Citizenship

1. On the question of how to interpret the figure of John Kwang, see Huang, "Citizen Kwang"; D. Kim, "Do I, Too, Sing America?"; J. Kim, "From *Mee-gook* to Gook"; Lee, "Where the Talented Tenth Meets the Model Minority"; Narkunas, "Surfing the Long Waves of Global Capital with Chang-rae Lee's *Native Speaker*"; Palumbo-Liu, *Asian/American;* and Song, *Strange Future.*

2. Strikingly, Henry identifies so insistently *with* immigrants that he seems to identify *as* an immigrant, although he was born in the United States. This identification indicates the power of Asian racial formation as foreign, as well as a psychic sense of solidarity with immigrants. Because of this strong identification, I interpret him as a central participant in the immigrant-nation romance.

3. L. Park, *Consuming Citizenship,* 5.

4. Berlant, *The Queen of America Goes to Washington City,* 195; emphasis in original.

5. *Time,* July 8, 1985, 101; quoted in Berlant, *The Queen of America Goes to Washington City,* 196.

6. Honig, *Democracy and the Foreigner.*

7. While this chapter focuses on the immigrant as the figure of political romance, the historic campaign of Barack Obama for president in 2008 similarly deployed his racial difference as signifying the fulfillment of a multiracial democracy for the nation.

8. Freud, *Group Psychology,* 111–16.

9. Habermas, *The Structural Transformation of the Public Sphere.*

10. Sollors, *Beyond Ethnicity,* offers one of the most well known discussions of the "tension" between consent (choosing American national identity) and descent (an ethnic identity that one inherits).

11. D. Kim, "Do I, Too, Sing America?" 242.

12. Ibid., 245.

13. This moment in the narrative recalls Benjamin's well-known quote on the revolutionary possibilities of the moment of arrest: "Thinking involves not only the flow of thoughts, but their arrest as well. Where thinking suddenly stops in a configuration pregnant with tensions, it gives that configuration a shock, by which it crystallizes into a monad. A historical materialist approaches a historical subject only where he encounters it as a monad. In this structure he recognizes the sign of a Messianic cessation of happening, or, put differently, a revolutionary chance in the fight for the oppressed past." *Illuminations*, 262–63. Kwang's constituents see in his political rise an opportunity to right the historic wrongs of racial exclusion.

14. Žižek, *The Sublime Object of Ideology*, 34.

15. See Bow, *Betrayal and Other Acts of Subversion*, 70–114, on this kind of feminist developmental narrative in Chinese North American women's writing; and Koshy, "*Jasmine*, by Bharati Mukherjee," 124–26, for a discussion of how Mukherjee's novel *Jasmine* is read as a similar kind of novel of Asian female emancipation in North America.

16. I focus my discussion on the character Ahjuhma, but the underage hostess with whom Kwang is found in a car crash is another pivotal, though minor, character in the novel's plot.

17. J. Lee, "Where the Talented Tenth Meets the Model Minority," 252; Y.-M. Park and Wald, "Native Daughters in the Promised Land," 620–23.

18. Manalansan, "Immigrant Domesticity and the Politics of Olfaction in the Global City."

19. Wolfe, *Animal Rites*, 2–5.

20. Ibid., 4; emphasis in original.

21. Kristeva, *The Powers of Horror*. For discussions of Asian American racialization as abjection, see Li, *Imagining the Nation*, 6–15; and Shimakawa, *National Abjection*.

22. It is possible of course for the reader to grant Ahjuhma human agency by reconsidering the narrative from her individual and cultural perspective. In this light, she is not simply refusing a Western liberal norm; she is also practicing and reinforcing her own ethical and cultural norms. However, I believe that such a reading of Ahjuhma is simply a more culturally sensitive version of Lelia's "rehumanization" project, one that still renders her an object of knowledge. My inclination is to de-privilege the "human" by accepting her "nonhuman" status as viable.

23. The Immigration and Naturalization Service, established in 1933, was responsible for investigating and deporting undocumented migrants. In 2003, its functions were transferred from the Department of Justice to several components within the newly created Department of Homeland Security.

24. Huang, "Citizen Kwang"; Lee, "Where the Talented Tenth Meets the Model Minority"; D. Kim, "Do I, Too, Sing America?"

25. R. Lee, "Reading Contests and Contesting Reading"; Huang, "Citizen Kwang."

26. See Light, Kwuon, and Zhong, "Korean Rotating Credit Associations in Los Angeles"; and Takaki, *Strangers from a Different Shore*, 275–76, on Korean immigrant rotating-credit associations.

27. Oliver and Shapiro, *Black Wealth, White Wealth.*

28. Eastern European migrants are in fact included in Kwang's coalition. Through this inclusion, Lee suggests that their incorporation into hegemonic or universal whiteness is incomplete.

29. One of the most common complaints made about students of color at various levels is that they "self-segregate." The title of Beverly Tatum's book, *Why Are All the Black Kids Sitting Together in the Cafeteria?,* articulates one of the common forms of this accusation. The concept of "self-segregation" posits the white subject as innocent and the racialized subject as guilty of practices antagonistic to social unity and cohesion. Moreover, this formulation also belies a sense of white entitlement and universalism, such that a feeling of personal exclusion translates into a wrong against society itself.

30. Palumbo-Liu, *Asian/American,* 317.

31. J. Lee, "Where the Talented Tenth Meets the Model Minority," 253.

32. Ludwig, "Ethnicity as Cognitive Identity," 235–36.

33. Critics such as Tina Chen and Crystal Parikh have written cogently on the ethnic and racial implications of Henry's work as a spy or double agent, gaining the other's trust in order ultimately to render him knowable. However, what if Lelia, not Henry, is the ultimate double agent, working undercover to discover secrets from the native informant? In this case, dissimulation is not necessary for her work; indeed, genuine emotion seems to be the most effective lever. My thanks to Stephen Sohn for suggesting this reading.

34. Koshy, *Sexual Naturalization,* 20–21.

35. D. Kim, "Do I, Too, Sing America?" 252.

36. Ibid., 253.

37. Ibid.

38. This poetic lyricism of Henry's narrative voice is perhaps the aspect of the novel that reviewers have most consistently commented on. The following excerpts from reviews are reprinted in the paperback edition's first pages: "A lyrical page turner" *(Seattle Weekly);* "The prose Lee writes is elliptical, riddling, poetic, often beautifully made" *(New Yorker);* "The book's narrative is lyrical, its plot compelling" *(Boston Globe);* "Thoughtful, elegant prose" *(San Francisco Bay Guardian);* "Lyrical, mysterious, and nuanced" *(Booklist);* "Elegant, highly wrought prose" *(New York Newsday);* "A first novel of impressive poetic and psychological accomplishment" *(Library Journal);* "Incandescent prose" *(The Sunday Times,* London). In *Strange Future,* Min Song refers to "Lee's self-conscious skill in his craft" and "his flawless prose": "We can never forget with Lee's prose that we are reading a work of literature, because it calls attention to itself through its self-consciously polished prose as a work of literature" (194–95).

4. Perverse Citizenship

1. As I mention in the endnotes to the introduction, I consider *The Interpreter* an antidomestic novel in the sense that its plot intriguingly rewrites the generic plot of

nineteenth-century domestic fiction, that of a heroine faced with the world's failures and looking inward for resolution.

2. Lacan, *Écrits*, 697.

3. Pease, *The New American Exceptionalism*, 158–59.

4. Lacan, *Seminar XI*, 185.

5. Feher-Gurewich, "A Lacanian Approach to the Logic of Perversion," 192.

6. Evans, *Dictionary of Lacanian Psychoanalysis*, 92.

7. We can understand Grace's abrupt conversion to born-again Christianity in adulthood as an attempt to find a higher Other that will separate her from the demands of her parents and of the nation-state.

8. Žižek, *The Ticklish Subject*, 284.

9. Ibid., 299.

10. Wong, *Reading Asian American Literature*.

11. L. Park, *Consuming Citizenship*, 43.

12. As Ninh points out, such a fantasy of paying off debt to one's Asian immigrant parents is indeed a fantasy. Paradoxically, the more one makes oneself into a valuable commodity, the more debt continues to accrue, because the acquisition of any asset is framed as the direct result of parental or ancestral sacrifice. Ninh, *Ingratitude*, 27–40.

13. Deleuze, "Coldness and Cruelty," 70.

14. Ibid., 71.

15. See Ninh, *Ingratitude*, for an analysis of Asian immigrant parental threats of disownment, and the "subterfuge" of Asian American daughters taking such disownment at its word by leaving home (101–5).

16. For Marx, alienation from work also means social alienation, or alienation between human subjects: "If then the product of labour is alienation, production itself must be active alienation, the alienation of activity, the activity of alienation. . . . An immediate consequence of the fact that man is estranged from the product of his labour, from his life activity, from his species being, is the *estrangement* of *man* from *man* . . . one man is estranged from the other, as each is estranged from man's essential nature." Marx, "Economic and Philosophic Manuscripts of 1844," 74–77; emphasis in original.

17. Ng, *Bone*, 16; Lee, *Native Speaker*, 83.

18. Wong, *Reading Asian American Literature*, 118–65.

19. Ng, *Bone*, 181.

20. Feher-Gurewich, "A Lacanian Approach to the Logic of Perversion," 192.

21. Ibid., 202.

22. Lacan, *The Ethics of Psychoanalysis*, 295.

23. A woman in love with DJ bitterly recounts his obsession with Grace: "All he talks about is how she's the victim, how she needs to be saved, how she's all alone." Suzy pieces it all together, wondering, "Was it all for Grace?" (280). The implication is that DJ believes that he will save Grace from her parents by killing them. Also suggestive is the phrase "all alone" to describe Grace; previously, Grace had described

Suzy as "all alone" (262). I argue later that Grace and Suzy are paradoxically together in their aloneness.

24. Koshy, *Sexual Naturalization*, 15.

25. Bow, *Betrayal and Other Acts of Subversion*, 37–69; Cheng, *The Melancholy of Race*, 45–59.

26. As I discuss in the introduction, Lisa Park refers to premature adulthood and prolonged childhood as developmental dynamics that result from the responsibilities of second-generation Asian American children in the family business: "Premature adulthood is the placement of an individual who is socially considered a child . . . in adult-like roles with adult responsibilities. Conversely, then, a prolonged childhood is the placement of an individual who is socially considered an adult into child-like roles with child-like responsibilities. The importance of both phenomena lies in the fact that they are out of synch with the larger, socially determined concept of adulthood and childhood." Park, *Consuming Citizenship*, 66.

27. There is something vampirelike about Suzy's lonely existence, a sense of temporal disjunction that she feels between herself and others. Like a vampire, she seems exiled from humanity, from "common mortals," in Feher-Gurewich's words. Although Suzy has two friends that she occasionally sees socially, she is not anchored by any routine. This is why she can devote her life to this investigation—it does not interrupt her life because there is nothing to interrupt. Suzy is also vampirelike or parasitic in feeding off other people's domestic spheres.

28. Suzy remembers vividly a mirror in the elevator of their apartment building in South Korea: "She always wanted to look at the mirror, but it hung so high that she could never reach it. . . . Sometimes Dad would give her a lift . . . but then she was too high up on his shoulders, and the mirror reflected only her dangling feet. Suzy was not sure why this mirror should stick so distinctly in her mind, but almost always she would look for a mirror upon entering elevators and would immediately feel a lack, or a pang of something distant and impossible to name" (43).

29. Dolar, "At First Sight," 139.

30. Ibid., 139, emphasis in original.

31. Lacan, *Seminar VII*, 217.

32. Ibid.

33. Ibid., 212.

34. Deleuze, "Coldness and Cruelty," 57–68.

35. Lacan, *Seminar XI*, 185.

36. Deleuze, "Coldness and Cruelty," 102.

37. Feher-Gurewich, "A Lacanian Approach to the Logic of Perversion," 194.

38. Copjec, *Read My Desire*, 190.

39. J.-M. Miller, "Commentary on Lacan's Text," 423–26.

40. J.-M. Miller, "On Perversion," 315.

41. Copjec, *Read My Desire*, 92; emphasis added.

42. *The Interpreter*, 294 (emphasis in original).

Coda

1. Cheng, *The Melancholy of Race*, 31.

2. *Flower Drum Song* was of course written by Richard Rodgers and Oscar Hammerstein, and in that sense my discussion of it here is a departure from my earlier focus on texts written by Asian American authors. However, following the lead of Celine Parreñas Shimizu, I consider performances by Asian American actresses such as Nancy Kwan as a kind of authorship. The ascription of performing agency is complicated in this case because Linda Low's musical numbers were sung by B. J. Baker, a white singer who also worked with Elvis Presley, Frank Sinatra, Bobby Darin, and Sam Cooke. Nevertheless, I would argue that Linda's bodily and musical performances are received by the audience as Asian American. Shimizu, *The Hypersexuality of Race*, 30–101.

3. Linda Low's enjoyment is too infectious to be harnessed for the business of reproducing the traditional family of Wang Chi Yang. However, her enjoyment does generate economic profit for the Fong family business of entertainment and spectacle, and she is finally rewarded for her longtime loyalty to the Fongs with marriage to Sammy Fong.

4. These lines are spoken by Sammy Fong, in his attempt to "sell" Mei Li, whom his mother has arranged for him to marry, to the Wang family.

5. Cheng, *The Melancholy of Race*, 58; emphasis in original.

6. Ngai, *Ugly Feelings*, 24–28; Massumi, *Parables for the Virtual*, 27–28.

7. Ahmed, "Affective Economies."

8. Ibid., 120–21.

9. Puar, *Terrorist Assemblages*, 206.

10. Chuh proposes this subjectlessness as a means to "create the conceptual space to prioritize difference by foregrounding the discursive constructedness of subjectivity. In other words, it points attention to the constraints on the liberatory potential of the achievement of subjectivity, by reminding us that a subject only becomes recognizable and can act as such by conforming to certain regulatory matrices." Chuh, *Imagine Otherwise*, 9.

Bibliography

Abraham, Nicolas, and Maria Torok. *The Shell and the Kernel, Volume 1*. Edited and translated by Nicholas T. Rand. Chicago: University of Chicago Press, 1994.

Ahmed, Sara. "Affective Economies." *Social Text* 22, no. 2 (Summer 2004): 117–39.

———. *The Cultural Politics of Emotion*. New York: Routledge, 2004.

———. *The Promise of Happiness*. Durham: Duke University Press, 2010.

Alexander, M. Jacqui. "Erotic Autonomy as a Politics of Decolonization: An Anatomy of Feminist and State Practice in the Bahamas Tourist Economy." In *Feminist Genealogies, Colonial Legacies, Democratic Futures*. Edited by M. Jacqui Alexander and Chandra Talpade Mohanty, 63–100. New York: Routledge, 1997.

Anderson, Benedict. *Imagined Communities*. London: Verso, 1991.

Arendt, Hannah. *The Human Condition*. Chicago: University of Chicago Press, 1958.

Armstrong, Nancy. *Desire and Domestic Fiction: A Political History of the Novel*. New York: Oxford University Press, 1987.

Austin, Regina. "'A Nation of Thieves': Consumption, Commerce, and the Black Public Sphere." In *The Black Public Sphere*. Edited by The Black Public Sphere Collective, 229–52. Chicago: University of Chicago Press, 1995.

Barthes, Roland. *A Lover's Discourse: Fragments*. Translated by Richard Howard. New York: Hill and Wang, 1978.

Bascara, Victor. *Model Minority Imperialism*. Minneapolis: University of Minnesota Press, 2006.

Baudrillard, Jean. *Seduction*. Translated by Brian Singer. New York: St. Martin's Press, 1990.

Behdad, Ali. *A Forgetful Nation: On Immigration and Cultural Identity in the United States*. Durham: Duke University Press, 2005.

Benjamin, Walter. *Illuminations*. Edited by Hannah Arendt. Translated by Harry Zohn. New York: Schocken Books, 1968.

Berlant, Lauren. "Citizenship." In *Keywords for American Cultural Studies*. Edited by Burgett and Hendler, 37–42.

———. *The Queen of America Goes to Washington City: Notes on Sex and Citizenship.* Durham: Duke University Press, 1997.

Bhabha, Homi K. *The Location of Culture.* New York: Routledge, 1994.

Bow, Leslie. *Betrayal and Other Acts of Subversion: Feminism, Sexual Politics, Asian American Women's Literature.* Princeton: Princeton University Press, 2001.

Brogan, Kathleen. *Cultural Haunting: Ghosts and Ethnicity in Recent American Literature.* Charlottesville: University Press of Virginia, 1998.

Brostrom, Jennifer. "Interview with Fae Myenne Ng." In *Contemporary Literary Criticism Yearbook,* 87–88. Detroit: Gale Research, 1994.

Brown, Gillian. *Domestic Individualism: Imagining Self in Nineteenth-Century America.* Berkeley and Los Angeles: University of California Press, 1990.

Burgett, Bruce, and Glenn Hendler, eds. *Keywords for American Cultural Studies.* New York: New York University Press, 2007.

Cacho, Lisa Marie. "The Violence of Value." American Studies Association. November 7, 2009.

Campomanes, Oscar. "Afterword: The New Empire's Forgetful and Forgotten Citizens: Unrepresentability and Unassimilability in Filipino-American Postcolonialities." *Critical Mass: A Journal of Asian American Cultural Criticism* 2, no. 2 (Spring 1995): 145–200.

Carbado, Devon. "Racial Naturalization." *American Quarterly* 57, no. 3 (September 2005): 633–58.

Carr, Brian. "At the Thresholds of the 'Human': Race, Psychoanalysis, and the Replication of Imperial Memory." *Cultural Critique* 39 (Spring 1998): 119–50.

Castronovo, Russ. *Necro Citizenship: Death, Eroticism, and the Public Sphere in the Nineteenth-Century United States.* Durham: Duke University Press, 2001.

Chakrabarty, Dipesh. *Provincializing Europe: Postcolonial Thought and Historical Difference.* Princeton: Princeton University Press, 2000.

———. "The Time of History and the Times of Gods." In *The Politics of Culture in the Shadow of Capital.* Edited by Lisa Lowe and David Lloyd, 35–60. Durham: Duke University Press, 1997.

Chan, Sucheng. *Asian Americans: An Interpretive History.* New York: Twayne, 1991.

———. "Exclusion of Chinese Women." In *Entry Denied: Exclusion and the Chinese Community in America, 1882–1943.* Edited by Sucheng Chan, 94–146. Philadelphia: Temple University Press, 1991.

Chang, Yoonmee. "Chinese Suicide: Political Desire and Queer Exogamy in Fae Myenne Ng's *Bone.*" *MFS: Modern Fiction Studies* 56, no. 1 (Spring 2010): 90–112.

Chen, Tina. *Double Agency: Acts of Impersonation in Asian American Literature and Culture.* Stanford: Stanford University Press, 2005.

Cheng, Anne Anlin. *The Melancholy of Race: Psychoanalysis, Assimilation, and Hidden Grief.* New York: Oxford University Press, 2000.

———. "Passing, Natural Selection, and Love's Failure: Ethics of Survival from Chang-rae Lee to Jacques Lacan." *American Literary History* 17, no. 3 (2005): 553–74.

———. "Wounded Beauty: An Exploratory Essay on Race, Feminism, and the Aesthetic Question." *Tulsa Studies in Women's Literature* 19, no. 2 (Fall 2000): 191–218.

Cherniavsky, Eva. *Incorporations: Race, Nation, and the Body Politics of Capital.* Minneapolis: University of Minnesota Press, 2006.

Cheung, King-kok. *Articulate Silences: Hisaye Yamamoto, Maxine Hong Kingston, Joy Kogawa.* Ithaca: Cornell University Press, 1993.

Chin, Frank, Jeffery Paul Chan, Lawson Fusao Inada, and Shawn Wong, eds. *Aiiieeeee! An Anthology of Asian-American Writers.* Washington, D.C.: Howard University Press, 1983.

Chin, Marilyn. *Revenge of the Mooncake Vixen.* New York: W. W. Norton, 2009.

Chin, Vivian Fumiko. "Finding the Right Gesture: Becoming Chinese American in Fae Myenne Ng's *Bone.*" In *The Chinese in America: From the Gold Mountain to the New Millennium.* Edited by Susie Lan Cassel, 365–77. Lanham, Md.: Altamira Press, 2002.

Cho, Grace M. *Haunting the Korean Diaspora: Shame, Secrecy, and the Forgotten War.* Minneapolis: University of Minnesota Press, 2008.

Cho, John. "Tracing the Vampire." *Hitting Critical Mass: A Journal of Asian American Cultural Criticism* 3, no. 2 (Spring 1997): 87–113.

Chu, Patricia. *Assimilating Asians: Gendered Strategies of Authorship in Asian America.* Durham: Duke University Press, 2000.

Chuh, Kandice. *Imagine Otherwise: On Asian Americanist Critique.* Durham: Duke University Press, 2003.

Comaroff, Jean, and John L. Comaroff, eds. *Millennial Capitalism and the Culture of Neoliberalism.* Durham: Duke University Press. 2001.

Copjec, Joan. *Read My Desire: Lacan Against the Historicists.* Cambridge, Mass.: MIT Press, 1994.

Dean, Tim. *Beyond Sexuality.* Chicago: University of Chicago Press, 2000.

Deleuze, Gilles. "Coldness and Cruelty." *Masochism.* New York: Zone Books, 1991.

Deleuze, Gilles, and Félix Guattari. *A Thousand Plateaus: Capitalism and Schizophrenia.* Translated by Brian Massumi. Minneapolis: University of Minnesota Press, 1987.

Derrida, Jacques. *Specters of Marx: The State of the Debt, the Work of Mourning, and the New International.* New York: Routledge, 1994.

Dolar, Mladen. "At First Sight." In *Gaze and Voice as Love Objects.* Edited by Renata Salecl and Slavoj Žižek, 129–53. Durham: Duke University Press, 1996.

Duggan, Lisa. *The Twilight of Equality: Neoliberalism, Cultural Politics, and the Attack on Democracy.* Boston: Beacon Press, 2003.

Edelman, Lee. *No Future: Queer Theory and the Death Drive.* Durham: Duke University Press, 2004.

Eng, David L. *The Feeling of Kinship: Queer Liberalism and the Racialization of Intimacy.* Durham: Duke University Press, 2010.

———. *Racial Castration: Managing Masculinity in Asian America.* Durham: Duke University Press, 2001.

Eng, David L., and Shinhee Han. "A Dialogue on Racial Melancholia." In *Loss*. Edited by Eng and Kazanjian, 343–71.

Eng, David L., and David Kazanjian, eds. *Loss*. Berkeley and Los Angeles: University of California Press, 2003.

Evans, Dylan. *Dictionary of Lacanian Psychoanalysis*. London: Routledge, 1996.

Feher-Gurewich, Judith. "A Lacanian Approach to the Logic of Perversion." In *The Cambridge Companion to Lacan*. Edited by Jean-Michel Rabaté, 191–207. Cambridge: Cambridge University Press, 2003.

Feldstein, Richard, Bruce Fink, and Maire Jaanus, eds. *Reading Seminars I and II: Lacan's Return to Freud*. Albany: State University of New York Press, 1996.

Fink, Bruce. *A Clinical Introduction to Lacanian Psychoanalysis: Theory and Technique*. Cambridge, Mass.: Harvard University Press, 1997.

Foucault, Michel. *A History of Sexuality, Volume 1: An Introduction*. Translated by Robert Hurley. New York: Vintage Books, 1978.

Fraser, Nancy. "Rethinking the Public Sphere: A Contribution to the Critique of Actually Existing Democracy." In *Habermas and the Public Sphere*. Edited by Craig Calhoun, 109–42. Cambridge, Mass.: MIT Press, 1992.

Freud, Sigmund. *Beyond the Pleasure Principle*. In *The Standard Edition of the Complete Psychological Works of Sigmund Freud, Volume XVIII*. Edited and translated by James Strachey, 1–64. London: Vintage, 1955.

———. "A Child Is Being Beaten." In *The Standard Edition of the Complete Psychological Works of Sigmund Freud, Volume XVII*. Edited and translated by James Strachey, 179–88. London: Vintage, 1955.

———. "Group Psychology and the Analysis of the Ego." *The Standard Edition of the Complete Psychological Works of Sigmund Freud, Volume XVIII*. Edited and translated by James Strachey, 65–143. London: Vintage, 1955.

———. "Mourning and Melancholia." In *General Psychological Theory*. Edited by Philip Rieff, 164–79. New York: Touchstone, 1963.

———. "The Uncanny." *The Standard Edition of the Complete Psychological Works of Sigmund Freud, Volume XVII*. Edited and translated by James Strachey, 217–56. London: Vintage, 1955.

Fromm, Erich. *Escape from Freedom*. New York: Holt, Rinehart, and Winston. 1941; 1976.

Fuss, Diana, ed. *Human, All Too Human*. New York: Routledge, 1996.

George, Rosemary. "Domesticity." In *Keywords for American Cultural Studies*. Edited by Burgett and Hendler, 88–91.

———, ed. *Burning Down the House: Recycling Domesticity*. Boulder, Colo.: Westview Press, 1998.

Gilroy, Paul. *Postcolonial Melancholia*. New York: Columbia University Press, 2005.

Glenn, Evelyn Nakano. "Split Household, Small Producer, and Dual Wage Earner: An Analysis of Chinese-American Family Strategies." *Journal of Marriage and the Family* 45, no. 1 (February 1983): 35–46.

Goellnicht, Donald. "Of Bones and Suicide: Sky Lee's *Disappearing Moon Café* and Fae Myenne Ng's *Bone.*" *Modern Fiction Studies* 46, no. 2 (Summer 2000): 300–330.

Gopinath, Gayatri. "Nostalgia, Desire, Diaspora: South Asian Sexualities in Motion." *positions* 5, no. 2 (Fall 1997): 467–89.

Gordon, Avery F. *Ghostly Matters: Haunting and the Sociological Imagination.* Minneapolis: University of Minnesota Press, 1997.

Grewal, Inderpal. *Transnational America: Feminisms, Diasporas, Neoliberalisms.* Durham: Duke University Press, 2005.

Gutiérrez-Jones, Carl. *Critical Race Narratives: A Study of Race, Rhetoric, and Injury.* New York: New York University Press, 2001.

Habermas, Jürgen. *The Structural Transformation of the Public Sphere: An Inquiry into a Category of Bourgeois Society.* Translated by Thomas Burger. Cambridge, Mass.: MIT Press, 1991.

Hagedorn, Jessica. "Ming the Merciless." In *Pet Food and Tropical Apparitions.* San Francisco: Momo's Press, 1981.

Harris, Cheryl I. "Whiteness as Property." In *Critical Race Theory: The Key Writings That Formed the Movement.* Edited by Kimberlé Crenshaw, Neil Gotanda, Gary Peller, and Kendall Thomas, 267–91. New York: New Press, 1995.

Hartman, Saidiya V. *Scenes of Subjection: Terror, Slavery, and Self-Making in Nineteenth-Century America.* New York: Oxford University Press, 1997.

Harvey, David. *A Brief History of Neoliberalism.* Oxford: Oxford University Press, 2005.

Hearne, Vicki. *Adam's Task: Calling Animals by Name.* New York: Random House, 1987.

Hicks, Heather J. "Hoodoo Economics: White Men's Work and Black Men's Magic in Contemporary American Film." *Camera Obscura* 18, no. 2 (2003): 27–55.

Hirsch, Marianne. *Family Frames: Photography, Narrative, and Postmemory.* Cambridge, Mass.: Harvard University Press, 1997.

Holland, Sharon. *Raising the Dead: Readings of Death and (Black) Subjectivity.* Durham: Duke University Press, 2000.

Homer, Sean. *Jacques Lacan.* London: Routledge, 2005.

Hong, Grace Kyungwon. *The Ruptures of American Capital: Women of Color Feminism and the Culture of Immigrant Labor.* Minneapolis: University of Minnesota Press, 2006.

Honig, Bonnie. *Democracy and the Foreigner.* Princeton: Princeton University Press, 2001.

Hsiao, Ruth. "Facing the Incurable: Patriarchy in *Eat a Bowl of Tea.*" In *Reading the Literatures of Asian America.* Edited by Shirley Geok-lin Lim and Amy Ling, 151–62. Philadelphia: Temple University Press, 1992.

Huang, Betsey. "Citizen Kwang: Chang-rae Lee's *Native Speaker* and the Politics of Consent." *Journal of Asian American Studies* 9, no. 3 (October 2006): 243–69.

Isaac, Allan Punzalan. *American Tropics: Articulating Filipino America.* Minneapolis: University of Minnesota Press, 2006.

Kain, Geoffrey. "Refracting Identity(ies) in *Eat a Bowl of Tea*: Insularity as Impotence." *MELUS* 26, no. 2 (Summer 2001): 187–98.

Kang, Laura Hyun Yi. *Compositional Subjects: Enfiguring Asian/American Women.* Durham: Duke University Press, 2002.

Kaplan, Amy. "'Left Alone with America': The Absence of Empire in the Study of American Culture." In *Cultures of United States Imperialism.* Edited by Amy Kaplan and Donald E. Pease, 3–21. Durham: Duke University Press, 1993.

———. "Manifest Domesticity." *American Literature* 70, no. 3 (September 1998): 581–606.

Kaufman, Gershen. "The Meaning of Shame: Toward Self-Affirming Identity." *Journal of Counseling Psychology* 21, no. 6 (November 1974): 568–74.

Khanna, Ranjanna. *Dark Continents: Psychoanalysis and Colonialism.* Durham: Duke University Press, 2003.

Kim, Daniel Y. "Do I, Too, Sing America? Vernacular Representations and Chang-rae Lee's *Native Speaker.*" *Journal of Asian American Studies* 6, no. 3 (October 2003): 231–60.

Kim, Elaine H. *Asian American Literature: An Introduction to the Writings and Their Social Context.* Philadelphia: Temple University Press, 1982.

Kim, Jodi. "From *Mee-Gook* to Gook": The Cold War and Racialized Undocumented Capital in Chang-rae Lee's *Native Speaker.*" *MELUS* 34, no. 1 (Spring 2009): 117–37.

Kim, Suki. *The Interpreter.* New York: Picador, 2003.

Kim, Thomas W. "'For a paper son, paper is blood': Subjectivation and Authenticity in Fae Myenne Ng's *Bone.*" *MELUS* 24, no. 4 (Winter 1999): 41–56.

Kingston, Maxine Hong. *The Woman Warrior.* New York: Vintage, 1977.

Koshy, Susan. "*Jasmine,* by Bharati Mukherjee." In *A Resource Guide to Asian American Literature.* Edited by Sau-ling Cynthia Wong and Stephen H. Sumida, 121–29. New York: Modern Language Association of America, 2001.

———. *Sexual Naturalization: Asian Americans and Miscegenation.* Stanford: Stanford University Press, 2004.

Kristeva, Julia. *Powers of Horror: An Essay on Abjection.* New York: Columbia University Press, 1982.

Kuzniar, Alice A. *Melancholia's Dog.* Chicago: University of Chicago Press, 2006.

Lacan, Jacques. *Écrits.* Edited and translated by Bruce Fink. New York: W. W. Norton, 2006.

———. *Écrits: A Selection.* Translated by Alan Sheridan. New York: W. W. Norton, 1977.

———. "Proposition du 9 octobre 1967 sur le psychoanalyst de l'École." *Scilicet* 1 (1968).

———. *The Seminar of Jacques Lacan, Book I. Freud's Papers on Technique, 1953–1954.* Edited by Jacques-Alain Miller. Translated by John Forrester. New York: W. W. Norton, 1988.

———. *The Seminar of Jacques Lacan, Book VII. The Ethics of Psychoanalysis, 1959–1960*. Edited by Jacques-Alain Miller. Translated by Sylvana Tomaselli. New York: W. W. Norton, 1992.

———. *The Seminar of Jacques Lacan, Book XI: The Four Fundamental Concepts of Psychoanalysis*. Edited and translated by Alan Sheridan. New York: W. W. Norton, 1977.

Lane, Christopher. "The Psychoanalysis of Race: An Introduction." In *The Psychoanalysis of Race*. Edited by Christopher Lane, 1–37. New York: Columbia University Press, 1998.

Langer, Adam. "Ten to Watch in 2003: Suki Kim: The New Electra." *Book Magazine*. January–February 2003. http://www.sukikim.com/reviews.html#2 (accessed October 6, 2010).

Lasch, Christopher. *Haven in a Heartless World: The Family Besieged*. New York: W. W. Norton, 1995.

Lee, Chang-rae. *Native Speaker*. New York: Riverhead, 1995.

Lee, James Kyung-Jin. "Where the Talented Tenth Meets the Model Minority: The Price of Privilege in Wideman's *Philadelphia Fire* and Lee's *Native Speaker*." *Novel: A Forum on Fiction* 35, nos. 2–3 (Spring–Summer 2002): 231–57.

Lee, Rachel. "Reading Contests and Contesting Reading: Chang-rae Lee's *Native Speaker* and Ethnic New York." *MELUS* 29, nos. 3–4 (Fall–Winter 2004): 341–52.

Levine, Andrea. "Joining the State: Sexuality and Citizenship in Junot Diaz and Chang-rae Lee." In *Racial Transformations: Latinos and Asians Remaking the United States*. Edited by Nicholas De Genova, 147–69. Durham: Duke University Press, 2006.

Lewis, Helen Block, "Introduction." In *The Role of Shame in Symptom Formation*. Edited by Helen Block Lewis. Hillsdale, N.J.: Lawrence Erlbaum, 1987.

Li, David Leiwei. *Imagining the Nation: Asian American Literature and Cultural Consent*. Stanford: Stanford University Press, 1998.

Light, Ivan, and Edna Bonacich. *Immigrant Entrepreneurs: Koreans in Los Angeles, 1965–1982*. Berkeley and Los Angeles: University of California Press, 1998.

Light, Ivan, Im Jung Kwuon, and Zhong Deng. "Korean Rotating Credit Associations in Los Angeles." *Amerasia* 16, no. 1 (1990): 35–54.

Ling, Jinqi. *Narrating Nationalisms: Ideology and Form in Asian American Literature*. New York: Oxford University Press, 1998.

Lloyd, David, and Abdul JanMohamed, eds. *The Nature and Context of Minority Discourse*. New York: Oxford University Press, 1990.

Lowe, Lisa. *Immigrant Acts: On Asian American Cultural Production*. Durham: Duke University Press, 1996.

———. "The Intimacies of Four Continents." In *Haunted by Empire: Geographies of Intimacy in North American History*. Edited by Ann Laura Stoler, 191–212. Durham: Duke University Press, 2006.

Ludwig, Sämi. "Ethnicity as Cognitive Identity: Private and Public Negotiations in Chang-rae Lee's *Native Speaker*." *Journal of Asian American Studies* 10, no. 3 (October 2007): 221–42.

Lye, Colleen. *America's Asia: Racial Form and American Literature, 1893–1945*. Princeton: Princeton University Press, 2005.

MacCannell, Juliet Flower. *The Hysteric's Guide to the Future Female Subject*. Minneapolis: University of Minnesota Press, 2000.

———. *The Regime of the Brother: After the Patriarchy*. London: Routledge, 1991.

Maeda, Daryl J. *Chains of Babylon: The Rise of Asian America*. Minneapolis: University of Minnesota Press, 2009.

Manalansan, Martin F., IV. "Immigrant Domesticity and the Politics of Olfaction in the Global City." In *The Smell Culture Reader*. Edited by Jim Drobnick, 41–52. New York: Berg, 2006.

Marx, Karl. "Economic and Philosophic Manuscripts of 1844." In *The Marx-Engels Reader*. 2nd ed. Edited by Robert C. Tucker, 66–125. New York: W. W. Norton, 1978.

Massumi, Brian. *Parables for the Virtual: Movement, Affect, Sensation*. Durham: Duke University Press, 2002.

McClintock, Anne. *Imperial Leather: Race, Gender, and Sexuality in the Colonial Contest*. New York: Routledge, 1993.

McHugh, Kathleen Anne. *American Domesticity: From How-to Manual to Hollywood Melodrama*. New York: Oxford University Press, 1999.

Melamed, Jodi. "The Spirit of Neoliberalism: From Racial Liberalism to Neoliberal Multiculturalism." *Social Text* 89, 24, no. 4 (Winter 2006): 1–24.

Miller, Jacques-Alain. "Commentary on Lacan's Text." *Reading Seminars I and II: Lacan's Return to Freud*. Edited by Richard Feldstein, Bruce Fink, and Maire Jaanus, 422–27. Albany: State University of New York Press, 1996.

———. "Extimité." In *Lacanian Theory of Discourse: Subject, Structure, and Society*. Edited by Mark Bracher, Marshall W. Alcorn Jr., Ronald J. Corthell, and Françoise Massardier-Kenney, 74–87. New York: New York University Press, 1994.

———. "On Perversion." In *Reading Seminars I and II: Lacan's Return to Freud*. Edited by Richard Feldstein, Bruce Fink, and Maire Jaanus, 306–20. Albany: State University of New York Press, 1996.

Miller, Toby. *Cultural Citizenship: Cosmopolitanism, Consumerism, and Television*. Philadelphia: Temple University Press, 2007.

Mitter, Swasti. *Common Fate, Common Bond: Women in the Global Economy*. London: Pluto Press, 1986.

Moraga, Cherríe, and Gloria Anzaldúa, eds. *This Bridge Called My Back: Writings by Radical Women of Color*. New York: Kitchen Table: Women of Color Press, 1981.

Mulvey, Laura. "Visual Pleasure and Narrative Cinema." In *Visual and Other Pleasures*, 14–26. Bloomington: Indiana University Press, 1989.

Muñoz, José Esteban. *Disidentifications: Queers of Color and the Performance of Politics*. Minneapolis: University of Minnesota Press, 1999.

Narkunas, J. Paul. "Surfing the Long Waves of Global Capital with Chang-rae Lee's *Native Speaker*: Ethnic Branding and the Humanization of Capital." *MFS: Modern Fiction Studies* 54, no. 2 (Summer 2008): 327–52.

Ng, Fae Myenne. *Bone*. New York: HarperPerennial, 1993.

————. Conference presentation. China Institute of America. New York, February 11, 1993.

Ngai, Mae. *Impossible Subjects: Illegal Aliens and the Making of America.* Princeton: Princeton University Press, 2004.

Ngai, Sianne. *Ugly Feelings.* Cambridge, Mass.: Harvard University Press, 2005.

Ninh, erin Khuë. "The Cautionary Tale: Sexual Discourse and the Asian American Daughter." Paper presented at the Modern Language Association, San Francisco, December 8, 2008.

————. *Ingratitude: The Debt-Bound Daughter in Asian American Literature.* New York: New York University Press, 2011.

Oh, Seung Ah. *Recontextualizing Asian American Domesticity: From "Madame Butterfly" to "My American Wife!"* Lanham, Md.: Lexington Books, 2008.

Oishi, Eve. "Bad Asians: New Film and Video by Queer Asian American Artists." In *Countervisions: Asian American Film Criticism.* Edited by Darrell Y. Hamamoto and Sandra Liu, 221–41. Philadelphia: Temple University Press, 2000.

Oliver, Melvin, and Thomas Shapiro. *Black Wealth, White Wealth: A New Perspective on Racial Inequality.* New York: Routledge, 1995.

Palumbo-Liu, David. *Asian/American: Historical Crossings of a Racial Frontier.* Stanford: Stanford University Press, 1999.

Parikh, Crystal. "Blue Hawaii: Asian Hawaiian Cultural Production and Racial Melancholia." *Journal of Asian American Studies* 5, no. 3 (October 2002): 199–216.

————. *An Ethics of Betrayal: The Politics of Otherness in Emergent U.S. Literatures and Culture.* New York: Fordham University Press, 2009.

Park, Lisa. *Consuming Citizenship: Children of Asian Immigrant Entrepreneurs.* Stanford: Stanford University Press, 2005.

Park, You-Me, and Gayle Wald. "Native Daughters in the Promised Land: Gender, Race, and the Question of Separate Spheres." *American Literature* 70, no. 3 (September 1998): 607–33.

Pateman, Carole. *The Sexual Contract.* Stanford: Stanford University Press, 1988.

Patterson, Orlando. *Slavery and Social Death: A Comparative Study.* Cambridge, Mass.: Harvard University Press, 1982.

Pease, Donald E. "Exceptionalism." In *Keywords for American Cultural Studies.* Edited by Burgett and Hendler, 108–12.

————. *The New American Exceptionalism.* Minneapolis: University of Minnesota Press, 2009.

————. "Re-thinking 'American Studies after U.S. Exceptionalism.'" *American Literary History* 21, no. 1 (Spring 2009): 19–27.

Peterson, Carla. "Family." In *Keywords for American Cultural Studies.* Edited by Burgett and Hendler, 112–16.

Peterson, Christopher. *Kindred Specters: Death, Mourning, and American Affinity.* Minneapolis: University of Minnesota Press, 2007.

Puar, Jasbir. *Terrorist Assemblages: Homonationalism in Queer Times.* Durham: Duke University Press, 2007.

Reddy, Chandan. "Asian Diasporas, Neoliberalism, and Family: Reviewing the Case for Homosexual Asylum in the Context of Family Rights." *Social Text* 23, nos. 3–4 (2005): 101–19.

Roach, Joseph. *Cities of the Dead: Circum-Atlantic Performance.* New York: Columbia University Press, 1996.

Roley, Brian Ascalon. *American Son.* New York: W. W. Norton, 2001.

Rosaldo, Renato. "Cultural Citizenship, Inequality, and Multiculturalism." In *Race, Identity, and Citizenship: A Reader.* Edited by Rodolfo D. Torres, Louis F. Mirrón, and Jonathan Xavier Inda, 253–61. Malden, Mass.: Blackwell, 1999.

Said, Edward. *Culture and Imperialism.* New York: Vintage, 1994.

Santa Ana, Jeffrey. "Affect-Identity: The Emotions of Assimilation, Multiraciality, and Asian American Subjectivity." In *Asian North American Identities: Beyond the Hyphen.* Edited by Eleanor Ty and Donald C. Goellnicht, 15–42. Bloomington: Indiana University Press, 2004.

Sartre, Jean-Paul. *Being and Nothingness.* Translated by Hazel E. Barnes. New York: Washington Square Press, 1956.

Sassen, Saskia. *Losing Control? Sovereignty in an Age of Globalization.* New York: Columbia University Press, 1996.

Savran, David. "The Sadomasochist in the Closet: White Masculinity and the Culture of Victimization." *differences: A Journal of Feminist Cultural Studies* 8, no. 2 (1996): 127–52.

Sedgwick, Eve Kosofsky. *Touching Feeling: Affect, Pedagogy, Performativity.* Durham: Duke University Press, 2003.

Sedgwick, Eve Kosofsky, and Adam Frank, eds. *Shame and Its Sisters: A Silvan Tomkins Reader.* Durham: Duke University Press, 1995.

See, Sarita Echavez. *The Decolonized Eye: Filipino American Art and Performance.* Minneapolis: University of Minnesota Press, 2009.

Seshadri-Crooks, Kalpana. *Desiring Whiteness: A Lacanian Analysis of Race.* New York: Routledge, 2000.

Shah, Nayan. *Contagious Divides: Epidemics and Race in San Francisco's Chinatown.* Berkeley and Los Angeles: University of California Press, 2001.

Shimikawa, Karen. *National Abjection: The Asian American Body Onstage.* Durham: Duke University Press, 2002.

Shimizu, Celine Parreñas. *The Hypersexuality of Race: Performing Asian American Women on Screen and Scene.* Durham: Duke University Press, 2007.

Shumway, David R. *Modern Love: Romance, Intimacy, and the Marriage Crisis.* New York: New York University Press, 2003.

Silverman, Kaja. *The Threshold of the Visible World.* New York: Routledge, 1996.

Sollors, Werner. *Beyond Ethnicity: Consent and Descent in American Culture.* New York: Oxford University Press, 1986.

Song, Min Hyoung. *Strange Future: Pessimism and the 1992 Los Angeles Riots.* Durham: Duke University Press, 2005.

Stoler, Ann Laura, ed. *Haunted by Empire: Geographies of Intimacy in North American History.* Durham: Duke University Press, 2006.

Takaki, Ronald. *Strangers from a Different Shore: A History of Asian Americans.* Boston: Little, Brown, 1989.

Tan, Amy. *The Joy Luck Club.* New York: Vintage, 1989.

Tate, Claudia. *Domestic Allegories of Political Desire.* New York: Oxford University Press, 1992.

Tatum, Beverly Daniel. *Why Are All the Black Kids Sitting Together in the Cafeteria?* New York: Basic Books, 1997.

Ting, Jennifer. "Bachelor Society: Deviant Heterosexuality and Asian American Historiography." In *Privileging Positions: The Sites of Asian American Studies.* Edited by Gary Okihiro et al., 271–79. Pullman: Washington State University Press, 1995.

Viego, Antonio. *Dead Subjects: Toward a Politics of Loss in Latino Studies.* Durham: Duke University Press, 2007.

Whang, Selena. "The White Heterosexual Couple: On Masculinity, Sadism and Racialized Lesbian Desire." *College Literature* 24, no. 1 (February 1997): 16–32.

Wolfe, Cary. *Animal Rites: American Culture, the Discourse of Species, and Posthumanist Theory.* Chicago: University of Chicago Press, 2003.

———. *What Is Posthumanism?* Minneapolis: University of Minnesota Press, 2010.

———, ed. *Zoontologies: The Question of the Animal.* Minneapolis: University of Minnesota Press, 2003.

Wong, Sau-ling Cynthia. "Autobiography as Guided Chinatown Tour? Maxine Hong Kingston's *The Woman Warrior* and the Chinese-American Autobiographical Controversy." In *Multicultural Autobiography: American Lives.* Edited by James Robert Payne, 248–79. Knoxville: University of Tennessee Press, 1992.

———. *Reading Asian American Literature: From Necessity to Extravagance.* Princeton: Princeton University Press, 1993.

Wynter, Sylvia. "On Disenchanting Discourse: 'Minority' Literary Criticism and Beyond." In *The Nature and Context of Minority Discourse.* Edited by Abdul R. JanMohamed and David Lloyd, 432–69. New York: Oxford University Press, 1991.

Young, Iris Marion. "Polity and Group Difference: A Critique of the Ideal of Universal Citizenship." *Ethics* 99, no. 2 (January 1989): 250–74.

Žižek, Slavoj. "Enjoy Your Nation as Yourself!" In *Theories of Race and Racism: A Reader.* Edited by Les Back and John Solomos, 594–606. New York: Routledge, 2000.

———. *Enjoy Your Symptom! Jacques Lacan in Hollywood and Out.* New York: Routledge, 1992.

———. *How to Read Lacan.* New York: W. W. Norton, 2006.

———. *The Metastases of Enjoyment.* London: Verso, 1994.

———. *The Plague of Fantasies.* London: Verso, 1997.

———. *The Sublime Object of Ideology.* London: Verso, 1989.

———. *The Ticklish Subject: The Absent Centre of Political Ontology.* London: Verso, 1999.

Index

abject: abjection of racial others, 85–91, 93, 95, 96, 104; La Malinche as colonial, 105; migrant woman worker in position of, 55, 124, 125–26

Abraham, Nicolas, 37–38, 44, 49, 193n11, 194n31

abstraction: capital as modern system of, 132, 134; as mode arising from Enlightenment, 135; as mode of money club, 135–36

affect: affect alien, Henry in Lee's *Native Speaker* as, 26, 142; affective labor of child, 41, 182; of alterity produced by Asian American racial formation, 19; charisma as ability to produce excess of, 114–15; emotion and, distinction between, 181–82; instinctual, produced by national citizenship, 16; lack of, in migrant woman worker, 122; marriage and exposure of intimate, consent to normative American culture and, 138, 141–42; of "Montauk fantasy" in Kim's *The Interpreter,* 155; recursive nature of, 43; of romance, 109, 145; second-generation Asian American, 28; shameful, of debt, 55; of traumatic enjoyment, 1; unconscious, as encrypted secrets, 29; *See also* jouissance(s); romance; shame

affective economies, notion of, 182

"Afterword: The New Empire's Forgetful and Forgotten Citizens" (Campomanes), 65

agency: ascribed to the enslaved, 100; ascription of, to the inhuman in vigilante violence, 93; of Asian immigrants and Asian Americans, 24; of liberal subjecthood, 128, 172; romantic love as trope for fully realized, 56–57, 58; of shaping the law, citizenship and, 26

Ahmed, Sara, 182, 192n56, 196n7, 203n7

AIDS, 133

Alexander, M. Jacqui, 193n14

alien, perception of Asian as, 15

alien abductions, vigilante violence and, 93–94

alienation: domestic spaces as spaces of, 179; into language, 163; Marx on, 201n16; perverse domesticity and experience of, 160–65

Alioto, Joseph, 192n3

America: failure to recognize racial migrant, 68, 69; as frontier, 84; as nation of nations, fetishistic structure of, 120–21; romance of, 109

Juliana Chang is associate professor of English at Santa Clara University. She is the editor of *Quiet Fire: A Historical Anthology of Asian American Poetry, 1892–1970*.